RANDOM HOUSE
LARGE PRINT

American Heart
Association®

Learn and Live™

Low-Fat, Low-Cholesterol

cookbook

Third Edition

Also by the American Heart Association

The New American Heart Association Cookbook, 6th Edition

American Heart Association Low-Calorie Cookbook

American Heart Association Low-Salt Cookbook, 2nd Edition

American Heart Association Quick & Easy Cookbook

American Heart Association Meals in Minutes

American Heart Association One-Dish Meals

American Heart Association Low-Fat & Luscious Desserts

American Heart Association To Your Health!
A Guide to Heart-Smart Living

American Heart Association 6 Weeks to Get Out the Fat

American Heart Association Fitting in Fitness

American Heart Association 365 Ways to Get Out the Fat

American Heart
Association®

Learn and Live ₅ₘ

Low-Fat,
Low-Cholesterol

cookbook delicious recipes to help lower your cholesterol

Third Edition

R A N D O M   H O U S E
L A R G E   P R I N T

Published in the United States of America by Random House Large Print in association with Crown Publishing, New York, and simultaneously in Canada by Random House of Canada Limited, Toronto. Distributed by Random House, Inc., New York.

Your contribution to the American Heart Association supports research that helps make publications like this possible. For more information, call 1-800-AHA-USA1 (1-800-242-8721) or contact us online at *www.americanheart.org*.

Printed in the United States of America

Design by Jan Derevjanik

The Library of Congress has established a Cataloging-in-Publication record for this title.

ISBN 0-375-43365-1

www.randomlargeprint.com

FIRST LARGE PRINT EDITION

Front cover: Spiced Shish Kebabs with Horseradish Cream (page 261); Photograph by Ben Fink

10 9 8 7 6 5 4 3 2 1

This Large Print edition published in accord with the standards of the N.A.V.H.

contents

acknowledgments

American Heart Association Consumer Publications
    Director: Jane Anneken Ruehl
    Senior Editor: Janice Roth Moss
    Editor: Jacqueline Fornerod Haigney
    Assistant Editor: Roberta Westcott Sullivan
    Senior Marketing Manager: Bharati Gaitonde
Recipe Developers for Third Edition
    Nancy S. Hughes
    Carol Ritchie
Recipe Developers for Previous Editions
    Carol Ritchie
    Linda Foley Woodrum
    Laureen Mody, R.D.
    Leni Reed, R.D.
    Sherry Ferguson
Nutrition Analyst
    Tammi Hancock, R.D.

preface

Welcome to the third edition of the *American Heart Association Low-Fat, Low-Cholesterol Cookbook*, one of the best-selling cookbooks in the American Heart Association library. This award-winning collection of recipes and useful health information is your invitation to a lifelong enjoyment of good food and good health. If you need to lower your cholesterol, this cookbook will help you enjoy the process!

The American Heart Association has long been a trusted authority on heart health. New information comes out of laboratories around the world with astonishing speed. We are pleased to be able to transform that information into useful resources for healthier living. By using this cookbook, you are taking full advantage of what we have learned from the latest scientific research on nutrition.

The more than 200 delicious recipes in this book fit the way you want to live today and the way you want to eat for the future. We offer old favorites such as Turkey Tetrazzini (page 232) to bring you comfort; we've added intriguing new dishes such as Thai Coconut Curry with Vegetables (page 324) to pique your interest. The completely revised information on heart health and cholesterol gives you an updated perspective on how healthy eating and exercise contribute to your well-being.

Most of all, we invite you to the table. With this book in your kitchen, you *can* take charge of your cholesterol and love every bite along the way.

Eat wisely, eat well!

Rose Marie Robertson

—Rose Marie Robertson, M.D., FAHA, FACC
Chief Science Officer
American Heart Association

introduction

How Cholesterol Affects Your Heart and Your Health

Most likely, you are reading this book because you are concerned about the effects of cholesterol on your health or the health of someone you love. Taking an active role in managing your diet is one of the best ways to control high cholesterol or prevent it from rising in the first place. The recipes and information in this book will help you do that. We want you to know just how important your decision to eat well can be.

RISK FACTORS FOR HEART DISEASE AND HEART ATTACK

A combination of risk factors makes up the equation that you and your doctor use to decide how best to protect your heart and your health. High blood cholesterol is one of the factors that can increase your risk of heart attack or stroke. The more risk factors you have, the greater your chance of developing heart disease. It is reassuring, however, to know that many parts of this equation—such as high blood cholesterol—are things that you can change to have better control of your own well-being.

Major Risk Factors That You Can Change

DIET

Several studies have shown a powerful link between diet and heart disease. What you eat has a strong effect on your blood cholesterol level. Changing your diet to reduce blood cholesterol can definitely reduce the risk of heart attack, other coronary events, and stroke in most people.

CIGARETTE/TOBACCO SMOKE

A smoker's risk of heart attack is more than twice that of a nonsmoker. Smokers also have two to four times the risk of sudden cardiac death. Your risk of heart disease also increases if you breathe in second-hand smoke at home or in the workplace. When a person stops smoking, no matter how long or how much he or she smoked, the risk of heart disease drops rapidly. Three years after quitting, the risk of death from heart disease and stroke for a person who smoked a pack a day or less is almost the same as for a person who never smoked.

HIGH BLOOD PRESSURE

High blood pressure has no symptoms, which is why it's called the "silent killer." High blood pressure increases the risk of stroke, heart attack, kidney failure, and congestive heart failure. Have your blood pressure checked regularly. If it's 140/90 millimeters of mercury (mm Hg) or above, your doctor can help you control it through proper diet, weight loss, regular exercise, reduced sodium intake, and medication.

PHYSICAL INACTIVITY

Physical inactivity is another major risk factor for heart disease. Regular exercise can help control levels of harmful cholesterol, raise levels of helpful cholesterol, and lower blood pressure in some people. Lack of exercise also increases the likelihood of being overweight or obese. It's easy to see that being physically active is an important part of lowering your risk for heart disease.

Major Risk Factors That You Cannot Change

HEREDITY

The tendency toward heart disease seems to run in families. Children of parents with heart disease are more likely to develop it themselves, particularly if heart disease was a cause of premature death in their parents or grandparents. Race is also a factor. Compared with whites, blacks develop high blood pressure earlier in life and their average blood pressures are much higher. As a result, their risk of heart disease is greater.

GENDER AND INCREASING AGE

Men have a greater risk than women of heart attack earlier in life. Men tend to have higher levels of low-density lipoprotein (LDL) cholesterol and lower levels of high-density lipoprotein (HDL) cholesterol than women (see pages 7 to 10 for more information on these types of cholesterol). However, women's death rate from heart disease increases after menopause. Most people who die of heart attack are age 65 or older. At older ages, women who have heart attacks are twice as likely as men to die within a few weeks of an attack.

Other Risk Factors

DIABETES

The 10.9 million Americans who have physician-diagnosed diabetes are major candidates for heart disease and stroke. Since the risk factors of having diabetes and being overweight often go hand in hand, it's especially important for diabetic patients to watch their diet and maintain proper weight.

METABOLIC SYNDROME

The term "metabolic syndrome" (also called insulin resistance or syndrome X) refers to a combination of any three of the following risk factors.

- Abdominal obesity defined as a waist measurement greater than 40 inches for men and greater than 35 inches for women

- Triglyceride level of 150 milligrams per deciliter (mg/dL) and higher

- High-density lipoprotein cholesterol level less than 40 mg/dL for men and less than 50 mg/dL for women

- Systolic blood pressure of 130 mm Hg and higher or diastolic blood pressure of 85 mm Hg and higher

- Fasting blood sugar of 110 mg/dL and higher

When a person has any three of these factors at the same time, the risk of heart disease that comes with high blood cholesterol is even greater. If you have three or more of these risk factors, discuss a treatment approach with your doctor.

OBESITY

People who are overweight or obese are more likely to develop heart disease and stroke even if they have no other risk factors. Excess weight can reduce levels of good cholesterol and may increase bad cholesterol. The way weight is distributed on your body may be a clue to your risk of heart disease. If a man's waist measurement exceeds his hip measurement, he has a significantly greater risk of heart disease. For a woman, the risk increases when the waist measurement is more than 80 percent of the hip measurement.

Obesity is determined by body mass index (BMI). Based on weight and height, BMI reflects the amount of your overall body fat. To find your BMI category:

- Weigh yourself without clothes or shoes. Measure your height without shoes.

- Find your height in the left-hand column of the chart below and see whether your weight falls into either range listed

HEIGHT	OVERWEIGHT (BMI 25.0-29.9)	OBESE (BMI 30.0 and above)
4'10"	119–142 LB	143 LB OR MORE
4'11"	124–147	148
5'0"	128–152	153
5'1"	132–157	158
5'2"	136–163	164
5'3"	141–168	169
5'4"	145–173	174
5'5"	150–179	180
5'6"	155–185	186
5'7"	159–190	191
5'8"	164–196	197
5'9"	169–202	203
5'10"	174–208	209
5'11"	179–214	215
6'0"	184–220	221
6'1"	189–226	227
6'2"	194–232	233
6'3"	200–239	240
6'4"	205–245	246

BELOW 25—A BMI from 18.5 to 24.9 is considered healthy. BMI values less than 18.5 are considered underweight.

25.0 TO 29.9—Overweight. A BMI in this range indicates a moderate risk of heart and blood vessel disease. A BMI of 25 translates to about 10 percent over ideal body weight.

30 OR MORE—Obesity. This means a high risk of heart and blood vessel disease, with 30 or more extra pounds.

40 OR MORE—Extreme obesity.

To calculate your exact BMI, multiply your weight in pounds by 705. Divide the product by your height in inches; divide again by your height in inches. If you have a BMI of 30 or above, discuss a weight loss plan with your doctor.

WHAT IS CHOLESTEROL AND WHAT DOES IT DO?

Your body needs some cholesterol—a waxy fat-like substance—to strengthen cell walls and for other body functions such as producing hormones. Your blood carries cholesterol and other fats through your body in distinct particles called lipoproteins. (Because lipids, or fats, do not mix with water, the body wraps them in protein to move them through the bloodstream.) Three types of lipoproteins make up the major part of your total blood cholesterol measurement: low-density lipoprotein (LDL), high-density lipoprotein (HDL), and very-low-density lipoprotein (VLDL).

Lipoproteins

As research continues, we learn more about how the different lipoproteins work. Harmful lipoproteins carry cholesterol to the inner walls of your arteries, allowing it to collect there and contribute to the buildup of plaque. That process is called atherosclerosis. Heavy plaque buildup on the artery walls slows the flow of blood to the heart. If the blood supply to a portion of the heart is completely blocked, usually by a blood clot that breaks away from the plaque, a heart attack results. On the other hand, helpful lipoproteins may prevent extra cholesterol from collecting in the arteries.

The cholesterol in your blood is measured in milligrams of cholesterol per deciliter of blood (mg/dL). The desirable total blood cholesterol level is less than 200 mg/dL. (See the chart on page 7 for more information on cholesterol levels.) The total cholesterol measurement is broken down further to determine how much "good" and "bad" lipoprotein cholesterol is in the blood.

LOW-DENSITY LIPOPROTEIN: THE "BAD" CHOLESTEROL

In most people, low-density lipoprotein (LDL) makes up about 60 to 70 percent of total blood cholesterol. There is a very clear relationship between LDL cholesterol level and risk of heart disease: the higher the level, the greater the risk. This is why LDL cholesterol is the primary target of efforts to lower cholesterol.

The optimal level for LDL cholesterol is less than 100 mg/dL. Near optimal is between 100 and 129 mg/dL. An LDL level between 130 and 159 mg/dL is considered a borderline high risk. If your LDL cholesterol is between 160 and 189 mg/dL, you are at high risk for heart disease. LDL cholesterol that is 190 mg/dL or above is considered very high.

HIGH-DENSITY LIPOPROTEIN:
THE "GOOD" CHOLESTEROL

Typically, one third to one fourth of the cholesterol in your blood is carried in high-density lipoprotein (HDL). HDL is considered the "good" cholesterol because a high HDL level seems to protect against heart attack. There is also strong evidence that low HDL levels are directly related to higher risk for heart disease. An HDL cholesterol level of 60 mg/dL and greater is considered high.

Low levels of HDL cholesterol can be caused by many factors. The most common are cigarette smoking, obesity, and lack of exercise. Fortunately, you can change all of these factors to increase your HDL level and reduce your risk of heart disease.

VLDLS AND TRIGLYCERIDES

Another lipoprotein that carries blood cholesterol is very-low-density lipoprotein (VLDL). VLDLs also carry most of the blood triglycerides. Triglycerides are other lipids found in the blood, as well as in the body's fat tissue. In fact, triglycerides make up most body fat. Fats found in foods—such as butter, margarine, and vegetable oil—are also triglycerides. As blood circulates, triglycerides are removed from VLDLs to be used for energy by cells or stored as body fat. The remaining lipoprotein particles are called VLDL remnants. These remnants can be taken up by the liver or transformed into low-density lipoprotein. Elevated VLDL cholesterol levels signal the potential need for cholesterol-lowering therapy.

High blood levels of triglycerides are associated with increased risk for heart disease. This is especially true when other risk factors are present, such as obesity, cigarette smoking, hypertension, diabetes, and low HDL cholesterol.

How Does Lowering Cholesterol Level Help Prevent Heart Disease?

High blood cholesterol plays a major role in heart disease. Many studies have shown that high blood cholesterol can be a cause of heart attack. We know that lowering blood cholesterol reduces both the risk of having a heart attack and the risk of dying from one. There is evidence that reducing blood cholesterol can slow, or sometimes even reverse, the accumulation of cholesterol in arteries in both men and women.

Many variables affect the amount of cholesterol your body produces and how much of it is in the form of LDL versus HDL cholesterol or triglycerides. By changing some of these variables, you can take control and reduce your level of blood cholesterol. If you make wise choices about the foods you eat and your lifestyle, you can lower your risk for heart disease. As a general rule, if you reduce your total cholesterol level by 1 percent, you reduce your heart attack risk by 2 percent. This means that if you reduce your blood cholesterol from 250 to 200 mg/dL (a 20 percent decrease), for example, you'd reduce your heart attack risk by 40 percent.

What's My Ideal Cholesterol Level?
Your physician has probably measured your levels of total blood cholesterol, LDL cholesterol, and HDL cholesterol. These blood cholesterol levels will show how you fit into the classifications on the following chart. These measurements help your doctor identify your risk of heart disease. In calculating your risk, he or she will also take into account your physical and medical history, as well as the presence of other risk factors.

Classification of Cholesterol Levels

TOTAL, IN MG/DL	LDL, IN MG/DL	TRIGLYCERIDES, IN MG/DL
Desirable: <200	Optimal: <100	Normal: <150
Borderline high: 200–239	Near optimal/ above optimal: 100–129	Borderline high: 150–199
High: ≥240		High: 200–499
	Borderline high: 130–159	Very high: ≥500
	High: ≥160–189	
	Very high: ≥190	

Your level of HDL, or "good," cholesterol may also be used to assess your risk of heart disease. An HDL level of 60 mg/dL and above is considered protective. Your doctor may be concerned if HDL is below 40 mg/dL.

If you've had a heart attack or have other major risk factors, lowering your LDL ("bad") cholesterol level to less than 100 mg/dL is extremely important. If you have two or more risk factors and don't have heart disease, you should try to reduce it to 130 mg/dL or less. If you have one or no risk factors and haven't had a heart attack, you should aim—at the very least—to reduce your total cholesterol level to below 240 and your LDL cholesterol level to below 160. The closer you can come to a total cholesterol level under 200, the better.

Talk with your doctor about your individual situation. If he or she recommends drug treatment, you will still need to modify your diet and lifestyle. The extent of those modifications will depend on how many other risk factors for heart disease are part of the equation.

How Diet and Exercise Affect Blood Cholesterol Levels

More and more studies show that you *can* take control of your blood cholesterol level by managing your diet and keeping active. How much you have to modify your diet and lifestyle to achieve these goals depends on several things, including your other risk factors and your individual response to changes in your diet. For many people, relatively minor changes can reduce their cholesterol levels significantly. Others need to make more extensive lifestyle changes.

The term "Therapeutic Lifestyle Changes" (TLC) refers to the specific things that you can do to help lower your LDL cholesterol. This term was coined by the panels of the National Cholesterol Education Program to identify their updated recommendations for cholesterol management for people at high risk for heart disease or those who already have it. The main components of these recommendations are described below

WHAT CAN INCREASE BLOOD CHOLESTEROL?

There are three main factors that increase your blood cholesterol level:

- Saturated fats and trans fats in your diet

- Cholesterol that your body makes and cholesterol from the food you eat

- Obesity

Saturated Fats and Trans Fats

Fats are composed of triglycerides and are more accurately called "fatty acids." These fatty acids fall into three categories: saturated (which includes trans fats), monounsaturated, and polyunsaturated. Of these three, only the saturated and trans fatty acids raise blood LDL cholesterol. In this book, the term "saturated fat" is used as shorthand for the more accurate term "saturated fatty acid." Likewise, we refer to monounsaturated and polyunsaturated fats rather than fatty acids.

Foods high in saturated fat come mostly from animal products and some plant products. The more saturated fat you eat, the greater the increase in blood LDL cholesterol levels. A high intake of saturated fat leads to a higher risk of heart disease.

Some people are unusually sensitive to saturated fat, and their blood cholesterol rises dramatically in response; others show less striking increases. Many people who already have high blood cholesterol seem to be especially sensitive to saturated fat, which may explain why their cholesterol levels are high. For people at high risk who need to lower their LDL cholesterol levels the most, we recommend that saturated fat make up less than 7 percent of the total calories consumed daily.

Trans fatty acids result from the process used to add hydrogen to oils to make them more solid. Some are found naturally in animal fats. Research has shown that intake of trans fat also raises blood LDL cholesterol. Therefore, it will also increase the risk of heart disease. For this reason, we recommend that intake of trans fats be kept as low as possible.

Cholesterol

Your body produces its own cholesterol, and you take in additional cholesterol by eating foods rich in cholesterol. It's important to distinguish between the cholesterol in your blood and the cholesterol in your food.

CHOLESTEROL IN YOUR BLOOD (SERUM CHOLESTEROL)

Cholesterol is made primarily by your liver, which manufactures enough to meet your body's needs. Some people's livers produce much more cholesterol than others. It is this cholesterol that is in your blood (called serum cholesterol) that is measured to determine your total cholesterol level and your LDL and HDL levels. The only way to determine these levels is to have them measured.

CHOLESTEROL IN YOUR FOOD
(DIETARY CHOLESTEROL)

The cholesterol in the foods you eat adds to the amount of cholesterol in your system. Most of this increase is in LDL cholesterol. Dietary cholesterol comes exclusively from animal products, such as egg yolks and organ meats. Some cholesterol is found in all meats, poultry, seafood, and animal fats, such as whole milk and lard. A high-cholesterol diet raises the blood cholesterol level—but the amount of that increase varies from person to person. If you are actively trying to reduce your blood cholesterol level or have heart disease, you should eat less than 200 mg cholesterol per day.

Overweight and Obesity

Overweight (BMI of 25 to 29.9) and obesity (BMI of 30 or more) predispose an individual to have high blood cholesterol. (See pages 5 to 7 for more information on BMI.) People who are overweight or obese are more likely to have heart disease and stroke. That's why it's important for anyone carrying excess weight to eat fewer calories and burn more calories in physical activity.

Studies show that most overweight and obese people have high levels of triglycerides and both LDL and VLDL cholesterol. In contrast, levels of HDL, or "good," cholesterol are usually low. When an overweight person eats a diet high in saturated fat and cholesterol, the level of blood LDL cholesterol usually rises even more. Sadly, this combination of overweight and a high-saturated-fat, high-cholesterol diet is common in this country. Losing weight—even as little as 10 pounds—can help reduce LDL cholesterol levels. If you or someone you love is overweight, discuss an appropriate weight-loss program with a health-care professional.

WHAT CAN LOWER YOUR BLOOD CHOLESTEROL?

There are three primary approaches to lowering your blood cholesterol levels:

• Diet

• Physical activity

• Drug therapy

Diet
As we have seen, the foods you eat definitely affect how much cholesterol circulates in your blood. By following a diet that includes less of the foods that contain cholesterol and saturated and trans fats and more of the foods that do not, most people will naturally reduce their blood choles-terol levels. Polyunsaturated and monounsaturated fats and complex carbohydrates are all helpful replacements for the harmful saturated and trans fats in your diet.

POLYUNSATURATED FATS

There are two types of polyunsaturated fatty acids. One type is composed of omega-6 fatty acids, found in many vegetable oils, such as safflower, sunflower, soybean, and corn. The other type is composed of omega-3 fatty acids, which are found in large amounts in some fish and fish oils in the form of eicosapentaenoic and docosahexaenoic acids (EPA and DHA), and in certain vegetable sources, such as soybean and canola oils and English walnuts, in the form of alpha linolenic acid.

Substituting polyunsaturated fats for saturated fats in your diet will help reduce your levels of LDL cholesterol and thereby reduce your risk of heart disease. Plan your meals so that you get up to 10 percent of your total calories from polyunsaturated fats.

MONOUNSATURATED FATS

Monounsaturated fat is present in plant oils and nuts. Research is ongoing, but studies have shown that when substituted for saturated fats, monounsaturated fats do lower blood LDL cholesterol and do not lower the protective HDL cholesterol. Monounsaturated fats can make up to 20 percent of your total calories.

CARBOHYDRATES

Studies show that when carbohydrates are used to replace saturated fats in the diet, LDL levels will fall. A diet very rich in carbohydrates, however, can reduce levels of helpful HDL cholesterol and increase triglycerides. Therefore, it is wise to limit your carbohydrate intake to 60 percent or less of total calories, or even less if you have the metabolic syndrome (see page 4 for information on this condition). Most important, your carbohydrates should come primarily from natural sources such as whole grains, vegetables, fruits, and fat-free dairy products, and not from highly processed baked goods.

OTHER DIETARY FACTORS TO CONSIDER

If the dietary changes above are not enough to lower LDL cholesterol to your target level, you may want to discuss other options with your doctor to find out how any of the following fit into your eating plan.

FIBER • Fiber is the part of food that we cannot digest. What is referred to as soluble fiber is really an indigestible complex carbohydrate, such as those found in oatmeal or oat bran. Studies show that eating between 5 and 10 grams of soluble fiber each day may help reduce LDL cholesterol by up to 5 percent when combined with a diet low in saturated fat and cholesterol. Insoluble fiber, however, does not significantly affect LDL cholesterol.

STANOLS/STEROLS • These substances are isolated from soybean and tall pine-tree oils. They are sometimes added to commercial margarines. Studies have shown that including stanols and/or sterols in your diet may help further reduce levels of blood LDL cholesterol.

SOY PROTEIN • Soy products are popular with many people looking for vegetarian options to replace food products that contain animal fats, which contain both saturated fat and dietary cholesterol. When included in a diet low in saturated fat and cholesterol, they can help lower blood levels of total and LDL cholesterol.

OMEGA-3 FATTY ACIDS • Research suggests that increased intake of omega-3 fatty acids—such as found in salmon, halibut, mackerel, and tuna—reduces the risk for coronary events. We recommend that you eat at least two servings per week of fish rich in omega-3 fatty acids. (For a list of recommended fish, see page 499.) For people who already have heart disease or high blood triglyceride levels, their healthcare professionals may recommend fish oil supplements to help increase their intake of omega-3 fatty acids.

Some types of fish may contain high levels of mercury, PCBs (polychlorinated biphenyls), dioxins, and other environmental contaminants. Shark, swordfish, tilefish (golden bass or golden snapper), and king mackerel are examples. Women who are pregnant, planning to become pregnant, or nursing — and young children—should avoid eating potentially contaminated fish.

ALCOHOL • Some studies have shown that *moderate* intake of alcohol may reduce risk for heart disease. At the same time, the many dangerous effects of *high* alcohol intake—such as high blood pressure, irregular heart beat, and weakened heart muscle—can far outweigh the benefits. If you do drink alcohol, do so in moderation (no more than one drink per day for women or two drinks per day for men). If you don't drink, don't start.

SODIUM • Often, people with high cholesterol also have high blood pressure. Reducing the amount of dietary sodium may help lower blood pressure or even prevent it from rising. Eating a healthy diet (see pages 17 to 19), being physically active, and limiting your sodium intake to 2,400 mg or less per day are the first steps to managing both high cholesterol and high blood pressure.

A STATEMENT ON HIGH-PROTEIN AND HIGH TOTAL-FAT WEIGHT-LOSS DIETS

Despite the surge in popularity of high-fat or high-protein diets, no clinical studies indicate that these diets lead to long-term weight loss. At the same time, there are concerns about the ill effects of these diets: High intake of saturated fats can raise harmful LDL cholesterol, and low intake of fruits, vegetables, and grains will not provide the important nutrients these foods offer.

Physical Activity

Regular, vigorous physical activity protects against heart disease. It increases the protective HDL cholesterol and, in some people, reduces LDL cholesterol and blood pressure. We recommend 30 to 60 minutes of moderate exercise on most days of the week. Even moderate levels of regular low-intensity physical activity, such as walking, dancing, and housework, are beneficial.

Talk with your physician before starting an exercise program, especially if you're middle-aged or older and haven't exercised for a long time. If you exercise in moderation, you will improve your overall health and help reduce your cholesterol levels.

Drug Therapy: When Diet and Exercise Are Not Enough

The best approach to managing cholesterol begins with a lifestyle that includes a diet low in saturated fat and cholesterol and adequate physical activity. Some people, however, cannot reduce their cholesterol to their target goal even after a period of carefully following an LDL-lowering diet, exercising as recommended, and losing excess weight. If you are in this situation, discuss your next options with your doctor.

Although diet is the best way to start, there are many drug treatments available that can act with a healthful diet to help you reduce your cholesterol and thereby your risk for heart disease. These drugs may be prescribed individually or in combination with other drugs. Some of the common types of cholesterol-lowering drugs include statins, resins, nicotinic acid (niacin), and fibric acids.

- **Statins** are very effective for lowering LDL ("bad") cholesterol levels and have few immediate short-term side effects. They work by interrupting the formation of cholesterol from the circulating blood.

- **Resins** are also called bile acid binding drugs. They work in the intestines by promoting increased disposal of cholesterol. There are three kinds of medications in this class: cholestyramine, colestipol, and coleseveiam.

- **Nicotinic acid** works in the liver by affecting the production of blood fats. It is used to lower triglycerides, lower LDL cholesterol, and raise HDL cholesterol.

- **Fibric acids** currently available include clofibrate and gemfibrozil. Clofibrate raises HDL cholesterol levels and lowers triglyceride levels. Gemfibrozil lowers blood fats and raises HDL cholesterol levels.

If your doctor does recommend cholesterol-lowering medications for you, be sure to take them as prescribed. Despite the known benefits of reducing blood cholesterol, many people with high cholesterol do not receive the treatment they need. Only half of the people who are given medications take them long enough to receive the full benefits. It can take from six months to one year for your cholesterol levels to show the effects of drug therapy. Be patient, continue to eat wisely, take your medication as needed, and know that you are doing your best to take care of your heart.

how to use these recipes

You have made the decision to eat wisely to take care of your heart health, and it is one of the best choices you can make. We invite you to use our recipes with creativity and common sense to build your own individual eating plan. Then if you eat too much of something one day, you can adjust your choices accordingly the next day.

Nutrition Analyses

With each recipe, you'll find a nutritional breakdown of the calorie count and the amounts of total fat, saturated fat, polyunsaturated fat, monounsaturated fat, cholesterol, sodium, carbohydrate, fiber, and protein. By reading this information carefully, you can choose the recipes that best meet your needs.

Keep the following information in mind as you review the nutrition analyses of these recipes:

- Each analysis is based on a single serving, unless otherwise indicated.

- Optional ingredients and garnishes are not included in any nutrition analysis unless noted. We encourage you to be creative with garnishes, especially with fruits and vegetables. If you eat them, however, remember to count them.

- Ingredients with a weight range (a 2- to 3-pound chicken, for example) were analyzed at the average weight.

- If a dash is used for a value, it means that accurate data for that nutrient were not available for at least one ingredient in the recipe.

- When a recipe lists two or more ingredient options (1 cup nonfat or low-fat yogurt, for example), the first was used in the nutrition analysis.

- The specific amounts of the ingredients listed, not the amounts sometimes shown in parentheses, were analyzed. The amounts in parentheses are guidelines to help you decide how much of an ingredient to purchase to prepare that recipe. For example, when a recipe calls for 3 tablespoons lime juice (about 2 limes), we analyzed the 3 tablespoons of juice, not the 2 limes. (We do not list the quantity in parentheses if only one, or part of one, item is needed.)

- Meat figures are based on cooked lean meat with all visible fat removed. For lean ground beef, we used 90 percent fat free.

- When a recipe calls for low-fat or reduced-fat cheese, we used cheese with no more than 3 grams of fat per serving. See "Understand Key Words on Food Packaging" (page 514) for more information on product labeling.

- The values for saturated, monounsaturated, and polyunsaturated fats may not add up to the total fat value. That's because numbers are rounded and values for other fatty substances, such as trans fat and glycerol, are not available.

- When a recipe calls for "acceptable stick margarine," we used corn oil margarine in the analysis. If you want an alternative, choose a margarine that lists liquid vegetable oil as the first ingredient.

- When a recipe calls for "acceptable vegetable oil," we used canola oil in the analysis. Polyunsaturated-rich oils such as corn, safflower, soybean, sunflower, sesame, and flaxseed are also acceptable. Acceptable monounsaturated-rich oils include olive, peanut, almond, and walnut oils.

- If a marinade was used for meat, poultry, or seafood, the nutrition analysis includes only the amount of marinade absorbed, based on U.S. Department of Agriculture (USDA) data on absorption. If the marinade is also used for basting or in a sauce or gravy, the nutrition analysis includes the full amounts of all ingredients. Absorption data is not available for vegetable marinades, so we added in the total amount of marinade used in the recipe.

- For recipes that include alcohol, we estimate that most of the alcohol calories have evaporated during cooking

- According to the USDA, there is virtually no difference in the nutritional values of fresh, frozen, and canned food when prepared for the table. When using frozen or canned foods, however, be sure to watch for added ingredients, such as salt or sugar, that will change the analysis. We call for no-salt products if available. If not, you can rinse and drain canned vegetables and beans to reduce the sodium content by 25 to 30 percent.

- The abbreviation for gram is "g"; the abbreviation for milligram is "mg." We also use "mg/dL" for "milligrams per deciliter."

Ingredients

We analyzed these recipes using the ingredients exactly as listed. Many ingredients, such as herbs, spices, and vinegars, can be interchanged for greater variety without substantially changing the nutritional value of the dish. We encourage you to experiment or substitute ingredients, as long as your choices do not add saturated fat, trans fat, cholesterol, or sodium.

Likewise, the nutrition analysis won't change if you use bottled or frozen lemon, lime, or orange juice versus fresh juice; dried versus fresh herbs; or packaged black pepper versus freshly ground. Fresh ingredients, however, almost always give you more flavor, so we have called for those in most cases.

To make shopping easier, we have listed commonly used ingredients and their weight and volume equivalents in Appendix E. For example, if you see "1 cup chopped onion" in a recipe, you'll know that you need to have one large onion on hand to prepare that dish.

◆

We hope you enjoy the delicious recipes and helpful information that follow. Whether you are reading this book to control your present cholesterol level or to prevent it from rising in the first place, we applaud your commitment to a lifetime of eating well to stay well.

Recipes

appetizers

Smoked Salmon Dip with Cucumber and Herbs

Creamy Caper Dip

Zucchini Spread

Southwestern Black Bean Spread

Crab Spring Rolls with Peanut Dipping Sauce

Toasted Ravioli with Italian Salsa

Canapés with Roasted Garlic, Artichoke, and Chèvre Spread

Orange-Ginger Chicken Skewers

Stuffed Chile Peppers

Stuffed Mushrooms

Zesty Potato Skins

Tomato Bursts

Tortilla Snacks

smoked salmon dip with cucumber and herbs

serves 16

Creamy and cool but with a slight smoky flavor, this dip is hard to resist. Surround it with bell peppers, carrots, jícama slices, and halved cherry tomatoes for a colorful presentation.

- 1 MEDIUM CUCUMBER, PEELED AND DICED
- 8 OUNCES FAT-FREE OR LIGHT SOUR CREAM
- 2 OUNCES SMOKED SALMON, RINSED, PATTED DRY WITH PAPER TOWELS, AND DICED
- 1 TABLESPOON FRESH SNIPPED DILLWEED OR 1 TEASPOON DRIED, CRUMBLED
- 1 TABLESPOON SNIPPED FRESH CHIVES OR 1 TEASPOON DRIED OR FINELY CHOPPED GREEN ONIONS (GREEN PART ONLY)
- 1 TEASPOON GRATED LEMON ZEST
- 1 TABLESPOON FRESH LEMON JUICE
- 1/4 TEASPOON PAPRIKA

PER SERVING

CALORIES 22	CHOLESTEROL 3 mg
TOTAL FAT 0.0 g	SODIUM 39 mg
SATURATED 0.0 g	CARBOHYDRATES 3 g
POLYUNSATURATED 0.0 g	FIBER 0 g
MONOUNSATURATED 0.0 g	PROTEIN 2 g

In a medium bowl, stir together all the ingredients except the paprika. Blend well. Transfer to a serving bowl. Smooth the top and sprinkle evenly with paprika.

Serve immediately, or cover and refrigerate for 30 minutes or up to two days to allow the flavors to blend.

Cook's Tip

Chives add a sophisticated look to a dish because they are fine and delicate. Green onions offer slightly more texture because of their larger size. When finely chopped, however, the tops of green onions offer the same mild onion flavor as chives.

Cook's Tip on Smoked Salmon

When shopping for smoked salmon, read nutrition labels and choose the product with the lowest sodium. Rinsing the salmon under cold water before use helps to remove some of the excess sodium.

creamy caper dip

serves 12

Pop everything in the blender and you'll have an elegant yet satisfying dip. You can serve it with chips or vegetables or as a topping for cucumber or tomato slices.

8 OUNCES FAT-FREE OR LOW-FAT PLAIN YOGURT
1/4 CUP FAT-FREE OR LIGHT MAYONNAISE DRESSING
3 TABLESPOONS CAPERS, RINSED AND DRAINED
2 TABLESPOONS DIJON MUSTARD
1 MEDIUM GARLIC CLOVE, MINCED
1 TABLESPOON OLIVE OIL (EXTRA-VIRGIN PREFERRED)

In a blender, process all the ingredients except the oil until smooth. Stir in the oil.

Cover and refrigerate until ready to serve, or up to 8 hours.

PER SERVING
CALORIES 29
TOTAL FAT 1.0 g
  SATURATED 0.0 g
  POLYUNSATURATED 0.0 g
  MONOUNSATURATED 1.0 g

CHOLESTEROL 0 mg
SODIUM 175 mg
CARBOHYDRATES 2 g
FIBER 0 g
PROTEIN 1 g

zucchini spread

serves 8

Serve this versatile spread with crackers, vegetable sticks, or rounds of crusty French bread. For an interesting sandwich, lightly coat the inside of a pita half with the spread, then stuff the pita with your favorite vegetables.

3 1/2 CUPS UNPEELED, SHREDDED ZUCCHINI (ABOUT 1 TO 1 1/4 POUNDS)

1/4 CUP FINELY SNIPPED FRESH PARSLEY OR CILANTRO

2 TABLESPOONS RED WINE VINEGAR

1 TABLESPOON OLIVE OIL

1 MEDIUM GARLIC CLOVE, MINCED

1/4 TEASPOON SALT

PEPPER TO TASTE

2 TABLESPOONS FINELY CHOPPED WALNUTS OR PECANS, DRY-ROASTED

Squeeze the zucchini to remove excess water. In a food processor or blender, process the zucchini and all other ingredients except the nuts until smooth, scraping the sides as needed.

Spoon the mixture into a serving bowl. Fold in the nuts. Cover and refrigerate before serving.

PER SERVING	
CALORIES 37	CHOLESTEROL 0 mg
TOTAL FAT 3.0 g	SODIUM 76 mg
SATURATED 0.5 g	CARBOHYDRATES 2 g
POLYUNSATURATED 1.0 g	FIBER 1 g
MONOUNSATURATED 1.5 g	PROTEIN 1 g

southwestern black bean spread

serves 12

Layered bean spreads are always popular at gather-
ings, so be sure you have plenty to go around. Serve
this zesty mixture on crisp jícama slices, toasted pita
bread, or baked tortilla chips. For a speedy snack,
spread on a warm tortilla, wrap, and go!

	15-OUNCE CAN NO-SALT-ADDED BLACK BEANS, RINSED IF DESIRED AND DRAINED
1/2	CUP ROASTED RED BELL PEPPERS, RINSED AND DRAINED IF BOTTLED
	4-OUNCE CAN DICED GREEN CHILES, RINSED AND DRAINED
2	TABLESPOONS FRESH LIME JUICE
2	MEDIUM GARLIC CLOVES, MINCED
1	TEASPOON GROUND CUMIN
1	TEASPOON ONION POWDER
1/4	TEASPOON SALT
1	LARGE TOMATO, DICED
1	SMALL AVOCADO, DICED (ABOUT 1/2 CUP)
1/2	CUP FAT-FREE SOUR CREAM
1	TABLESPOON FRESH LIME JUICE

In a food processor or blender, process the black
beans, peppers, chiles, 2 tablespoons lime juice,
garlic, cumin, onion powder, and salt for 15 to 20
seconds, or until the mixture is slightly chunky.

Process for 10 to 20 seconds more for a smoother texture. (Or, in a medium bowl, mash the ingredients with a potato masher to the desired texture.)

Spread the mixture evenly on a serving plate or in a shallow bowl. Top with the tomato and avocado.

In a small bowl, stir together the sour cream and 1 tablespoon lime juice. Drop by spoonfuls over the surface of the black bean spread for a decorative "dolloped" look, or smooth out the top surface.

Cook's Tip on Avocados

Avocados actually are fruits, not vegetables. They are high in fat, but most of that is monounsaturated, the same kind as in olive oil. Avocados contain more beta carotene than many other fruits and vegetables, are high in potassium, and are a fair source of dietary fiber. They are, however, high in calories. Look for avocados that are heavy for their size and yield to gentle pressure. If you have an avocado that feels too firm, let it ripen on the counter for a couple of days, or put it in a brown paper sack with a tomato or an apple to speed the process.

PER SERVING

CALORIES 60	CHOLESTEROL 2 mg
TOTAL FAT 1.0 g	SODIUM 100 mg
SATURATED 0.0 g	CARBOHYDRATES 10 g
POLYUNSATURATED 0.0 g	FIBER 2 g
MONOUNSATURATED 0.5 g	PROTEIN 3 g

crab spring rolls with peanut dipping sauce

serves 10

These golden-brown, crispy spring rolls are a treat in themselves—the sauce is a rich, fragrant bonus! Experiment with lean cooked chicken, ham, or beef instead of crab for variety. Find spring roll wrappers in an Asian grocery store (usually in the freezer section) or substitute egg roll wrappers.

SPRING ROLLS

VEGETABLE OIL SPRAY

4 CUPS SHREDDED CABBAGE (ABOUT 1 POUND)

1 MEDIUM CARROT, SHREDDED

2 GREEN ONIONS (GREEN AND WHITE PARTS), THINLY SLICED

4 OUNCES IMITATION CRABMEAT

2 TEASPOONS PLAIN RICE VINEGAR

1 TEASPOON LOW-SALT SOY SAUCE

10 SPRING ROLL WRAPPERS (8 X 8 INCH)

WHITE OF 1 LARGE EGG, LIGHTLY BEATEN

DIPPING SAUCE

3 TABLESPOONS REDUCED-FAT PEANUT BUTTER

3 TABLESPOONS PLAIN RICE VINEGAR

2 TABLESPOONS LOW-SALT SOY SAUCE

2 TABLESPOONS WATER

1/2 TEASPOON TOASTED SESAME OIL

1 GREEN ONION (GREEN PART ONLY), THINLY SLICED

Heat a large skillet over medium-high heat for 1 or 2 minutes. Remove from the heat and lightly spray with vegetable oil spray (being careful not to spray near a gas flame). Return the skillet to the heat and cook the cabbage for 1 to 2 minutes, stirring occasionally.

Add the carrot and green onions; cook for 1 minute, stirring occasionally.

Stir in the crabmeat, vinegar, and soy sauce; cook for about 30 seconds, or until the crabmeat is warmed through. Remove from the heat and refrigerate for at least 30 minutes.

Preheat the oven to 400°F.

To assemble the spring rolls, place a spring roll wrapper on a flat surface, with one point of the wrapper pointing toward you. Spoon about 1/3 cup of the filling up the middle of the wrapper. Bring the bottom point of the wrapper over

PER SERVING	
CALORIES 80	
TOTAL FAT 2.0 g	CHOLESTEROL 6 mg
	SODIUM 144 mg
SATURATED 0.5 g	CARBOHYDRATES 11 g
POLYUNSATURATED 0.5 g	FIBER 2 g
MONOUNSATURATED 1.0 g	PROTEIN 5 g

the filling. Lightly brush the two side points of the wrapper with egg white. Bring the side points into the center of the wrapper (wrapper will look like an unsealed envelope). Starting from the bottom, roll the wrapper up to the top point so the filling is enclosed. Lightly brush the top point with egg white and press to make sure the spring roll is sealed. Lightly spray the outside of the spring roll with vegetable oil spray and put on a baking sheet. Repeat with the remaining wrappers.

Bake for 25 to 30 minutes, or until the wrappers turn a light golden-brown.

Meanwhile, in a medium bowl, whisk together the dipping sauce ingredients except the green onion. Sprinkle the dipping sauce with the green onion and serve with the baked spring rolls.

Cook's Tip

You can assemble spring rolls and keep them in the refrigerator for up to eight hours before baking or for up to two months in the freezer. (Do not thaw before baking.) The dipping sauce will keep for up to two days in the refrigerator, the filling for up to four days.

toasted ravioli with italian salsa

These tempting tidbits, traditionally deep-fried but baked in this recipe, boast an interesting fusion twist—a salsa flavored with herbs common to the Italian kitchen.

1	POUND FROZEN BEEF RAVIOLI (30 PIECES)
	VEGETABLE OIL SPRAY
1/4	CUP FAT-FREE OR LIGHT ITALIAN SALAD DRESSING
1/2	CUP PLAIN DRY BREAD CRUMBS
1 1/2	TEASPOONS SALT-FREE ITALIAN HERB SEASONING

ITALIAN SALSA

	14.5-OUNCE CAN NO-SALT-ADDED TOMATOES WITH JUICE
1/2	SMALL RED ONION, QUARTERED
1	HOT BANANA PEPPER OR 1/2 SMALL GREEN BELL PEPPER, SEEDS AND RIBS DISCARDED
1	TABLESPOON CHOPPED FRESH OREGANO OR 1 TEASPOON DRIED, CRUMBLED
1	TABLESPOON FRESH BASIL OR 1 TEASPOON DRIED, CRUMBLED
1	MEDIUM GARLIC CLOVE, HALVED
1	TEASPOON BALSAMIC OR RED WINE VINEGAR
1/4	TEASPOON SUGAR

Prepare the ravioli using the package directions, omitting the salt and oil. Drain in a colander. Cool for at least 10 minutes.

Meanwhile, lightly spray two baking sheets with vegetable oil spray. Using a pastry brush, lightly coat the top of each ravioli with the dressing. Put the ravioli on the baking sheets.

In a small bowl or cup, combine the bread crumbs and herb seasoning. Sprinkle over the ravioli. (The ravioli can be refrigerated for up to 8 hours at this point.)

In a food processor or blender, process the salsa ingredients for 15 to 20 seconds. (Salsa will keep in the refrigerator for up to four days.)

Preheat the oven to 400°F.

Lightly spray the tops of the ravioli with vegetable oil spray. Bake the ravioli for 9 to 11 minutes. Drizzle the salsa over the ravioli or use the salsa for dipping.

Cook's Tip

Some prepared ravioli may be high in sodium and saturated fat. When shopping, select the one with the lowest sodium and fat values.

PER SERVING	
CALORIES 133	CHOLESTEROL 8 mg
TOTAL FAT 2.0 g	SODIUM 259 mg
SATURATED 1.0 g	CARBOHYDRATES 24 g
POLYUNSATURATED 0.0 g	FIBER 2 g
MONOUNSATURATED 0.0 g	PROTEIN 6 g

canapés with roasted garlic, artichoke, and chèvre spread

serves 18

Planning is the secret to easy entertaining! Make the spread for these canapés up to three days in advance for quick and easy assembly shortly before guests arrive.

6	7-INCH PITA BREADS
6	MEDIUM GARLIC CLOVES, UNPEELED
	14-OUNCE CAN ARTICHOKE HEARTS, RINSED, DRAINED, AND CHOPPED
1/2	CUP FAT-FREE OR LIGHT MAYONNAISE DRESSING
2	OUNCES SOFT CHÈVRE OR GOAT CHEESE
1/8	TEASPOON WHITE PEPPER
2	TABLESPOONS SNIPPED FRESH CHIVES OR THINLY SLICED GREEN ONIONS (GREEN PART ONLY)
18	CHERRY TOMATOES, HALVED

Preheat the oven to 350°F.

Cut each pita into sixths. (Don't separate the bottoms from the tops.) Put the pita pieces in a single layer on an ungreased baking sheet.

PER SERVING

CALORIES 80	CHOLESTEROL 1 mg
TOTAL FAT 1.0 g	SODIUM 212 mg
SATURATED 0.5 g	CARBOHYDRATES 14 g
POLYUNSATURATED 0.0 g	FIBER 1 g
MONOUNSATURATED 0.0 g	PROTEIN 3 g

Put the garlic in a garlic roaster or any small ovenproof pan and place on the bottom oven rack. Bake for 5 minutes.

Put the pita pieces on a rack in the middle of the oven. Bake for 10 minutes. Remove the garlic and pitas from the oven. (Leave the oven on.) Let cool for 10 minutes.

Cut off the stem ends of the garlic. Squeeze the garlic out onto a cutting board, discarding the peel. Mince the garlic.

In a medium bowl, stir together the garlic, artichokes, mayonnaise, chèvre, and pepper.

To assemble the canapés, spread about 1 teaspoon of the artichoke mixture on each slice of pita. Sprinkle with the chives. Press a cherry tomato half with cut side up into the artichoke mixture. Put the canapés on an ungreased baking sheet.

Bake for 5 minutes and serve.

Cook's Tip on Roasted Garlic

Add roasted and peeled garlic cloves to your favorite spaghetti sauce or stew, mashed potatoes, or cold pasta salad. Puree roasted and peeled garlic and brush it on toast, corn on the cob, or pizza dough before you add the sauce and toppings.

orange-ginger chicken skewers

serves 10

A delightful variation from backyard barbecue, these standouts on a stick get their tangy flavor from fruit and ginger.

VEGETABLE OIL SPRAY

12 OUNCES BONELESS, SKINLESS CHICKEN BREASTS, ALL VISIBLE FAT DISCARDED

1/2 CUP PREPARED BARBECUE SAUCE

1/4 CUP BLACKBERRY ALL-FRUIT SPREAD

2 TEASPOONS GRATED ORANGE ZEST

1 TEASPOON GRATED PEELED GINGERROOT

Soak twenty 6- to 8-inch bamboo skewers in cold water for at least 10 minutes.

Preheat the broiler. Lightly spray the broiler pan and rack with vegetable oil spray.

Cut the chicken into 40 thin strips. Thread 2 strips onto each skewer in an "s" shape.

In a small bowl, whisk together the remaining ingredients until smooth. (If the spread is too

PER SERVING	
CALORIES 79	CHOLESTEROL 20 mg
TOTAL FAT 0.5 g	SODIUM 108 mg
SATURATED 0.0 g	CARBOHYDRATES 9 g
POLYUNSATURATED 0.0 g	FIBER 0 g
MONOUNSATURATED 0.0 g	PROTEIN 0 g

lumpy, microwave on high for 15 seconds, stir, and microwave for another 15 seconds, or until smooth.) Pour a quarter of the sauce into a separate bowl to serve separately. Baste the chicken with about 1/4 cup sauce.

Broil the skewers for 2 minutes. Turn and baste with about 1/4 cup sauce. Broil for 2 minutes, or until the chicken is no longer pink in the center. Baste with the remaining sauce.

Place the skewers on a platter. Serve with the extra sauce for dipping on the side.

stuffed chile peppers

serves 7

Jalapeños, the most popular and readily available chile peppers, range from hot to very hot. Lessen the intensity of these short green peppers by removing the ribs, or membranes, and the seeds.

- 8 OUNCES FAT-FREE OR LOW-FAT COTTAGE CHEESE, RINSED AND DRAINED
- 2 TABLESPOONS FINELY CHOPPED RED BELL PEPPER
- 2 TABLESPOONS SNIPPED CHIVES OR FINELY CHOPPED GREEN ONIONS (GREEN PART ONLY)
- 1 MEDIUM GARLIC CLOVE, MINCED
- 1/8 TEASPOON SALT
- 14 JALAPEÑO PEPPERS, HALVED LENGTHWISE, SEEDS AND RIBS DISCARDED

In a food processor or blender, process the cottage cheese until smooth, scraping the sides as necessary.

Transfer the cottage cheese to a small bowl. Stir in the remaining ingredients except the jalapeños.

Spoon the mixture into the jalapeño halves. (A small spoon, such as a baby spoon, works best.) Cover and refrigerate until serving time.

PER SERVING	
CALORIES 63	
TOTAL FAT 0.0 g	CHOLESTEROL 3 mg
SATURATED 0.0 g	SODIUM 127 mg
POLYUNSATURATED 0.0 g	CARBOHYDRATES 10 g
MONOUNSATURATED 0.0 g	FIBER 0 g
	PROTEIN 6 g

Cook's Tip on Hot Peppers

Hot chile peppers contain oils that can burn your skin, lips, and eyes. Wear rubber gloves or wash your hands thoroughly with warm, soapy water immediately after handling peppers.

stuffed mushrooms

These hot appetizers are an ideal party food. Prepare them an hour in advance and pop them in the oven as your guests arrive. The aroma is mouthwatering!

18	LARGE FRESH MUSHROOMS
1	TEASPOON OLIVE OIL
1/4	CUP MINCED ONION
1/4	CUP FINELY CHOPPED WALNUTS
1	MEDIUM GARLIC CLOVE, MINCED
1	SHREDDED WHEAT BISCUIT, CRUSHED
1	TABLESPOON GRATED OR SHREDDED PARMESAN CHEESE
1/2	TEASPOON SALT-FREE ITALIAN SEASONING
	PEPPER TO TASTE
1/2	TEASPOON PAPRIKA

Preheat the oven to 350°F.

Cut and discard a thin slice from the stem end of each mushroom. Remove and finely chop the remainder of the stems.

PER SERVING

CALORIES 80	CHOLESTEROL 1 mg
TOTAL FAT 4.5 g	SODIUM 23 mg
SATURATED 0.5 g	CARBOHYDRATES 8 g
POLYUNSATURATED 2.5 g	FIBER 2 g
MONOUNSATURATED 1.0 g	PROTEIN 4 g

Heat a nonstick skillet over medium-high heat. Pour the oil into the skillet and swirl to coat the bottom. Cook the mushroom stems, onion, walnuts, and garlic for 4 to 5 minutes, or until the onion is tender, stirring occasionally.

Remove from the heat. Stir in the remaining ingredients except the paprika.

Spoon the stuffing into the mushroom caps, packing the mixture firmly. Place the mushrooms in a shallow baking dish. Sprinkle tops lightly with the paprika.

Bake for 20 to 25 minutes, or until the mushrooms are tender and heated through.

zesty potato skins

serves 8

Visually appealing and delicious, these filled potato skins are perfect for entertaining or snacking. Spiced with Southwestern flair, they're a great alternative to the usual chips and dip.

6	MEDIUM RED POTATOES, BAKED (ABOUT 1 1/4 POUNDS)
	VEGETABLE OIL SPRAY
1/2	TEASPOON GARLIC POWDER
1/2	TEASPOON CHILI POWDER
1/2	TEASPOON GROUND CUMIN
1/8	TEASPOON PEPPER
8	OUNCES FAT-FREE OR LOW-FAT COTTAGE CHEESE, UNDRAINED
1/2	TEASPOON GRATED LIME ZEST
1 1/2	TABLESPOONS FRESH LIME JUICE
1	TEASPOON DRIED CHIVES
1/4	TEASPOON CHILI POWDER
24	BLACK OLIVE SLICES (4 LARGE OLIVES)

Preheat the oven to 450°F.

PER SERVING

CALORIES 73	CHOLESTEROL 1 mg
TOTAL FAT 0.5 g	SODIUM 117 mg
SATURATED 0.0 g	CARBOHYDRATES 14 g
POLYUNSATURATED 0.0 g	FIBER 2 g
MONOUNSATURATED 0.0 g	PROTEIN 6 g

Cut each potato in half. Scoop out the center, leaving about 1/4 inch of potato on the inside of each skin. Cut the skins into quarters. Lightly spray the insides of the skins with vegetable oil spray.

In a small bowl, combine the garlic powder, 1/2 teaspoon chili powder, cumin, and pepper. Sprinkle the mixture evenly on the insides of the potatoes. Place the skins with skin side down on a baking sheet.

Bake for 15 to 20 minutes, or until lightly browned.

Meanwhile, in a food processor or blender, process the remaining ingredients except the olives until smooth.

Spoon about 1 teaspoon of the cottage cheese mixture onto each potato skin and top with an olive slice.

tomato bursts

These tasty little tomato bites are stuffed with zesty kalamata olives, herbs, and fresh garlic.

- 2 OUNCES FAT-FREE OR REDUCED-FAT CREAM CHEESE
- 12 KALAMATA OLIVES, DRAINED AND FINELY CHOPPED
- 3 TABLESPOONS MINCED GREEN ONIONS (GREEN AND WHITE PARTS)
- 1 TEASPOON DRIED BASIL, CRUMBLED
- 1 MEDIUM GARLIC CLOVE, MINCED
- 1/8 TEASPOON SALT
- 32 CHERRY TOMATOES (ABOUT 1 POUND)

In a small bowl, stir together all the ingredients except the tomatoes to blend thoroughly.

Cut a slice from the top of each tomato. Using a 1/4-teaspoon measuring spoon, scoop out the pulp. (To remove any remaining seeds or loose pulp, run the tomatoes under cold water and drain upside down on paper towels.)

Fill each tomato with 1 teaspoon of the cream-cheese mixture. Cover and refrigerate until ready to serve, or up to 8 hours.

PER SERVING	
CALORIES 40	CHOLESTEROL 1 mg
TOTAL FAT 1.5 g	SODIUM 170 mg
SATURATED 0.0 g	CARBOHYDRATES 5 g
POLYUNSATURATED 0.5 g	FIBER 1 g
MONOUNSATURATED 1.0 g	PROTEIN 2 g

tortilla snacks

Whether you're watching a video or sporting event or having an impromptu get-together, this heart-healthy version of a classic snack is quick to assemble and oh–so–easy to eat.

1	CUP FINELY CHOPPED TOMATOES
1/4	CUP FINELY SNIPPED FRESH CILANTRO
2	TABLESPOONS MINCED GREEN ONIONS (GREEN AND WHITE PARTS)
1	TABLESPOON FRESH LIME JUICE
1/4	TEASPOON SALT
1/8	TEASPOON CAYENNE
1/3	CUP FAT-FREE SOUR CREAM
1/2	TEASPOON GROUND CUMIN
4	6-INCH CORN TORTILLAS
1/2	CUP SHREDDED REDUCED-FAT SHARP CHEDDAR CHEESE

Preheat the oven to 475°F.

In a medium bowl, stir together the tomatoes, cilantro, green onions, lime juice, salt, and cayenne. Set aside.

PER SERVING	
CALORIES 57	CHOLESTEROL 5 mg
TOTAL FAT 1.5 g	SODIUM 143 mg
SATURATED 1.0 g	CARBOHYDRATES 8 g
POLYUNSATURATED 0.0 g	FIBER 1 g
MONOUNSATURATED 0.5 g	PROTEIN 3 g

In a small bowl, stir together the sour cream and cumin. Set aside.

Put the tortillas on a baking sheet. Sprinkle with the cheese.

Bake for 3 minutes. Cut each tortilla into fourths.

To assemble, drain the tomato mixture in a sieve or colander. Spoon about 1 tablespoon of the tomato mixture onto each wedge. Top each with 1 teaspoon sour-cream mixture. Serve immediately.

Cook's Tip

Both the tomato mixture and the sour-cream mixture may be made up to four hours in advance.

soups

Light and Lemony Spinach Soup

Country-Style Vegetable Soup

Tomato, Orange, and Tarragon Soup

Creamy Wild Rice and Wheat Berry Soup

Silky Winter Squash Soup

Summertime Soup

Clam and Potato Chowder with Fresh Herbs

Lobster Bisque with Leeks and Shallots

Chicken and Spinach Enchilada Soup

Lentil-Spinach Soup

Hot and Sour Soup with Exotic Mushrooms

Gumbo with Greens and Ham

light and lemony spinach soup

serves 2

The intriguing flavor combination makes this soup a wonderful choice for entertaining. It looks beautiful, and it's so easy to prepare!

- 2 CUPS FAT-FREE, LOW-SODIUM CHICKEN BROTH
- 2 TEASPOONS FRESH LEMON JUICE
- 1/4 TEASPOON DRIED THYME, CRUMBLED
- 1/8 TEASPOON SALT (OPTIONAL)
- 4 LEAVES SPINACH OR OTHER GREENS, SUCH AS ESCAROLE, TORN
- 1 GREEN ONION (GREEN PART ONLY), THINLY SLICED

In a 1–quart saucepan, bring the broth, lemon juice, thyme, and salt to a boil over high heat.

Meanwhile, put the spinach in bowls.

Pour the hot soup over the spinach. Top the soup with the green onion. Serve immediately.

PER SERVING

CALORIES 18	CHOLESTEROL 0 mg
TOTAL FAT 0.0 g	SODIUM 77 mg
SATURATED 0.0 g	CARBOHYDRATES 2 g
POLYUNSATURATED 0.0 g	FIBER 1 g
MONOUNSATURATED 0.0 g	PROTEIN 3 g

country-style vegetable soup

A great anytime dish, this hearty soup contains an abundance of fresh vegetables.

- **1 POUND WHITE OR RED POTATOES, CHOPPED**
- **4 LARGE CARROTS, CHOPPED**
- **3 MEDIUM RIBS OF CELERY WITH LEAVES, CHOPPED**
- **2 MEDIUM ZUCCHINI, CHOPPED**
- **1 MEDIUM ONION, CHOPPED**
- **1/4 CUP MINCED FRESH PARSLEY**
- **2 BAY LEAVES**
- **1/4 TEASPOON SALT (OPTIONAL)**
- **PEPPER TO TASTE**
- **6 CUPS FAT-FREE, LOW-SODIUM CHICKEN BROTH**
- **3/4 CUP SHREDDED FAT-FREE OR REDUCED-FAT CHEDDAR CHEESE**

In a large, heavy saucepan or Dutch oven, combine the potatoes, carrots, celery, zucchini, onion, parsley, bay leaves, salt, and pepper.

PER SERVING

CALORIES 80	CHOLESTEROL 1 mg
TOTAL FAT 0.0 g	SODIUM 128 mg
SATURATED 0.0 g	CARBOHYDRATES 15 g
POLYUNSATURATED 0.0 g	FIBER 3 g
MONOUNSATURATED 0.0 g	PROTEIN 7 g

Stir in the broth. Bring to a boil over high heat. Reduce the heat and simmer, covered, for 45 to 60 minutes, or until the vegetables are very tender. Remove the bay leaves.

Ladle the soup into bowls and top with the cheese.

Cook's Tip

If you like the crunch of celery, don't add it to the soup until about 10 minutes before serving.

tomato, orange, and tarragon soup

Establish your culinary reputation with this unusual and refreshing soup that can be served hot or cold.

1	TEASPOON ACCEPTABLE VEGETABLE OIL
12	OUNCES WHITE OR RED POTATOES, PEELED AND DICED
1	MEDIUM ONION, SLICED
3	LARGE TOMATOES, CHOPPED
2	CUPS FAT-FREE, LOW-SODIUM CHICKEN BROTH
2	TABLESPOONS CHOPPED FRESH TARRAGON OR 2 TEASPOONS DRIED, CRUMBLED
1	MEDIUM GARLIC CLOVE, CRUSHED
1/4	TEASPOON SALT
	PEPPER TO TASTE
1	TEASPOON GRATED ORANGE ZEST
1	CUP FRESH ORANGE JUICE
	FRESH TARRAGON OR PARSLEY SPRIGS (OPTIONAL)

PER SERVING

CALORIES 98

TOTAL FAT 1.0 g

  SATURATED 0.0 g

  POLYUNSATURATED 0.5 g

  MONOUNSATURATED 0.5 g

CHOLESTEROL 0 mg

SODIUM 127 mg

CARBOHYDRATES 21 g

FIBER 3 g

PROTEIN 4 g

Heat a heavy nonstick saucepan over medium-high heat. Pour the oil into the saucepan and swirl to coat the bottom. Cook the potatoes and onion for 2 to 3 minutes, or until the onion is tender.

Stir in the tomatoes, broth, tarragon, garlic, salt, and pepper. Bring to a boil over high heat. Reduce the heat and simmer, covered, for 20 to 25 minutes, or until the vegetables are tender.

In a food processor or blender, process the soup in small batches until liquefied. Pour through a sieve to remove coarse skins. Discard the skins.

Stir the orange zest and juice into the strained soup. Reheat or serve chilled. Garnish with the fresh tarragon if desired.

Cook's Tip on Grated Orange Zest

Use a tool called a rasp zester or citrus zester to grate citrus rind easily. Be careful not to cut into the bitter pith, or white part, of the skin. An average medium orange yields 1 to 2 tablespoons of grated zest. Since this recipe uses only 1 teaspoon, you'll have some to freeze for another dish.

creamy wild rice and wheat berry soup

serves 4

Wild rice isn't a rice at all—it's the nutty-flavored seed of an annual marsh grass. If you can't locate wheat berries or millet, use an additional 1/4 cup of wild rice instead.

1/4	**CUP WILD RICE**
1/4	**CUP WHEAT BERRIES OR MILLET**
2	**CUPS WATER**
1	**CUP FAT-FREE, LOW-SODIUM CHICKEN BROTH**
1	**CUP CHOPPED ONION**
1	**CUP CHOPPED CELERY**
2	**MEDIUM GARLIC CLOVES, MINCED**
1/2	**TEASPOON CURRY POWDER**
1/4	**TEASPOON PEPPER**
	12-OUNCE CAN FAT-FREE EVAPORATED MILK
2	**TABLESPOONS DRY SHERRY (OPTIONAL)**
4	**VERY THIN LEMON SLICES (OPTIONAL)**
2	**TABLESPOONS SNIPPED FRESH PARSLEY (OPTIONAL)**

PER SERVING

CALORIES 178	CHOLESTEROL 4 mg
TOTAL FAT 0.5 g	SODIUM 158 mg
SATURATED 0.0 g	CARBOHYDRATES 33 g
POLYUNSATURATED 0.0 g	FIBER 4 g
MONOUNSATURATED 0.0 g	PROTEIN 12 g

Put the rice and wheat berries in a colander. Rinse under running water and drain well.

In a large saucepan, bring the rice, wheat berries, water, broth, onion, celery, garlic, curry powder, and pepper to a boil over high heat. Reduce the heat and simmer, covered, for 1 hour, or until the rice is tender.

Stir in the milk and sherry if desired. Heat through.

Ladle the soup into bowls and garnish with lemon slices and parsley if desired.

Cook's Tip on Reducing the Sodium in Canned Broth

If all you have on hand is canned broth that is high in sodium, here is an easy fix: Substitute water for a little less than half the can of broth.

Cook's Tip on Sprouted Wheat Berries

Look for sprouted wheat berries in the produce section of large supermarkets or at health food stores. Use them instead of nuts for crunch in salads or sandwiches, or lightly cook them in a skillet and toss with cooked vegetables.

silky winter squash soup

Chase away a winter chill with this soothing soup. Acorn squash and aromatic vegetables are roasted and then pureed until smooth as silk.

- 1 POUND ACORN SQUASH
- 1 MEDIUM ONION, HALVED
- 2 MEDIUM RIBS OF CELERY, CUT INTO 2-INCH PIECES
- 1/2 CUP BABY CARROTS
- OLIVE OIL SPRAY
- 4 MEDIUM GARLIC CLOVES, WHOLE AND UNPEELED
- 3 CUPS FAT-FREE, LOW-SODIUM CHICKEN BROTH, DIVIDED USE
- 1/4 CUP FAT-FREE HALF-AND-HALF
- 1/4 TEASPOON GROUND CUMIN
- 1/4 TEASPOON SALT
- 1/4 TEASPOON PEPPER

Preheat the oven to 350°F.

Cut the squash in half lengthwise. Using a spoon, scoop out and discard the seeds.

PER SERVING	
CALORIES 82	CHOLESTEROL 0 mg
TOTAL FAT 0.5 g	SODIUM 234 mg
SATURATED 0.0 g	CARBOHYDRATES 18 g
POLYUNSATURATED 0.0 g	FIBER 3 g
MONOUNSATURATED 0.0 g	PROTEIN 4 g

Place the squash with flesh side up and the onion halves with cut side up in a nonstick 13 x 9 x 2-inch baking pan. Add the celery and carrots. Lightly spray the vegetables with olive oil spray.

Bake, uncovered, for 45 minutes, or until the vegetables are almost done (just past tender-crisp).

Add the garlic cloves.

Bake for 15 minutes, or until the vegetables are tender when pierced with a sharp knife. Put the pan on a cooling rack and let cool for 10 minutes.

Using a spoon, scoop the flesh from the squash. Peel the garlic.

In a food processor or blender, process the squash, onion, celery, carrots, garlic, and 1 cup chicken broth for 1 to 2 minutes, or until smooth, scraping down the sides of the work bowl occasionally.

In a medium saucepan, bring the squash mixture, 2 cups chicken broth, and the remaining ingredients to a simmer over medium-high heat, stirring occasionally. Reduce the heat and simmer, uncovered, for 5 to 6 minutes, or until the flavors have blended and the soup is warmed through, stirring occasionally.

Cook's Tip on Defatting Broth

To defat homemade or canned broth, refrigerate it to allow the fat to harden. (Leave commercially prepared broth in the unopened can.) Remove and discard the fat before using the broth.

summertime soup

Soup made with melons? You bet! Serve this chilled creation in pretty bowls at your next summertime brunch—its refreshing taste will delight your guests.

- 1   SMALL RIPE CANTALOUPE, PEELED, SEEDED, AND CUBED
- 2   LARGE RIPE MANGOES, PEELED AND CUBED
- 2   MEDIUM PEACHES, PEELED AND CUBED
- 3   CUPS FRESH OR FROZEN UNSWEETENED STRAWBERRIES (ABOUT 16 OUNCES)
- 1/2   CUP FAT-FREE OR LOW-FAT PLAIN YOGURT
- 1/3   CUP FROZEN ORANGE JUICE CONCENTRATE
- 1/3   CUP PORT
- 2   TABLESPOONS ORANGE LIQUEUR
- 1   TABLESPOON FRESH LIME JUICE
- 1 1/2   TEASPOONS RASPBERRY VINEGAR
- 1/2   CUP FAT-FREE OR LOW-FAT PLAIN YOGURT, WELL CHILLED

In a food processor or blender, process all the ingredients except 1/2 cup yogurt until thick and

PER SERVING	
CALORIES 192	CHOLESTEROL 1 mg
TOTAL FAT 0.5 g	SODIUM 48 mg
SATURATED 0.0 g	CARBOHYDRATES 40 g
POLYUNSATURATED 0.0 g	FIBER 4 g
MONOUNSATURATED 0.0 g	PROTEIN 4 g

creamy. Pour into a serving bowl and freeze for about 20 minutes.

Spoon into individual bowls and top each serving with a heaping teaspoon of yogurt. Serve immediately.

Cook's Tip on Cutting Mangoes

Place the mango on its flattest side. Using a sharp knife, make a horizontal cut to slice off approximately the top half of the mango. (You won't be able to cut the fruit exactly in half because of the large pit.) Turn the mango over, pit side down. Slice off the top part of the second side. Remove the peel from all three pieces. Trim any remaining fruit from the pit.

clam and potato chowder with fresh herbs

Our good-for-your-heart chowder boasts an abundance of fresh herbs and tastes as rich as the New England original.

1/2	PINT SHUCKED FRESH CLAMS (8 OUNCES) OR 6.5-OUNCE CAN MINCED CLAMS
	WATER IF NEEDED
1	MEDIUM POTATO, PEELED AND FINELY CHOPPED
1	MEDIUM TURNIP, PEELED AND FINELY CHOPPED
4	MEDIUM SHALLOTS OR 1 MEDIUM ONION, CHOPPED
1/2	TEASPOON LOW-SODIUM CHICKEN BOUILLON GRANULES
1/8	TEASPOON PEPPER
2	12-OUNCE CANS FAT-FREE EVAPORATED MILK, DIVIDED USE
2	TABLESPOONS ALL-PURPOSE FLOUR
2	TEASPOONS CHOPPED FRESH MARJORAM OR OREGANO
1	TEASPOON CHOPPED FRESH THYME

Chop the fresh clams, reserving the juice. Set aside. Strain the clam juice to remove bits of shell. If using canned clams, drain the clams and reserve the juice. If necessary, add water to the clam juice to equal 1 cup.

In a medium saucepan, bring the clam juice, potato, turnip, shallots, bouillon granules, and pepper to a boil over high heat. Reduce the heat and simmer, covered, for 10 minutes, or until the vegetables are tender.

Stir in 2 1/2 cups evaporated milk.

In a jar with a tight-fitting lid, combine the remaining evaporated milk and the flour. Cover and shake until completely blended. Stir into the potato mixture. Cook over medium heat for 5 minutes, or until thickened and bubbly, stirring frequently.

Add the clams. Cook, for 1 minute, stirring frequently. Stir in the marjoram and thyme just before serving.

PER SERVING

CALORIES 256	CHOLESTEROL 19 mg
TOTAL FAT 0.5 g	SODIUM 295 mg
SATURATED 0.0 g	CARBOHYDRATES 41 g
POLYUNSATURATED 0.0 g	FIBER 2 g
MONOUNSATURATED 0.0 g	PROTEIN 22 g

lobster bisque with leeks and shallots

serves 4

A restaurant-quality, heart-healthy soup that is creamy, rich-tasting, and full of chunks of delicate lobster meat—this elegant soup is a dream come true! Cooking the lobster in the shell adds flavor to the base of the soup. Serve with dainty oyster crackers for a bit of crunch.

1/2	CUP DRY WHITE WINE (REGULAR OR NONALCOHOLIC), VERMOUTH, OR FAT-FREE, LOW-SODIUM CHICKEN BROTH
1/2	CUP FAT-FREE, LOW-SODIUM CHICKEN BROTH
2	FRESH OR FROZEN LOBSTER TAILS (ABOUT 4 OUNCES EACH), THAWED IF FROZEN
2	TEASPOONS LIGHT TUB MARGARINE
2	LEEKS (WHITE PART ONLY), FINELY CHOPPED
2	MEDIUM RIBS OF CELERY, FINELY CHOPPED
4	MEDIUM SHALLOTS, PEELED AND FINELY CHOPPED
1 1/2	CUPS FAT-FREE, LOW-SODIUM CHICKEN BROTH
1	CUP FAT-FREE HALF-AND-HALF
1/3	CUP ALL-PURPOSE FLOUR
1/4	TEASPOON WHITE PEPPER
2	TABLESPOONS DRY SHERRY (OPTIONAL)
2	TABLESPOONS SNIPPED FRESH CHIVES OR GREEN ONIONS (GREEN PART ONLY) (OPTIONAL)

In a medium saucepan, bring the wine and 1/2 cup broth to a boil over high heat.

Add the lobster tails. Reduce the heat and simmer, covered, for 6 to 8 minutes, or until the lobster is cooked through. Set a colander over a medium bowl. Pour the lobster and the cooking liquid into the colander, reserving the liquid. Let cool for 10 minutes.

Meanwhile, in the same saucepan, melt the margarine. Stir in the leeks, celery, and shallots. Cook over medium heat for 4 to 5 minutes, or until the vegetables are tender, stirring occasionally.

Stir in 1 1/2 cups broth and the reserved lobster cooking liquid. Bring to a simmer over medium-high heat, stirring occasionally. Simmer for 2 to 3 minutes to allow the flavors to blend, stirring occasionally.

In a small bowl or cup, whisk together the half-and-half and flour until smooth. Pour into the soup. Simmer for 1 to 2 minutes, or until thick-

PER SERVING

CALORIES 166	CHOLESTEROL 11 mg
TOTAL FAT 1.0 g	SODIUM 190 mg
SATURATED 0.0 g	CARBOHYDRATES 26 g
POLYUNSATURATED 0.5 g	FIBER 2 g
MONOUNSATURATED 0.5 g	PROTEIN 10 g

ened, stirring occasionally. Keep soup warm over medium-low heat while preparing the lobster meat, stirring occasionally.

Using kitchen scissors or a sharp knife, split the lobster shells in half. Remove and coarsely chop the meat.

Stir the lobster meat and pepper into the soup. Add the sherry if desired. Simmer over medium-low heat for 2 to 3 minutes, or until the lobster is warmed through and flavors have blended, stirring occasionally.

Ladle into serving bowls. Top with chives if desired.

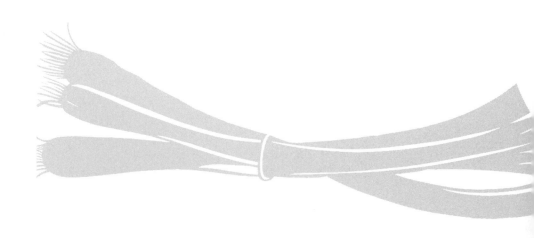

chicken and spinach enchilada soup

serves 4

Chock-full of chicken and spinach, this entrée soup captures the essence of enchiladas without the fuss. Serve up steaming bowls of this soup with warmed corn muffins or tortillas on the side.

2 TEASPOONS OLIVE OIL

1 POUND BONELESS, SKINLESS CHICKEN BREASTS, ALL VISIBLE FAT DISCARDED, CUT INTO 3/4-INCH PIECES

1/2 MEDIUM ONION, CHOPPED

2 CUPS FAT-FREE, LOW-SODIUM CHICKEN BROTH

1 1/2 CUPS FAT-FREE MILK

10.5-OUNCE CAN LOW-FAT, REDUCED-SODIUM CONDENSED CREAM OF CHICKEN SOUP

10-OUNCE PACKAGE FROZEN CHOPPED SPINACH, THAWED AND SQUEEZED DRY

1/2 TEASPOON CHILI POWDER

1/2 TEASPOON GROUND CUMIN

1/4 CUP SHREDDED FAT-FREE OR REDUCED-FAT CHEDDAR CHEESE

PER SERVING

CALORIES 266

TOTAL FAT 5.5 g

  SATURATED 1.5 g

  POLYUNSATURATED 0.5 g

  MONOUNSATURATED 2.0 g

CHOLESTEROL 75 mg

SODIUM 564 mg

CARBOHYDRATES 17 g

FIBER 3 g

PROTEIN 36 g

Heat a large nonstick saucepan over medium-high heat. Pour the oil into the saucepan and swirl to coat the bottom. Cook the chicken for 6 to 8 minutes, or until no longer pink in the center, stirring occasionally. Add the onion; cook for 1 to 2 minutes, or until tender-crisp, stirring occasionally.

Stir in the broth, milk, soup, spinach, chili powder, and cumin. Bring to a boil over high heat, stirring occasionally. Reduce the heat and simmer, uncovered, for 6 to 8 minutes, or until flavors have blended, stirring occasionally.

To serve, ladle the soup into bowls and sprinkle with the cheese.

lentil-spinach soup

The cheese or yogurt completes the protein in the lentils, making this delicious soup a nourishing main dish. This is a good recipe to double and freeze, but do not add the cheese or yogurt until serving time.

VEGETABLE OIL SPRAY

1 TEASPOON OLIVE OIL

1 LARGE ONION, CHOPPED

1 POUND DRIED LENTILS, SORTED FOR STONES AND SHRIVELED LENTILS AND RINSED (ABOUT 2 1/4 CUPS)

4 CUPS FAT-FREE, LOW-SODIUM CHICKEN BROTH

4 CUPS WATER

1 POUND FRESH SPINACH, STEMS REMOVED AND TORN INTO BITE-SIZE PIECES, OR 10-OUNCE PACKAGE FROZEN CHOPPED SPINACH, THAWED AND SQUEEZED DRY

1/2 TEASPOON PEPPER, OR TO TASTE

1/8 TEASPOON GROUND ALLSPICE

BROTH OR WATER IF NEEDED

1 CUP SHREDDED FAT-FREE OR PART-SKIM MOZZARELLA CHEESE OR 1/2 CUP FAT-FREE OR LOW-FAT PLAIN YOGURT, LIGHTLY BEATEN WITH A FORK

Heat a large stockpot or Dutch oven over medium-high heat. Remove from the heat and lightly spray with vegetable oil spray (being careful not to spray near a gas flame). Pour the oil into the stockpot and swirl to coat the bottom. Return the stockpot to the heat and cook the onion for 3 to 4 minutes, or until golden brown.

Stir in the lentils, broth, and water. Bring to a boil over high heat. Reduce the heat and simmer, covered, for 45 to 60 minutes, or until the lentils are tender, stirring occasionally.

Stir in the spinach, pepper, and allspice. Simmer, covered, for 15 minutes. Thin the soup with additional broth or water if needed.

To serve, ladle the soup into bowls and sprinkle with the cheese.

PER SERVING

CALORIES 247	CHOLESTEROL 3 mg
TOTAL FAT 1.0 g	SODIUM 255 mg
SATURATED 0.0 g	CARBOHYDRATES 38 g
POLYUNSATURATED 0.5 g	FIBER 20 g
MONOUNSATURATED 0.5 g	PROTEIN 23 g

hot and sour soup with exotic mushrooms

serves 8

Make the most of the variety of fresh mushrooms available at your local market. Their earthy flavors and textures enhance this tangy and peppery soup. Have some Asian-style soup spoons handy—they make eating the soup twice as fun!

4 CUPS FAT-FREE, LOW-SODIUM CHICKEN BROTH

1 POUND MIXED FRESH MUSHROOMS, SUCH AS WHITE BUTTON, ENOKI, OYSTER, PORTOBELLO, SHIITAKE, AND WOOD EAR, CUT INTO 1/4-INCH SLICES

2 BONELESS CENTER-CUT PORK CHOPS (ABOUT 4 OUNCES EACH), ALL VISIBLE FAT DISCARDED, CUT INTO 1/8-INCH-THICK STRIPS

1/4 CUP CIDER VINEGAR

1 1/2 TABLESPOONS LOW-SALT SOY SAUCE

2 TEASPOONS TOASTED SESAME OIL

1 TEASPOON SUGAR

1/4 TO 1/2 TEASPOON WHITE OR BLACK PEPPER

3 TABLESPOONS CORNSTARCH

1/4 CUP WATER

2 CUPS SNOW PEAS, ENDS TRIMMED (ABOUT 6 OUNCES)

8-OUNCE CAN SLICED WATER CHESTNUTS, RINSED AND DRAINED

EGG SUBSTITUTE EQUIVALENT TO 1 EGG, OR WHITES OF 2 EGGS, LIGHTLY BEATEN

In a medium saucepan, bring the broth, mushrooms, pork, vinegar, soy sauce, sesame oil, sugar, and pepper to a boil over high heat, stirring occasionally. Reduce the heat and simmer, uncovered, for 10 minutes, or until the mushrooms are tender and the pork is no longer pink in the center, stirring occasionally.

Put the cornstarch in a cup. Add the water, stirring to dissolve. Stir into the soup. Cook over medium-high heat for 2 to 3 minutes, or until thickened, stirring occasionally.

Add the snow peas and water chestnuts. Cook for 1 to 2 minutes, or until the snow peas are tender-crisp, stirring occasionally. Slowly drizzle the egg substitute into the soup. Cook for 1 minute, stirring gently, or until the egg is cooked through.

Remove from the heat and serve.

PER SERVING

CALORIES 105	CHOLESTEROL 18 mg
TOTAL FAT 3.0 g	SODIUM 143 mg
SATURATED 0.5 g	CARBOHYDRATES 10 g
POLYUNSATURATED 0.5 g	FIBER 2 g
MONOUNSATURATED 1.0 g	PROTEIN 10 g

Cook's Tip on Dried Mushrooms

Can't find your favorite fresh mushroom? Feel free to substitute dried mushrooms. Cover them with hot tap water by 1 inch and soak for 10 minutes, or until softened. Drain, squeeze out any excess water, and proceed with the recipe. Keep in mind that 1 ounce of dried mushrooms equals about 1 cup of rehydrated mushrooms.

Cook's Tip on Sesame Oil

Fragrant toasted sesame oil, also called toasted sesame oil or Asian sesame oil, is darker, stronger, and more fragrant than sesame oil. Fragrant toasted sesame oil is widely used in Asian and Indian foods. Because it is so flavorful, you get a lot of taste for just a little fat.

gumbo with greens and ham

serves 8

Gumbo typically starts with a high-fat roux made of oil and flour that is cooked until it browns. We eliminate the oil but still brown the flour to give this Southern soup an authentic Cajun taste.

1/2	CUP ALL-PURPOSE FLOUR
	VEGETABLE OIL SPRAY
2	MEDIUM ONIONS, CHOPPED
2	MEDIUM RIBS OF CELERY, CHOPPED
1	MEDIUM YELLOW OR GREEN BELL PEPPER, CHOPPED
1	MEDIUM RED BELL PEPPER, CHOPPED
6	MEDIUM GARLIC CLOVES, MINCED
6	OUNCES FRESH COLLARD GREENS, MUSTARD GREENS, KALE, OR SPINACH, COARSELY CHOPPED
3	CUPS WATER
2	CUPS CHOPPED LOWER-SODIUM, LOW-FAT HAM
1 1/2	CUPS SLICED FRESH OR FROZEN OKRA
2	BUNCHES WATERCRESS, COARSELY CHOPPED
1	BUNCH PARSLEY, COARSELY SNIPPED
1/4	TO 1/2 TEASPOON BLACK PEPPER
1/8	TO 1/4 TEASPOON CAYENNE
	RED HOT-PEPPER SAUCE TO TASTE
4	CUPS COOKED BROWN RICE

In a Dutch oven, cook the flour over medium-high heat for 5 minutes, stirring occasionally. Reduce the heat to medium; cook for 5 to 7 minutes, or until the flour is evenly browned, stirring constantly. Remove the flour and set aside. Allow the pot to cool. When cool, rinse the pot and dry.

Heat the Dutch oven over medium heat. Remove from the heat and lightly spray with vegetable oil spray (being careful not to spray near a gas flame). Return the Dutch oven to the heat and cook the onions, celery, bell peppers, and garlic for 15 minutes, stirring occasionally.

Stir in the browned flour and remaining ingredients except the brown rice. Bring to a boil over high heat. Reduce the heat and simmer, covered, for 30 minutes. Serve over the brown rice.

Cook's Tip on Fresh Greens

Be sure to rinse fresh greens well under running water to remove any dirt and sandy grit between the leaves.

PER SERVING	
CALORIES 222	
TOTAL FAT 2.5 g	CHOLESTEROL 15 mg
SATURATED 0.5 g	SODIUM 333 mg
POLYUNSATURATED 0.5 g	CARBOHYDRATES 40 g
MONOUNSATURATED 1.0 g	FIBER 5 g
	PROTEIN 12 g

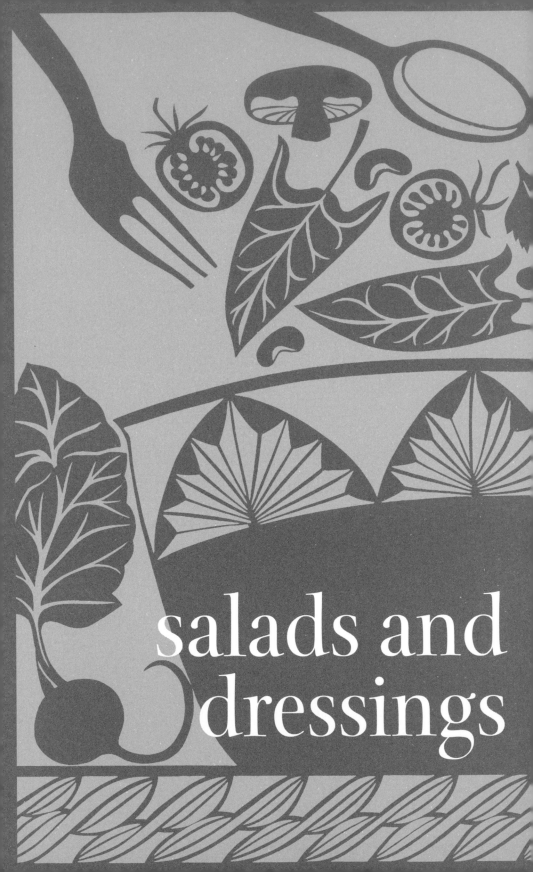

salads and dressings

Salad with Creamy Mustard Vinaigrette

Boston Citrus Salad

Green Bean and Toasted Pecan Salad

Warm Mushroom Salad

Pickled Cucumbers

Cucumber-Melon Salad with Raspberry Vinegar

Jícama and Grapefruit Salad with Ancho-Honey Dressing

Fresh Fruit Salad with Poppy Seed and Yogurt Dressing

Marinated Vegetable Salad

Lemon-Curried Black-Eyed Pea Salad

Tabbouleh

Crispy Tortilla Salad

Salmon and Pasta Salad

Seafood Pasta Salad

Artichoke Rotini Salad with Chicken

Roasted Potato and Chicken Salad with Greek Dressing

Herbed Chicken Salad

Ham and Rice Salad

Creamy Herb Dressing

Tomatillo-Avocado Dressing

Gazpacho Dressing

Parmesan-Peppercorn Ranch Dressing

Feta Cheese Vinaigrette with Dijon Mustard

Creamy Artichoke Dressing

salad with creamy mustard vinaigrette

serves 8

This recipe makes a double batch of dressing. Use half now and save the rest for another salad. In addition to providing iron and protein, tofu makes this dressing creamy and rich.

4 TEASPOONS SHELLED SUNFLOWER SEEDS

DRESSING

1/2 CUP FIRM REDUCED-FAT TOFU, WELL DRAINED (4 OUNCES)

1/2 CUP FAT-FREE OR LOW-FAT VINAIGRETTE DRESSING

2 TABLESPOONS WATER

1/2 TEASPOON HONEY

1/2 TEASPOON DIJON MUSTARD

1 HEAD LEAF LETTUCE, TORN INTO BITE-SIZE PIECES, OR ABOUT 8 OUNCES MIXED SALAD GREENS

3 DRIED APRICOT HALVES, SLIVERED

Preheat the oven to 300°F.

PER SERVING	
CALORIES 28	CHOLESTEROL 0 mg
TOTAL FAT 1.0 G	SODIUM 86 mg
SATURATED 0.0 g	CARBOHYDRATES 4 g
POLYUNSATURATED 0.5 g	FIBER 1 g
MONOUNSATURATED 0.0 g	PROTEIN 1 g

Put the sunflower seeds in a baking pan. Bake for 12 minutes, or until very lightly browned. Remove from the pan and let cool.

Meanwhile, in a food processor or blender, process the dressing ingredients until creamy.

Toss the lettuce with 5 tablespoons of the dressing. (Refrigerate the remainder of the dressing for later use.) Top with the apricots and sunflower seeds.

boston citrus salad

Delicate, pale-green Boston lettuce is the perfect backdrop for juicy citrus fruit. The orange-flower water, found at Middle Eastern markets and most gourmet-type grocery stores, gives an aromatic touch to this salad.

1	LARGE HEAD BOSTON, BUTTER, OR BIBB LETTUCE
2	LARGE NAVEL ORANGES
2	MEDIUM GRAPEFRUIT
1 1/2	TABLESPOONS FRESH LEMON JUICE
1 1/2	TABLESPOONS HONEY
1/2	TEASPOON ORANGE-FLOWER WATER OR ORANGE LIQUEUR (OPTIONAL)
3	TABLESPOONS SLIVERED ALMONDS, DRY-ROASTED

Tear the lettuce leaves into bite-size pieces.

Remove the peel and pith from the oranges. Cut the oranges into 1/4-inch slices. Cut the slices into quarters and put in a medium bowl.

Peel and section the grapefruit. Cut the grapefruit into bite-size pieces and add to the oranges.

PER SERVING	
CALORIES 102	CHOLESTEROL 0 mg
TOTAL FAT 2.0 g	SODIUM 3 mg
SATURATED 0.0 g	CARBOHYDRATES 22 g
POLYUNSATURATED 0.5 g	FIBER 6 g
MONOUNSATURATED 1.0 g	PROTEIN 2 g

Drain the fruit, reserving the juice in a small bowl.

Add the lemon juice, honey, and orange-flower water to the reserved fruit juice. Pour the juice mixture over the lettuce. Toss to coat evenly.

Arrange the lettuce on salad plates. Top each serving with grapefruit and orange pieces and a sprinkling of almonds.

Cook's Tip

Orange-flower water is also wonderful in cakes, cookies, puddings, and beverages.

green bean and toasted pecan salad

serves 4

This pretty combination is a refreshing break from the usual lettuce or slaw salads.

2	TABLESPOONS PECAN PIECES
12	OUNCES WHOLE GREEN BEANS, TRIMMED
1/2	TO 1 OUNCE THINLY SLICED RED ONION
1 1/2	TABLESPOONS WHITE BALSAMIC VINEGAR
2 1/4	TEASPOONS SUGAR
1/4	TEASPOON SALT
1/2	OUNCE BLUE CHEESE, CRUMBLED

Heat an 8-inch skillet over medium-high heat. Dry-roast the pecans for 2 to 3 minutes, or until fragrant and beginning to lightly brown, stirring frequently. Set aside.

Set a steamer basket in a small amount of simmering water in a medium saucepan. Put the green beans in the basket. Cook, covered, for 4 minutes, or until just tender-crisp.

PER SERVING

CALORIES 80	CHOLESTEROL 3 mg
TOTAL FAT 3.5 g	SODIUM 202 mg
SATURATED 1.0 g	CARBOHYDRATES 11 g
POLYUNSATURATED 1.0 g	FIBER 3 g
MONOUNSATURATED 1.5 g	PROTEIN 3 g

Transfer the beans to a colander; rinse with cold water to stop the cooking, and let the beans cool to room temperature. Drain well and dry on paper towels.

In a medium bowl, toss the green beans with the onion, vinegar, sugar, and salt to blend thoroughly. Sprinkle with the pecans and blue cheese.

Cook's Tip on Dry-Roasting Nuts

Don't be tempted to skip the dry-roasting step—even though a small amount of nuts is used, the toasting brings out a tremendous amount of flavor.

warm mushroom salad

Balsamic vinegar gives mushrooms a deep, rich flavor. If you wish, you can use meaty-textured portobello mushrooms and serve this salad as part of a meatless meal.

1/4	CUP PORT, SWEET RED WINE, OR FROZEN UNSWEETENED APPLE JUICE CONCENTRATE
3	TO 3 1/2 TABLESPOONS BALSAMIC VINEGAR OR RICE VINEGAR
2	TABLESPOONS WATER
3	MEDIUM GARLIC CLOVES, FINELY MINCED
12	OUNCES FRESH MUSHROOMS, CUT INTO 1/4-INCH-THICK SLICES
1	TEASPOON LIGHT STICK MARGARINE
1/8	TEASPOON PEPPER, OR TO TASTE
4	LEAVES BOSTON LETTUCE
1	TEASPOON SNIPPED FRESH PARSLEY

In a nonstick skillet, heat the port, vinegar, water, and garlic over medium-high heat until small bubbles begin to form.

PER SERVING	
CALORIES 64	CHOLESTEROL 0 mg
TOTAL FAT 1.0 g	SODIUM 15 mg
SATURATED 0.0 g	CARBOHYDRATES 9 g
POLYUNSATURATED 0.5 g	FIBER 1 g
MONOUNSATURATED 0.0 g	PROTEIN 3 g

Add the mushrooms; cook for 8 to 10 minutes, or until all the liquid evaporates, stirring frequently.

Stir in the margarine and pepper to coat evenly.

Arrange the mushrooms on the lettuce leaves and sprinkle with the parsley. Serve warm.

pickled cucumbers

These easy-to-make sweet-and-sour tidbits go well with almost any lunch or dinner. They're especially good on Open-Face Turkey Sandwiches (page 234).

- **1/4** CUP CIDER VINEGAR
- **1/4** CUP WATER
- **2** TABLESPOONS SUGAR
- **1/2** TEASPOON WHOLE CLOVES OR 1/2 TEASPOON DRIED DILLWEED, CRUMBLED
- **1/4** TEASPOON SALT
- **1/8** TEASPOON WHITE PEPPER
- **2** MEDIUM CUCUMBERS, THINLY SLICED

In a medium nonmetallic bowl, combine all the ingredients except the cucumbers. Stir in the cucumbers. Cover the bowl and refrigerate for at least 1 hour. Drain well before serving.

For longer storage, drain the cucumbers and refrigerate in a covered container for up to one week.

PER SERVING

CALORIES 49	CHOLESTEROL 0 mg
TOTAL FAT 0.0 g	SODIUM 146 mg
SATURATED 0.0 g	CARBOHYDRATES 12 g
POLYUNSATURATED 0.0 g	FIBER 2 g
MONOUNSATURATED 0.0 g	PROTEIN 2 g

Cook's Tip

For a decorative look, score each whole cucumber by running a fork lengthwise down the surface in several places. Then thinly slice the cucumber crosswise with a knife, or use the slicing disk of a food processor.

cucumber-melon salad with raspberry vinegar

serves 4

Serve this refreshingly different dish as a salad, or turn it into a relish by finely chopping the ingredients.

- **1 MEDIUM CUCUMBER**
- **1/2 LARGE CANTALOUPE, SEEDS DISCARDED**
- **1 BUNCH RADISHES**
- **1/4 CUP RASPBERRY VINEGAR**
  PEPPER (OPTIONAL)
- **4 LETTUCE LEAVES**

Partially peel the cucumber in strips, leaving some of the dark green to add color. Cut the cucumber into bite-size pieces and put in a medium bowl.

Cut the cantaloupe into cubes or use a melon baller to scoop out small balls. Add to the cucumber pieces.

Thinly slice the radishes. Add to the cucumber and cantaloupe.

PER SERVING

CALORIES 50	CHOLESTEROL 0 mg
TOTAL FAT 0.0 g	SODIUM 24 mg
SATURATED 0.0 g	CARBOHYDRATES 11 g
POLYUNSATURATED 0.0 g	FIBER 2 g
MONOUNSATURATED 0.0 g	PROTEIN 2 g

Toss the salad with the vinegar. Sprinkle with the pepper if desired.

Refrigerate, covered, until chilled, about 30 minutes to 1 hour. Serve on four plates lined with the lettuce.

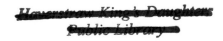

jícama and grapefruit salad with ancho-honey dressing

serves 4

Ancho peppers are dried poblano peppers. Wrinkled and dark reddish brown, they add a medium-hot boost to this salad dressing.

DRESSING

1/2	CUP WATER
2	ANCHO PEPPERS, HALVED LENGTHWISE, SEEDS AND RIBS DISCARDED
2	MEDIUM GARLIC CLOVES, QUARTERED
2	TABLESPOONS WHITE WINE VINEGAR
2	TABLESPOONS HONEY
1	TABLESPOON ACCEPTABLE VEGETABLE OIL
1	TABLESPOON FRESH LIME JUICE

◆

1	POUND JÍCAMA, PEELED AND CUT INTO VERY THIN SLICES (ABOUT 3 1/2 CUPS)
1/2	CUP CHOPPED RED ONION
1/4	CUP SNIPPED FRESH CILANTRO
1	LARGE RED OR PINK GRAPEFRUIT

In a small saucepan, bring the water, peppers, and garlic to a boil over high heat. Reduce the heat and simmer for 10 minutes.

In a food processor or blender, process the mixture until smooth.

Add the remaining dressing ingredients. Process until smooth.

In a medium bowl, combine the jícama, onion, and cilantro. Pour the dressing over the jícama mixture, stirring to coat.

Cover and marinate in the refrigerator for 2 to 24 hours.

Shortly before serving, peel and section the grapefruit. Drain well. Gently stir the grapefruit sections into the jícama mixture.

Cook's Tip on Jícama

Also called Mexican potato, this root vegetable has a thin brown skin and crunchy cream-colored flesh. Jícama has a sweet, nutty flavor and can be eaten raw or cooked. Use jícama as you would carrot and celery sticks, or chop or shred jícama

PER SERVING	
CALORIES 204	CHOLESTEROL 0 mg
TOTAL FAT 4.5 g	SODIUM 12 mg
SATURATED 0.5 g	CARBOHYDRATES 42 g
POLYUNSATURATED 1.5 g	FIBER 14 g
MONOUNSATURATED 2.0 g	PROTEIN 3 g

to add to a fresh green salad. Choose bulbs that are firm and free of blemishes. Store whole jícama, unwrapped, in the refrigerator for up to five days. Peel the skin just before using. Wrap leftover jícama in plastic wrap and store for two to three days in the refrigerator.

fresh fruit salad with poppy seed and yogurt dressing

serves 6

As you select a variety of fresh fruit for this salad, aim for pleasing combinations of color and texture, as well as taste.

- 3 MEDIUM ORANGES
- 3 CUPS ASSORTED FRESH FRUIT, CUT INTO BITE-SIZE PIECES
- 1 CUP FAT-FREE OR LOW-FAT LEMON YOGURT
- 1/4 TEASPOON POPPY SEEDS
- 6 FRESH SPRIGS OF MINT OR EDIBLE FLOWERS

Cut each orange in half. Cut a thin slice from the bottom of each half so the oranges will sit upright. Remove the flesh from each half. Coarsely chop the orange flesh and put the pieces in a large bowl.

Stir the other fruit into the orange pieces.

PER SERVING

CALORIES 104	CHOLESTEROL 1 mg
TOTAL FAT 0.5 g	SODIUM 31 mg
SATURATED 0.0 g	CARBOHYDRATES 25 g
POLYUNSATURATED 0.0 g	FIBER 5 g
MONOUNSATURATED 0.0 g	PROTEIN 3 g

Place each orange "bowl" on a small plate. Spoon the fruit into the orange bowls, letting any extra fruit cascade onto the plate.

In a small bowl, whisk together the yogurt and poppy seeds. Pour over the fruit, using 2 to 3 tablespoons per serving. Top each serving with a sprig of mint or a flower.

marinated vegetable salad

For a delicious sandwich, drain any leftovers and use the vegetables to stuff a pita. Garnish with a little fat-free or low-fat Cheddar cheese and your favorite variety of lettuce.

16-OUNCE PACKAGE FROZEN MIXED VEGETABLES, THAWED

15-OUNCE CAN NO-SALT-ADDED CHICK-PEAS, RINSED IF DESIRED AND DRAINED

MARINADE

1/3 **CUP FAT-FREE OR LOW-FAT ITALIAN SALAD DRESSING**

1/4 **CUP FROZEN UNSWEETENED APPLE JUICE CONCENTRATE, THAWED**

2 **TABLESPOONS FRESH LEMON JUICE**

2 **TEASPOONS ACCEPTABLE VEGETABLE OIL**

1 **TABLESPOON PLAIN RICE VINEGAR OR WHITE WINE VINEGAR**

2 **MEDIUM GARLIC CLOVES, FINELY MINCED, OR 1/4 TEASPOON GARLIC POWDER**

1/8 **TEASPOON PEPPER, OR TO TASTE**

8 **LETTUCE LEAVES**

In a large bowl, combine the frozen vegetables and chick-peas.

In a jar with a tight-fitting lid, combine the marinade ingredients. Shake well. Pour over the vegetable-bean mixture; stir gently to coat thoroughly. Cover and refrigerate for several hours. Serve over the lettuce leaves.

PER SERVING

CALORIES 169	CHOLESTEROL 0 mg
TOTAL FAT 3.0 g	SODIUM 144 mg
SATURATED 0.0 g	CARBOHYDRATES 30 g
POLYUNSATURATED 1.0 g	FIBER 7 g
MONOUNSATURATED 1.5 g	PROTEIN 7 g

lemon-curried black-eyed pea salad

The zesty lemon in this colorful salad delivers a mouthful of flavors. Best of all, this salad comes together in a snap thanks to canned peas and corn. Rinsing the peas reduces their sodium content.

SALAD

- **15-OUNCE CAN NO-SALT-ADDED BLACK-EYED PEAS, RINSED AND DRAINED**
- **11-OUNCE CAN NO-SALT-ADDED WHOLE-KERNEL CORN, DRAINED**
- 1/2 **CUP CHOPPED RED ONION**
- 1/2 **CUP THINLY SLICED CELERY**
- 1 **TEASPOON FINELY SHREDDED LEMON ZEST**

DRESSING

- 2 **TABLESPOONS FRESH LEMON JUICE**
- 1 **TABLESPOON WATER**
- 1 **TEASPOON OLIVE OIL**
- 1 **MEDIUM GARLIC CLOVE, MINCED**
- 1/2 **TEASPOON CURRY POWDER**
- 1/2 **TEASPOON DIJON MUSTARD**
- 1/8 **TEASPOON PEPPER**

In a medium bowl, stir together the salad ingredients.

In a jar with a tight-fitting lid, combine the dressing ingredients. Cover and shake well.

Pour the dressing over the black-eyed pea mixture, stirring until well coated.

Cover and refrigerate for 1 to 24 hours, or until serving time.

Cook's Tip

Look for canned no-salt-added "fresh" black-eyed peas. They will offer more flavor than canned "dried" peas. If you want to use dried black-eyed peas, soak 1 cup of them overnight in enough water to cover. Drain and add 3 cups fresh water. Bring to a boil over high heat. Reduce the heat and simmer, covered, for 50 to 60 minutes, or until just tender. Drain well and continue with the recipe.

PER SERVING

CALORIES 82	CHOLESTEROL 0 mg
TOTAL FAT 1.0 g	SODIUM 19 mg
SATURATED 0.0 g	CARBOHYDRATES 16 g
POLYUNSATURATED 0.0 g	FIBER 3 g
MONOUNSATURATED 0.5 g	PROTEIN 4 g

tabbouleh

Make this dish well in advance—the flavors improve with age. Bulgur, a finely cracked wheat, is available at most supermarkets and health food stores. To serve, place a scoop of the salad on a leaf of lettuce or use it to stuff hollowed-out tomatoes, zucchini halves, or bell peppers.

- 2 **CUPS WATER**
- 2 **CUPS LOW SODIUM VEGETABLE BROTH**
- 1 **CUP UNCOOKED BULGUR (5 TO 6 OUNCES)**
- 1/4 **CUP FRESH LEMON JUICE**
- 1 **TABLESPOON OLIVE OIL**
- 2 **MEDIUM TOMATOES, FINELY CHOPPED**
- 3 **GREEN ONIONS (GREEN AND WHITE PARTS), FINELY CHOPPED**
- 1/4 **CUP FINELY CHOPPED FRESH MINT OR 1 TABLESPOON DRIED, CRUMBLED**
- 1/4 **CUP MINCED FRESH PARSLEY**
  PEPPER TO TASTE

In a medium saucepan, bring the water and broth to a boil over high heat.

PER SERVING	
CALORIES 121	CHOLESTEROL 0 mg
TOTAL FAT 2.5 g	SODIUM 30 mg
SATURATED 0.5 g	CARBOHYDRATES 22 g
POLYUNSATURATED 0.5 g	FIBER 5 g
MONOUNSATURATED 1.5 g	PROTEIN 4 g

Put the bulgur in a large heatproof bowl. Stir in the boiling water and broth. Cover and let stand for 1 hour, or until most of the liquid is absorbed.

Drain the bulgur in a colander or sieve. Squeeze out excess moisture with your hands or by placing bulgur in cheesecloth or a dish towel, gathering the ends together, and squeezing. Return the bulgur to the large bowl.

In a small bowl, whisk together the lemon juice and oil. Stir gently into the bulgur with the remaining ingredients.

Cover and refrigerate for at least 1 hour. Serve chilled or at room temperature.

crispy tortilla salad

serves 6

You can bake the tortillas and make the salsa for this crispy, light, Mexican-style salad in advance, then assemble the salad just before serving.

- 6 6-INCH CORN TORTILLAS
- VEGETABLE OIL SPRAY
- 1/2 TEASPOON CHILI POWDER
- 1 HEAD ICEBERG LETTUCE, SHREDDED (ABOUT 6 CUPS)
- 19-OUNCE CAN NO-SALT-ADDED KIDNEY BEANS, RINSED IF DESIRED AND DRAINED
- 2 OUNCES FAT-FREE OR PART-SKIM MOZZARELLA CHEESE, GRATED
- 2 OUNCES FAT-FREE OR REDUCED-FAT CHEDDAR CHEESE, GRATED
- 3 MEDIUM TOMATOES (2 RED AND 1 YELLOW PREFERRED), CHOPPED
- 6 TABLESPOONS SALSA

Preheat the oven to 350°F.

Lightly spray both sides of each tortilla with vegetable oil spray. Sprinkle the top side lightly with chili powder.

PER SERVING	
CALORIES 166	CHOLESTEROL 3 mg
TOTAL FAT 1.0 g	SODIUM 298 mg
SATURATED 0.0 g	CARBOHYDRATES 27 g
POLYUNSATURATED 0.5 g	FIBER 7 g
MONOUNSATURATED 0.0 g	PROTEIN 14 g

Bake the tortillas in a single layer on a baking sheet for 10 to 15 minutes, or until crisp and lightly browned.

Top each tortilla with layers of the remaining ingredients in the order listed.

salmon and pasta salad

serves 5

This easy-to-fix salad is great for hot summer days, when tomatoes and cucumbers are at their best.

SALMON SALAD

1	CUP DRIED ELBOW MACARONI (4 OUNCES)
2 1/2	TABLESPOONS FAT-FREE OR LIGHT ITALIAN SALAD DRESSING
	10-OUNCE PACKAGE FROZEN ASPARAGUS
	7.66-OUNCE CAN SALMON, DRAINED, BONES DISCARDED IF DESIRED AND SKIN DISCARDED
1	LARGE RED BELL PEPPER, DICED
1/2	MEDIUM WHITE ONION, MINCED
1	TABLESPOON VERY LOW SODIUM OR LOW-SODIUM WORCESTERSHIRE SAUCE

DRESSING

8	OUNCES FAT-FREE OR LOW-FAT COTTAGE CHEESE
2	TABLESPOONS FRESH LEMON JUICE
2 TO 3	DASHES RED HOT-PEPPER SAUCE
1 TO 2	TABLESPOONS CHOPPED FRESH DILLWEED OR 1 TO 2 TEASPOONS DRIED, CRUMBLED

◆

15	CHERRY TOMATOES, 5 ITALIAN PLUM TOMATOES, OR 3 TO 4 TOMATOES (OPTIONAL)
3	MEDIUM CUCUMBERS (OPTIONAL)

Prepare the macaroni using the package directions, omitting the salt and oil. Drain in a colander and return to the saucepan.

Stir the salad dressing into the macaroni. Set aside.

Meanwhile, set a steamer basket in a small amount of simmering water in a medium saucepan. Put the asparagus in the basket. Cook, covered, for 3 to 5 minutes, or until tender-crisp. Cut diagonally into bite-size pieces.

In a large bowl, mash the salmon, including the bones. Stir in the dressed macaroni, asparagus, and remaining salad ingredients.

In a food processor or blender, process the dressing ingredients except the dillweed until creamy.

Stir the dillweed into the dressing. Pour over the salmon mixture and stir. Cover and refrigerate.

Cut the cherry tomatoes in half or slice the other tomatoes. Cut the cucumbers into spears.

To serve, mound the salmon salad in the center of five plates. Arrange the tomato and cucumber pieces around it if desired.

PER SERVING

CALORIES 217

TOTAL FAT 3.0 g

    SATURATED 0.5 g

    POLYUNSATURATED 1.0 g

    MONOUNSATURATED 1.0 g

CHOLESTEROL 19 mg

SODIUM 466 mg

CARBOHYDRATES 27 g

FIBER 3 g

PROTEIN 20 g

seafood pasta salad

Try poached fish, tuna packed in spring water, canned salmon, fresh or frozen shrimp, fat-free imitation crabmeat. . . . The possibilities for this recipe go on and on.

SALAD

	10-OUNCE PACKAGE DRIED PASTA SHELLS
2	CUPS COOKED SEAFOOD, SKIN AND BONES DISCARDED
1	SMALL RED ONION, FINELY CHOPPED
1	MEDIUM RED, GREEN, OR YELLOW BELL PEPPER, CHOPPED
1	CUP FROZEN GREEN PEAS, THAWED
4	TO 5 RADISHES, FINELY CHOPPED
1/4	CUP MINCED FRESH BASIL OR 4 TEASPOONS DRIED, CRUMBLED
1/4	CUP MINCED FRESH PARSLEY

◆

1/2	CUP FAT-FREE OR LIGHT ITALIAN SALAD DRESSING
1/2	TEASPOON DIJON MUSTARD
1	SMALL HEAD ROMAINE LETTUCE (OPTIONAL)
2	SMALL TOMATOES, EACH CUT INTO 6 WEDGES (OPTIONAL)

Prepare the pasta using the package directions, omitting the salt and oil. Drain well and put in a large bowl.

Stir the remaining salad ingredients into the pasta.

In a small bowl, whisk together the salad dressing and mustard. Stir gently into the pasta mixture.

Cover and refrigerate for several hours. Serve at room temperature or chilled.

For an attractive presentation, line a serving bowl or a platter with lettuce, fill with the pasta, and top with tomato wedges if desired.

PER SERVING

CALORIES 279	CHOLESTEROL 56 mg
TOTAL FAT 2.0 g	SODIUM 399 mg
SATURATED 0.5 g	CARBOHYDRATES 44 g
POLYUNSATURATED 0.5 g	FIBER 3 g
MONOUNSATURATED 0.5 g	PROTEIN 19 g

artichoke rotini salad with chicken

serves 4

Get double the flavor boost from the artichokes in this one-dish meal by using them in the lively dressing.

- 4 OUNCES DRIED ROTINI PASTA
- 14-OUNCE CAN ARTICHOKE HEARTS, DRAINED WITH 1/4 CUP LIQUID RESERVED
- 1/4 CUP FRESH LEMON JUICE
- 2 TABLESPOONS DRIED BASIL, CRUMBLED
- 2 MEDIUM GARLIC CLOVES, MINCED
- 1/4 TEASPOON CRUSHED RED PEPPER FLAKES
- 12 OUNCES FROZEN DICED COOKED CHICKEN, THAWED, OR 2 CUPS DICED COOKED CHICKEN, COOKED WITHOUT SALT, SKIN AND ALL VISIBLE FAT DISCARDED
- 1 MEDIUM RED BELL PEPPER, CUT INTO THIN STRIPS 2 INCHES LONG
- 2 TABLESPOONS OLIVE OIL (EXTRA-VIRGIN PREFERRED)
- 1/4 TEASPOON SALT
- 4 LARGE LETTUCE LEAVES (OPTIONAL)

PER SERVING	
CALORIES 298	
TOTAL FAT 8.5 g	CHOLESTEROL 46 mg
SATURATED 1.0 g	SODIUM 569 mg
POLYUNSATURATED 1.0 g	CARBOHYDRATES 31 g
MONOUNSATURATED 5.5 g	FIBER 3 g
	PROTEIN 26 g

Prepare the pasta using the package directions, omitting the salt and oil. Drain in a colander and run under cold water to cool completely. Drain well.

Meanwhile, in a food processor or blender, process half of the artichokes, the reserved artichoke liquid, the lemon juice, basil, garlic, and red pepper flakes until smooth.

Coarsely chop the remaining artichokes. In a medium bowl, combine the artichokes, chicken, and bell pepper.

Add the pasta to the chicken mixture. Pour in the artichoke dressing; toss gently yet thoroughly to coat. Gently stir in the olive oil and salt.

Arrange on a bed of lettuce if desired. Serve immediately for peak flavor.

roasted potato and chicken salad with greek dressing

Warm from the oven, roasted potatoes are tossed with a colorful mix of chicken, green beans, roasted bell peppers, and a lemony dressing. Serve this entrée salad immediately, or chill it in the refrigerator.

OLIVE OIL SPRAY

1 POUND UNPEELED SMALL RED POTATOES (ABOUT 6)

1 1/2 POUNDS FRESH OR FROZEN GREEN BEANS, TRIMMED IF FRESH

2 CUPS DICED COOKED CHICKEN BREAST, COOKED WITHOUT SALT, SKIN AND ALL VISIBLE FAT DISCARDED

1/2 CUP ROASTED RED BELL PEPPERS, DRAINED AND RINSED IF BOTTLED, COARSELY CHOPPED

1/4 CUP KALAMATA OLIVES, DRAINED AND COARSELY CHOPPED

DRESSING

2 TABLESPOONS WHITE WINE VINEGAR

2 TABLESPOONS FRESH LEMON JUICE

2 MEDIUM GARLIC CLOVES, MINCED

2 TEASPOONS OLIVE OIL

2 TEASPOONS LIGHT BROWN SUGAR

1 TEASPOON GRATED LEMON ZEST

1/2 TEASPOON DRIED OREGANO, CRUMBLED

Preheat the oven to 400°F. Lightly spray a baking sheet with olive oil spray.

Cut the potatoes into 3/4-inch cubes. Place them in a single layer on the baking sheet. Lightly spray the potatoes with olive oil spray.

Bake, uncovered, for 35 to 40 minutes, or until the potatoes are golden brown and tender when pierced with a sharp knife.

Meanwhile, in a large saucepan, bring enough water to cover the green beans to a boil over high heat. Add the green beans. Cook, uncovered, over medium-high heat for 6 to 8 minutes, or until the beans are tender, stirring occasionally. Drain well and pat dry with paper towels.

In a large bowl, combine the beans, potatoes, chicken, peppers, and olives.

In a small bowl, whisk together the dressing ingredients until well blended. Pour the dressing over the salad and toss to coat.

PER SERVING	
CALORIES 203	CHOLESTEROL 40 mg
TOTAL FAT 4.5 g	SODIUM 144 mg
SATURATED 1.0 g	CARBOHYDRATES 24 g
POLYUNSATURATED 0.5 g	FIBER 6 g
MONOUNSATURATED 3.0 g	PROTEIN 18 g

Cook's Tip

Roasted bell peppers add color, flavor, and texture to food. Prepare several at one time so you'll have some to use in this salad, plus plenty to enhance other salads, casseroles, sandwiches—you name it! (See Asparagus-Chicken à la King with Roasted Peppers, page 225, for how to roast peppers.)

herbed chicken salad

In addition to being an entrée salad, this dish is excellent when used as stuffing for tomatoes, bell peppers, or zucchini.

CHICKEN SALAD

2	CUPS DICED COOKED CHICKEN, COOKED WITHOUT SALT, SKIN AND ALL VISIBLE FAT DISCARDED
1/4	CUP FAT-FREE OR LOW-FAT PLAIN YOGURT
1/4	CUP FAT-FREE OR LIGHT MAYONNAISE DRESSING
2	GREEN ONIONS (GREEN AND WHITE PARTS), THINLY SLICED
1	SMALL CARROT, GRATED
2	RADISHES, GRATED
3	TABLESPOONS CHOPPED CELERY
2	TABLESPOONS CHOPPED GREEN BELL PEPPER
2	TABLESPOONS SNIPPED FRESH PARSLEY
1 1/2	TABLESPOONS TARRAGON VINEGAR, OR 1 1/2 TABLESPOONS RICE VINEGAR OR WHITE WINE VINEGAR PLUS 1/8 TEASPOON DRIED TARRAGON, CRUMBLED
1	TEASPOON VERY LOW SODIUM OR LOW-SODIUM WORCESTERSHIRE SAUCE
1	TEASPOON SALT-FREE ITALIAN HERB SEASONING
1/4	TEASPOON PEPPER, OR TO TASTE

◆

6 **LETTUCE LEAVES**

8-OUNCE CAN MANDARIN ORANGES IN WATER OR LIGHT SYRUP, DRAINED, OR 3 SMALL TOMATOES, SLICED

In a large bowl, stir together the chicken salad ingredients.

Cover and refrigerate for at least 1 hour.

To serve, place a scoop of chicken salad on a lettuce leaf and top with mandarin orange segments.

PER SERVING	
CALORIES 121	CHOLESTEROL 40 mg
TOTAL FAT 2.0 g	SODIUM 136 mg
SATURATED 0.5 g	CARBOHYDRATES 10 g
POLYUNSATURATED 0.5 g	FIBER 1 g
MONOUNSATURATED 0.5 g	PROTEIN 16 g

ham and rice salad

serves 8

Team this pretty entrée salad with fresh fruit and crusty bread.

HAM SALAD

- 1 CUP UNCOOKED BROWN OR LONG-GRAIN RICE
- 1 CUP FAT-FREE, LOW-SODIUM CHICKEN BROTH
- 6 OUNCES LOW-FAT, LOW-SODIUM HAM, ALL VISIBLE FAT DISCARDED, CUT INTO 1/4-INCH CUBES
- 1 CUP FRESH OR FROZEN WHOLE-KERNEL CORN, THAWED IF FROZEN
- 1 CUP FROZEN GREEN PEAS, THAWED
- 4 GREEN ONIONS (GREEN AND WHITE PARTS), THINLY SLICED
- 1 MEDIUM RED, YELLOW, OR GREEN BELL PEPPER, FINELY CHOPPED
- 4 TO 5 RADISHES, FINELY CHOPPED
- 1/4 CUP MINCED FRESH PARSLEY
- 1 TABLESPOON FRESH DILLWEED OR 1 TEASPOON DRIED, CRUMBLED

DRESSING

- 1/2 CUP FAT-FREE OR LIGHT ITALIAN SALAD DRESSING
- 1/2 TEASPOON DIJON MUSTARD

- 1 SMALL HEAD LETTUCE, (RED LEAF PREFERRED)

  FRESH MINT OR PARSLEY SPRIGS

Prepare the rice using the package instructions, substituting broth for 1 cup of the liquid and omitting the salt. Let cool.

In a large bowl, combine the rice with the remaining ham salad ingredients.

In a small bowl, whisk together the salad dressing and mustard. Pour the dressing into the rice and ham mixture, stirring to coat. Cover and refrigerate.

Serve at room temperature or chilled. Place a scoop of salad on a bed of lettuce and top with the mint.

PER SERVING

CALORIES 160	CHOLESTEROL 10 mg
TOTAL FAT 2.0 g	SODIUM 435 mg
SATURATED 0.5 g	CARBOHYDRATES 28 g
POLYUNSATURATED 0.5 g	FIBER 3 g
MONOUNSATURATED 0.5 g	PROTEIN 8 g

creamy herb dressing

makes about 1 1/4 cups;
2 tablespoons per serving

Serve this dressing hot or cold. It can be used as a dip or on poultry, baked potatoes, or cold seafood. It keeps well when covered and refrigerated.

1/2	CUP FAT-FREE OR LOW-FAT PLAIN YOGURT
1/2	CUP FAT-FREE OR LIGHT SOUR CREAM
1	GREEN ONION (GREEN AND WHITE PARTS), MINCED
2	TABLESPOONS FINELY SNIPPED FRESH PARSLEY OR CILANTRO
1/2	TEASPOON SALT-FREE LEMON-HERB SEASONING
1/2	TEASPOON HONEY OR SUGAR
1/4	TEASPOON SALT-FREE ITALIAN SEASONING (OPTIONAL)

In a small bowl, using a hand beater, whip together the yogurt and sour cream.

Stir in the remaining ingredients.

To serve cold, cover and refrigerate until ready to use. To serve hot, gently warm over medium heat, stirring until heated throughout. Do not boil.

PER SERVING

CALORIES 23

TOTAL FAT 0.0 g

  SATURATED 0.0 g

  POLYUNSATURATED 0.0 g

  MONOUNSATURATED 0.0 g

CHOLESTEROL 0 mg

SODIUM 20 mg

CARBOHYDRATES 4 g

FIBER 0 g

PROTEIN 2 g

tomatillo-avocado dressing

makes about 1 cup;
2 tablespoons per serving

You can use this guacamole-like recipe as a salad dressing, condiment, or dip. The flavor of the avocado is enhanced by the broiled tomatillos, which look like small green tomatoes enclosed in thin, papery husks.

VEGETABLE OIL SPRAY

6 TOMATILLOS, HUSKS DISCARDED (ABOUT 8 OUNCES), RINSED IN COLD WATER

1 MEDIUM RIPE AVOCADO, PEELED AND CHOPPED (ABOUT 1 CUP)

1 GREEN ONION (GREEN AND WHITE PARTS), CHOPPED

2 MEDIUM GARLIC CLOVES, MINCED

1/2 FRESH JALAPEÑO PEPPER, SEEDS AND RIBS DISCARDED, CHOPPED

1 TEASPOON SUGAR

1 TEASPOON FRESH LEMON JUICE

1/2 TEASPOON GROUND CUMIN

1/2 TEASPOON CHILI POWDER

1/4 TEASPOON SALT

1/8 TEASPOON PEPPER

Preheat the broiler. Lightly spray the broiler pan with vegetable oil spray.

Cut the tomatillos in half with a sharp knife. Put with the skin side up on the prepared pan.

Broil 4 to 6 inches from the heat for 5 minutes. Turn and broil for 2 to 3 minutes, or until the tomatillos are slightly tender. Put the tomatillos in a covered container and refrigerate for at least 10 minutes to cool.

In a food processor or blender, process the tomatillos with the remaining ingredients for 1 minute, or until the mixture is smooth.

PER SERVING

CALORIES 55	CHOLESTEROL 0 mg
TOTAL FAT 4.0 g	SODIUM 78 mg
SATURATED 0.5 g	CARBOHYDRATES 5 g
POLYUNSATURATED 0.5 g	FIBER 2 g
MONOUNSATURATED 2.5 g	PROTEIN 1 g

gazpacho dressing

makes about 3/4 cup;
2 tablespoons per serving

Substituting other herbs, such as parsley, mint, oregano, or tarragon, or salt-free herb seasoning for the cilantro will give you a range of flavored salad dressings.

- **6 OUNCES LOW-SODIUM VEGETABLE OR TOMATO JUICE**
- **1 TABLESPOON VERY FINELY CHOPPED ONION, ANY VARIETY**
- **1 TABLESPOON VERY FINELY CHOPPED CELERY**
- **1 TABLESPOON VERY FINELY CHOPPED BELL PEPPER, ANY VARIETY**
- **1 TABLESPOON GRATED CARROT**
- **1 TABLESPOON FINELY SNIPPED FRESH CILANTRO OR 1 TEASPOON DRIED, CRUMBLED**
- **1 TEASPOON FRESH LEMON JUICE**
- **1/2 TEASPOON SUGAR**
- **1/4 TEASPOON RED HOT-PEPPER SAUCE OR 1/2 TEASPOON WORCESTERSHIRE SAUCE**
- **PEPPER TO TASTE**

In a jar with a tight-fitting lid, combine all the ingredients. Shake well and refrigerate for at least 2 hours, allowing the flavors to blend.

PER SERVING	
CALORIES 66	CHOLESTEROL 0 mg
TOTAL FAT 0.0 g	SODIUM 124 mg
SATURATED 0.0 g	CARBOHYDRATES 13 g
POLYUNSATURATED 0.0 g	FIBER 2 g
MONOUNSATURATED 0.0 g	PROTEIN 2 g

parmesan-peppercorn ranch dressing

makes about 1 cup; 2 tablespoons per serving

Cool and creamy, this dressing puts the finishing touch on your favorite salad greens. Pack some in a small airtight container along with some raw vegetables for lunchtime dipping!

3/4	CUP FAT-FREE OR LOW-FAT BUTTERMILK
1/4	CUP FAT-FREE OR LIGHT SOUR CREAM
2	TABLESPOONS FAT-FREE OR LIGHT MAYONNAISE DRESSING
2	TABLESPOONS GRATED OR SHREDDED PARMESAN CHEESE
1/2	TEASPOON DRIED PARSLEY, CRUMBLED
1/2	TEASPOON DRIED CHIVES
1/4	TEASPOON DRIED OREGANO, CRUMBLED
1/4	TEASPOON GARLIC POWDER
1/8	TEASPOON SALT
1/8	TEASPOON PEPPER

In a medium bowl, gently whisk together all the ingredients.

For the best flavor, cover and refrigerate for at least 30 minutes before serving. Dressing can be refrigerated in an airtight container for up to five days.

PER SERVING

CALORIES 28	
TOTAL FAT 0.5 g	CHOLESTEROL 2 mg
SATURATED 0.5 g	SODIUM 126 mg
POLYUNSATURATED 0.0 g	CARBOHYDRATES 4 g
MONOUNSATURATED 0.0 g	FIBER 0 g
	PROTEIN 2 g

feta cheese vinaigrette with dijon mustard

makes about 1 cup;
2 tablespoons per serving

The flavor of this zesty vinaigrette will surprise you! Feta cheese mixed with honey provides a tang to this dressing, which is especially delicious over crisp romaine lettuce.

1	TABLESPOON CORNSTARCH
3/4	CUP WATER
1	OUNCE FETA CHEESE, CRUMBLED
2	TABLESPOONS WHITE WINE VINEGAR
4	TEASPOONS OLIVE OIL (EXTRA-VIRGIN PREFERRED)
1	TABLESPOON DIJON MUSTARD
2	TEASPOONS HONEY
1	MEDIUM GARLIC CLOVE, MINCED
1/8	TEASPOON SALT
1/8	TEASPOON PEPPER

Put the cornstarch in a cup. Add the water, stirring to dissolve.

PER SERVING

CALORIES 42	CHOLESTEROL 3 mg
TOTAL FAT 3.0 g	SODIUM 122 mg
SATURATED 1.0 g	CARBOHYDRATES 3 g
POLYUNSATURATED 0.0 g	FIBER 0 g
MONOUNSATURATED 2.0 g	PROTEIN 1 g

In a 1-quart saucepan, bring the cornstarch mixture to a boil over high heat, stirring occasionally. Cook for 2 to 3 minutes, or until thick and bubbly. Transfer the mixture to a medium bowl. Cover and refrigerate for at least 15 minutes.

Stir in the remaining ingredients. You can refrigerate this vinaigrette, covered, for up to five days.

creamy artichoke dressing

makes about 3/4 cup;
2 tablespoons per serving

Pureeing the artichoke hearts makes this dressing wonderfully smooth. Toss the remaining artichokes into your salad.

1/2	14-OUNCE CAN ARTICHOKE HEARTS
2	TABLESPOONS FAT-FREE, LOW-SODIUM CHICKEN BROTH
2	TABLESPOONS FRESH LEMON JUICE
1	TABLESPOON OLIVE OIL
2	MEDIUM GARLIC CLOVES, MINCED
1/2	TEASPOON DIJON MUSTARD
1/4	TEASPOON PEPPER

Pour off and reserve the liquid from the artichoke hearts. Rinse and drain the artichokes.

In a food processor or blender, process all the ingredients and 1 tablespoon of the reserved artichoke liquid until very smooth.

Cover and refrigerate. Serve over salad greens.

PER SERVING	
CALORIES 31	CHOLESTEROL 0 mg
TOTAL FAT 2.5 g	SODIUM 66 mg
SATURATED 0.5 g	CARBOHYDRATES 2 g
POLYUNSATURATED 0.0 g	FIBER 0 g
MONOUNSATURATED 1.5 g	PROTEIN 1 g

seafood

Stuffed Fish Fillets

Fish in a Package

Poached Fish in Asian Broth

Fish with Mustard Sauce over Spinach

Halibut Kebabs

Grilled Catfish with Mustard-Lemon Sauce

Grilled Cod with Artichoke Horseradish Sauce

Mesquite-Grilled Red Snapper with Gingered Black Bean Salsa

Mediterranean Grilled Salmon

Broiled Salmon with Pesto and Olives

Tilapia with Roasted Red Bell Peppers and Olives

Bulgur-Stuffed Trout

Tuna-Pasta Casserole

Tuna Salad Pita Sandwiches

Baked Crabmeat

California Bowls

Mussels with Yogurt-Caper Sauce

Shrimp Rémoulade

Seafood and Lemon Risotto

Cajun Red Scallops

Cioppino

stuffed fish fillets

You can prepare this elegant dish several hours before baking. Stuff the fillets, then cover and refrigerate them until shortly before baking time.

6	MILD FISH FILLETS, SUCH AS SOLE OR FLOUNDER (ABOUT 4 OUNCES EACH)
	VEGETABLE OIL SPRAY
1/2	TEASPOON WHITE PEPPER
1/2	TEASPOON PAPRIKA
1	TEASPOON ACCEPTABLE VEGETABLE OIL
6	OUNCES FRESH MUSHROOMS, FINELY CHOPPED
4	GREEN ONIONS (GREEN AND WHITE PARTS), FINELY CHOPPED
1/4	CUP PLAIN DRY BREAD CRUMBS
1/4	CUP SNIPPED FRESH PARSLEY
3	TABLESPOONS CHOPPED ALMONDS, DRY-ROASTED
1 1/2	TEASPOONS ACCEPTABLE VEGETABLE OIL
2	TABLESPOONS SNIPPED FRESH PARSLEY

Preheat the oven to 375°F.

Rinse the fish and pat dry with paper towels.

PER SERVING

CALORIES 162	CHOLESTEROL 53 mg
TOTAL FAT 5.5 g	SODIUM 124 mg
SATURATED 0.5 g	CARBOHYDRATES 6 g
POLYUNSATURATED 1.5 g	FIBER 1 g
MONOUNSATURATED 3.0 g	PROTEIN 22 g

Lightly spray six 6-ounce ovenproof custard cups or one 6-chamber muffin pan with 2 1/2 x 1 1/4-inch cups with vegetable oil spray. Curl each fillet inside a custard or muffin cup. Sprinkle with the pepper and paprika.

Heat a nonstick skillet over medium-high heat. Pour 1 teaspoon oil into the skillet and swirl to coat the bottom. Cook the mushrooms and green onions for 2 minutes, or until tender. Remove the skillet from the heat.

Stir in the bread crumbs, 1/4 cup parsley, and almonds.

Spoon equal amounts of the mixture into the center of the fish in each container. Brush the tops with the 1 1/2 teaspoons oil.

Bake for 15 minutes, or until the fish flakes easily when tested with a fork.

Carefully remove each stuffed fillet from the cups and place on serving plates. Spoon the cooking juices over the top. Garnish with 2 tablespoons parsley.

Cook's Tip

If your muffin pan has chambers that you aren't using, spray only the ones you need (cleanup will be easier). Put about 2 tablespoons of water in the unused chambers to keep your muffin pan from warping.

fish in a package

Dazzle your guests with these stuffed fish fillets, served with Green Beans Amandine (page 359), wild and white rice, and a fresh fruit dessert, such as Apple-Rhubarb Crisp (page 453).

10 THIN FISH FILLETS, SUCH AS TILAPIA OR FLOUNDER (ABOUT 4 OUNCES EACH)

STUFFING

1 TEASPOON ACCEPTABLE VEGETABLE OIL

1 SMALL ONION, CHOPPED

8 OUNCES FRESH MUSHROOMS, SLICED

1/2 CUP PLAIN DRY BREAD CRUMBS

1/4 CUP FINELY SNIPPED FRESH PARSLEY

2 TABLESPOONS SNIPPED FRESH DILLWEED OR 2 TEASPOONS DRIED, CRUMBLED

1/2 TEASPOON SALT

PEPPER TO TASTE

1/2 MEDIUM LEMON

◆

1/2 CUP DRY WHITE WINE (REGULAR OR NONALCOHOLIC) OR FAT-FREE, LOW-SODIUM CHICKEN BROTH

1 MEDIUM LEMON, SLICED (OPTIONAL)

FRESH PARSLEY SPRIGS (OPTIONAL)

Preheat the oven to 350°F.

Rinse the fish and pat dry with paper towels.

Heat a heavy nonstick skillet over medium-high heat. Pour the oil into the skillet and swirl to coat the bottom. Cook the onion for 2 to 3 minutes, or until tender.

Add the mushrooms; cook for 5 minutes, stirring occasionally. Remove the skillet from the heat.

Stir in the remaining stuffing ingredients except the lemon. Squeeze the lemon over the stuffing. Set aside to cool and to allow the bread crumbs to absorb the lemon juice.

Meanwhile, line a baking sheet with a piece of heavy-duty aluminum foil long enough to wrap and seal around the fish.

Place five fish fillets with skin side down in the center of the foil. Spoon equal amounts of the stuffing onto each fillet. Place one of the remaining fillets with skin side up on each "stuffed" fillet. Use toothpicks to secure the fish. Drizzle with the wine. Wrap the foil over fish; seal tightly to prevent steam and flavor from escaping.

Bake for 45 minutes, or until the fish flakes easily when tested with a fork. Open the foil package carefully to prevent a steam burn. Slide the fish onto a platter. Garnish with the lemon slices and parsley sprigs if desired.

PER SERVING	
CALORIES 115	CHOLESTEROL 43 mg
TOTAL FAT 1.5 g	SODIUM 190 mg
SATURATED 0.0 g	CARBOHYDRATES 6 g
POLYUNSATURATED 0.0 g	FIBER 1 g
MONOUNSATURATED 0.5 g	PROTEIN 18 g

poached fish in asian broth

serves 4

Packed with spices and seasonings, this broth gives the fish a delicate flavor. The grated carrot confetti makes the dish pretty enough for company.

BROTH

3	CUPS FAT-FREE, LOW-SODIUM CHICKEN BROTH
2	TABLESPOONS DRY SHERRY
2	TABLESPOONS LOW-SALT SOY SAUCE
2	LEMON SLICES
3	THIN SLICES PEELED GINGERROOT
1/8	TEASPOON CAYENNE

1	POUND THICK, MILD FISH FILLETS, SUCH AS ORANGE ROUGHY
5	TO 6 GREEN ONIONS (GREEN PART ONLY), CUT INTO 1-INCH PIECES
1	MEDIUM RED BELL PEPPER, CUT INTO 1/4 X 1-INCH PIECES
1	MEDIUM RIB OF CELERY, CUT INTO 1/4 X 1-INCH PIECES
1/2	TEASPOON TOASTED SESAME OIL
1	MEDIUM CARROT, GRATED
	BLACK PEPPER TO TASTE

In a nonaluminum fish poacher, a wok, or a large skillet, bring the broth ingredients to a boil over high heat.

Rinse the fish and pat dry with paper towels. Reduce the heat and put the fish in the broth. Add a small amount of water, if needed, to just cover the fish. Simmer the fish for about 10 minutes per inch of thickness at the thickest point, or just until the fish flakes easily when tested with a fork and is no longer translucent. Do not overcook.

Using a slotted spatula, remove the fish. Place equal portions in four soup bowls.

Return the liquid to a boil. Stir in the green onions, bell pepper, and celery. Cook for 2 to 3 minutes, or until the vegetables are tender-crisp. Remove and discard the lemon and gingerroot. Using a slotted spoon, remove the vegetables and arrange over the fish.

Stir the sesame oil into the broth. Pour equal amounts of broth into the soup bowls.

PER SERVING

CALORIES 123	CHOLESTEROL 23 mg
TOTAL FAT 1.5 g	SODIUM 330 mg
SATURATED 0 g	CARBOHYDRATES 6 g
POLYUNSATURATED 0.5 g	FIBER 2 g
MONOUNSATURATED 1.0 g	PROTEIN 20 g

Sprinkle each serving with the grated carrot and black pepper. Serve immediately.

Cook's Tip on Soy Sauce

When buying soy sauce, be sure to check the nutrition labels. Some brands of regular soy sauce actually contain less sodium than do those labeled as "light."

fish with mustard sauce over spinach

serves 4

Golden mustard sauce, white fish, and dark green spinach make a picture-perfect plate that is incredibly easy to prepare.

- **4 MILD FISH FILLETS, SUCH AS SOLE OR FLOUNDER (ABOUT 4 OUNCES EACH)**
- **1/4 CUP FAT-FREE OR LIGHT RANCH SALAD DRESSING**
- **3 TABLESPOONS FAT-FREE OR LOW-FAT PLAIN YOGURT**
- **1 1/2 TABLESPOONS PREPARED MUSTARD**
- **8 OUNCES FRESH SPINACH**

Preheat the oven to 400°F.

Rinse the fish and pat dry with paper towels. Place in a 12 x 8 x 2-inch glass baking dish.

In a small bowl, stir together the salad dressing, yogurt, and mustard. Spoon evenly over the fish.

Bake for 8 to 10 minutes, or until the fish flakes easily with a fork.

Meanwhile, remove the stems from the spinach. Rinse the spinach thoroughly. Drain well.

PER SERVING	
CALORIES 138	CHOLESTEROL 54 mg
TOTAL FAT 2.0 g	SODIUM 376 mg
SATURATED 0.5 g	CARBOHYDRATES 9 g
POLYUNSATURATED 0.5 g	FIBER 2 g
MONOUNSATURATED 0.5 g	PROTEIN 22 g

Heat a nonstick skillet over medium-high heat. Cook the spinach for 30 seconds, or just until wilted, stirring constantly.

Arrange the spinach in a single layer on serving plates. Top with the baked fish. Serve immediately.

halibut kebabs

Kebabs are an easy-to-prepare and fun way to enjoy mild-flavored halibut. For a simple but festive meal, serve with rice or pita bread and a fresh green salad.

1	POUND HALIBUT STEAK (ABOUT 1 INCH THICK)
1/4	CUP FRESH LEMON JUICE
1/4	CUP OLIVE OIL
3	MEDIUM SHALLOTS, THINLY SLICED
1	TEASPOON SALT-FREE ITALIAN HERB SEASONING
1/2	TEASPOON DRIED THYME, CRUMBLED
	VEGETABLE OIL SPRAY
1/2	LARGE RED ONION, CUT LENGTHWISE INTO THIRDS
1	LEMON, CUT INTO WEDGES

Rinse the fish and pat dry with paper towels. Remove the skin. Cut the fish into 16 cubes.

In a large bowl, stir together the lemon juice, oil, shallots, herb seasoning, and thyme. Add the fish and stir to coat. Cover and refrigerate for at least 5 minutes but no more than 1 hour.

PER SERVING

CALORIES 135	
TOTAL FAT 2.5 g	CHOLESTEROL 36 mg
SATURATED 0.5 g	SODIUM 62 mg
POLYUNSATURATED 1.0 g	CARBOHYDRATES 2 g
MONOUNSATURATED 1.0 g	FIBER 1 g
	PROTEIN 24 g

Soak four wooden skewers in water for at least 30 minutes to keep the wood from charring.

Meanwhile, preheat the broiler. Lightly spray the broiler rack with vegetable oil spray.

Peel the onion apart into single layers. Thread each skewer, alternating onion and fish, using four pieces of fish and five pieces of onion per skewer. Put the kebabs on the prepared rack.

Broil the kebabs about 4 inches from the heat for 2 to 2 1/2 minutes on each side, or until the fish flakes easily with a fork.

To serve, garnish with the lemon wedges.

grilled catfish with mustard-lemon sauce

serves 4

This creamy mustard sauce is an easy way to dress up fish or chicken. You can substitute honey mustard for the Dijon mustard if you prefer a sweeter sauce.

VEGETABLE OIL SPRAY

4 SMALL CATFISH FILLETS (ABOUT 1 POUND)

1/2 TEASPOON PEPPER

SAUCE

2 MEDIUM GARLIC CLOVES, MINCED

1 TABLESPOON ALL-PURPOSE FLOUR

1 1/4 CUPS FAT-FREE EVAPORATED MILK

1 TABLESPOON DIJON MUSTARD

2 TEASPOONS FINELY SHREDDED LEMON ZEST

1 TEASPOON CHOPPED FRESH BASIL, THYME, DILLWEED, PARSLEY, OR OREGANO OR 1/2 TEASPOON DRIED HERBS

FRESH HERBS FOR GARNISH (OPTIONAL)

PER SERVING	
CALORIES 184	CHOLESTEROL 69 mg
TOTAL FAT 3.5 g	SODIUM 231 mg
SATURATED 1.0 g	CARBOHYDRATES 11 g
POLYUNSATURATED 1.0 g	FIBER 0 g
MONOUNSATURATED 1.0 g	PROTEIN 25 g

Preheat the grill on medium–high. Lightly spray a grill basket or grill rack with vegetable oil spray.

Rinse the fish and pat dry with paper towels. Sprinkle both sides of the fish with pepper.

Grill the fish, uncovered, for 5 minutes per side, or until the fish flakes easily when tested with a fork.

Meanwhile, for the sauce, heat a small saucepan over medium heat. Remove the skillet from the heat and lightly spray with vegetable oil spray (being careful not to spray near a gas flame). Return the skillet to the heat and cook the garlic for 2 minutes, stirring occasionally.

Stir in the flour.

Stir in the milk all at once, stirring constantly (a wire whisk works best for this).

Stir in the mustard and lemon zest. Cook for 3 to 5 minutes, or until thickened and bubbly, stirring constantly.

Stir in 1 teaspoon herbs. Cook for 1 minute, stirring constantly.

Serve the fish with the sauce. Garnish with additional herbs if desired.

grilled cod with artichoke-horseradish sauce

California's artichoke industry started at the end of the 19th century. Today, this thistly plant is grown on thousands of acres throughout that state's mid-coastal region. This recipe uses artichoke hearts in a horseradish sauce served with grilled or broiled fish.

	14-OUNCE CAN ARTICHOKE HEARTS, RINSED AND DRAINED, OR 9-OUNCE PACKAGE FROZEN ARTICHOKE HEARTS, THAWED AND DRAINED
1	TABLESPOON LIGHT TUB MARGARINE
1/2	CUP CHOPPED SHALLOT OR ONION (ABOUT 4 MEDIUM SHALLOTS OR 1 MEDIUM ONION)
2	MEDIUM GARLIC CLOVES, MINCED
2	TABLESPOONS ALL-PURPOSE FLOUR
1/8	TEASPOON SALT
1/8	TEASPOON PEPPER
	12-OUNCE CAN FAT-FREE EVAPORATED MILK
1	TO 2 TABLESPOONS GRATED FRESH OR PREPARED WHITE HORSERADISH
1	TABLESPOON CHOPPED FRESH OREGANO OR 1 TEASPOON DRIED, CRUMBLED
	VEGETABLE OIL SPRAY
4	SMALL OR 2 MEDIUM COD FILLETS OR HALIBUT STEAKS (ABOUT 1 POUND)

Cut each artichoke heart into quarters. Set aside.

In a medium saucepan, melt the margarine over medium heat. Cook the shallot and garlic for 5 minutes, or until the shallot is tender.

Stir in the flour, salt, and pepper. Stir in the milk all at once. Cook for 5 to 10 minutes, or until the sauce is thickened and bubbly, stirring constantly. Cook and stir for 1 minute.

Stir in the artichoke hearts, horseradish, and oregano. Cook for 3 to 5 minutes, or until heated through, stirring constantly. Keep warm.

Preheat the grill on medium-high. Lightly spray the grill rack with vegetable oil spray.

Rinse the fish and pat dry with paper towels.

Grill the fish, uncovered, for 7 minutes. Turn and grill for 5 to 7 minutes, or until the fish flakes easily when tested with a fork. Or to broil, preheat the broiler. Lightly spray the broiler pan and rack with vegetable oil spray. Broil the fish about

PER SERVING

CALORIES 225	CHOLESTEROL 41 mg
TOTAL FAT 2.0 g	SODIUM 443 mg
SATURATED 0 g	CARBOHYDRATES 23 g
POLYUNSATURATED 0.5 g	FIBER 1 g
MONOUNSATURATED 1.0 g	PROTEIN 28 g

4 inches from the heat for 7 minutes. Turn and broil for 5 to 7 minutes, or until the fish flakes easily when tested with a fork.

To serve, spoon the artichoke sauce over the fish.

mesquite-grilled red snapper with gingered black bean salsa

serves 4

Chunks of mesquite wood give this grilled snapper recipe its distinctive smoky taste. Look for bags of mesquite chunks at your supermarket near the charcoal and lighter fluid.

VEGETABLE OIL SPRAY

SALSA

1/4	CUP CHOPPED ONION
1/4	CUP CHOPPED CARROT
1	TO 2 JALAPEÑO PEPPERS, SEEDS AND RIBS DISCARDED, CHOPPED
2	TABLESPOONS FINELY CHOPPED PEELED GINGERROOT
2	TO 3 MEDIUM GARLIC CLOVES, MINCED
	15-OUNCE CAN NO-SALT-ADDED BLACK BEANS, RINSED IF DESIRED AND DRAINED, 3 TABLESPOONS LIQUID RESERVED
1/4	TEASPOON SALT
1	MEDIUM TOMATO, SEEDS DISCARDED, CHOPPED

◆

1 POUND RED SNAPPER FILLETS (ABOUT 1/2 INCH THICK)

At least 1 hour before cooking, soak four to six mesquite wood chunks in enough water to cover.

Lightly spray the grill rack with vegetable oil spray and prepare the grill for heating.

For the salsa, heat a medium saucepan over medium-low heat. Remove from the heat and lightly spray with vegetable oil spray (being careful not to spray near a gas flame). Return the pan to the heat and cook the onion, carrot, jalapeños, gingerroot, and garlic for 5 minutes, or until the onion is tender.

Stir the black beans, reserved bean liquid, and salt into the onion mixture. Cook for 1 to 2 minutes, or until heated through. Stir in the tomatoes.

Drain the wood chunks and put them directly on the medium-hot coals.

Rinse the fish and pat dry with paper towels. Put the fish on the prepared rack.

Grill the fish, uncovered, directly over medium-hot coals for 5 minutes. Turn and grill for 5 to 7 minutes, or until the fish flakes easily

PER SERVING

CALORIES 229	CHOLESTEROL 42 mg
TOTAL FAT 1.5 g	SODIUM 225 mg
SATURATED 0.5 g	CARBOHYDRATES 22 g
POLYUNSATURATED 0.5 g	FIBER 5 g
MONOUNSATURATED 0.5 g	PROTEIN 30 g

when tested with a fork. Or to broil, preheat the broiler. Lightly spray the broiler pan and rack with vegetable oil spray. Broil the fish about 4 inches from the heat for 5 minutes. Turn and broil for 5 to 7 minutes, or until the fish flakes easily when tested with a fork.

Serve the fish with the salsa.

mediterranean grilled salmon

serves 6

The heady aroma of fresh herbs and the zing of lemon turn this salmon into a feast for the senses. Serve with crusty bread, risotto, and asparagus, such as Asparagus with Dill and Pine Nuts (page 346), on the side. When it's too cold outside for grilling, use the instructions for broiling instead.

MARINADE

- 1 **ITALIAN PLUM TOMATO, FINELY CHOPPED**
- 2 **TABLESPOONS RED WINE VINEGAR**
- 1 **TABLESPOON CHOPPED FRESH ROSEMARY OR 1 TEASPOON DRIED, CRUSHED**
- 1 **TABLESPOON CHOPPED FRESH SAGE OR 1 TEASPOON DRIED**
- 2 **TEASPOONS OLIVE OIL**
- 1 **TEASPOON GRATED LEMON ZEST**
- 1/4 **TEASPOON PEPPER**

◆

- 6 **SALMON FILLETS (ABOUT 4 OUNCES EACH)**
  VEGETABLE OIL SPRAY

In an airtight plastic bag or glass baking dish, combine the marinade ingredients. Seal the bag and shake gently to mix ingredients, or stir together if using a baking dish.

Rinse the fish and pat dry with paper towels. Add the fish to the marinade and seal the bag, turning gently to coat the fish. If using a glass baking dish, turn the fish to coat both sides and cover with plastic wrap. Refrigerate for 30 minutes or up to 2 hours. (Turn the fish every 15 minutes, if desired, to recoat with marinade.)

Preheat the grill on medium–high. Lightly spray the grill rack with vegetable oil spray.

Remove the fish from the bag and discard the marinade. Put the fish on the prepared rack.

Grill the fish for 5 to 6 minutes. Turn and grill for 4 to 5 minutes, or until the fish flakes easily when tested with a fork.

To broil the fish, preheat the broiler. Lightly spray a broiler-safe baking pan with vegetable oil spray. Put the fish in the prepared pan. Broil the fish about 4 inches from the heat for 4 to 5 minutes on each side, or until the fish flakes easily when tested with a fork.

PER SERVING

CALORIES 144	CHOLESTEROL 65 mg
TOTAL FAT 4.5 g	SODIUM 83 mg
SATURATED 0.5 g	CARBOHYDRATES 0 g
POLYUNSATURATED 1.5 g	FIBER 0 g
MONOUNSATURATED 1.0 g	PROTEIN 25 g

broiled salmon with pesto and olives

serves 4

An aromatic paste of fresh basil flecked with olives and pine nuts makes this salmon entrée very elegant yet incredibly easy to prepare. There's no need to wait for company—treat yourself.

VEGETABLE OIL SPRAY

4 SALMON FILLETS (ABOUT 4 OUNCES EACH)

1 CUP LOOSELY PACKED FRESH BASIL

2 TABLESPOONS PINE NUTS

2 TABLESPOONS SLICED BLACK OLIVES

1 TABLESPOON FAT-FREE OR LIGHT MAYONNAISE DRESSING

2 MEDIUM GARLIC CLOVES, MINCED

2 TEASPOONS OLIVE OIL

1 TEASPOON GRATED ORANGE ZEST

2 TABLESPOONS FRESH ORANGE JUICE

Preheat the broiler. Lightly spray a broiler-safe baking sheet with vegetable oil spray. Rinse the

PER SERVING

CALORIES 206	CHOLESTEROL 66 mg
TOTAL FAT 9.5 g	SODIUM 153 mg
SATURATED 1.5 g	CARBOHYDRATES 3 g
POLYUNSATURATED 2.5 g	FIBER 1 g
MONOUNSATURATED 4.0 g	PROTEIN 26 g

fish, pat dry with paper towels, and put on the baking sheet.

In a food processor or blender, process the remaining ingredients for 15 to 20 seconds, or until slightly chunky.

Using a pastry brush or spoon, spread the pesto mixture evenly over both sides of the fish. (The salmon can be covered and refrigerated for up to 4 hours at this point.)

Broil the fish about 4 inches from the heat for 4 to 5 minutes. Turn and broil for 4 to 5 minutes, or until the fish flakes easily when tested with a fork.

tilapia with roasted red bell peppers and olives

serves 4

You can count on this dish for a picture-perfect presentation. Because most tilapia is farm-raised, these fillets are usually evenly sized.

VEGETABLE OIL SPRAY

4 TILAPIA FILLETS (ABOUT 4 OUNCES EACH)

1/4 TEASPOON BLACK PEPPER

PAPRIKA TO TASTE

3/4 CUP DICED ROASTED RED BELL PEPPERS, RINSED AND DRAINED IF BOTTLED (ABOUT 6 OUNCES)

12 PIMIENTO-STUFFED GREEN OLIVES, CHOPPED

2 TABLESPOONS MINCED GREEN ONIONS (GREEN AND WHITE PARTS)

2 TABLESPOONS FINELY SNIPPED PARSLEY

2 TEASPOONS OLIVE OIL (EXTRA-VIRGIN PREFERRED)

1 1/2 TEASPOONS DRIED BASIL, CRUMBLED

1 TO 2 MEDIUM LEMONS, QUARTERED

PER SERVING

CALORIES 120	CHOLESTEROL 43 mg
TOTAL FAT 4.5 g	SODIUM 435 mg
SATURATED 0.5 g	CARBOHYDRATES 5 g
POLYUNSATURATED 0.5 g	FIBER 1 g
MONOUNSATURATED 2.5 g	PROTEIN 17 g

Preheat the oven to 350°F. Lightly spray a baking sheet with vegetable oil spray.

Rinse the fish and pat dry with paper towels, and put on the baking sheet. Lightly spray with vegetable oil spray. Sprinkle with black pepper and paprika.

Bake for 10 to 12 minutes, or until the fish flakes easily when tested with a fork.

Meanwhile, in a small bowl, stir together the remaining ingredients except the lemons.

To serve, squeeze a lemon wedge over each fillet. Top with equal amounts of the pepper-olive mixture. Serve with additional lemon wedges if desired.

bulgur-stuffed trout

The clear, crisp waters of the Rocky Mountains are known for their abundance of trout. This version features these flavorful fish stuffed with a mixture of bulgur, vegetables, seasonings, and lemon.

STUFFING

- 1/2 **CUP BOILING WATER**
- 1/4 **CUP UNCOOKED BULGUR**
- **VEGETABLE OIL SPRAY**
- 1/2 **CUP CHOPPED ONION OR SHALLOT (ABOUT 1 MEDIUM ONION OR 4 MEDIUM SHALLOTS)**
- 1/2 **CUP CHOPPED CELERY**
- 3 **MEDIUM GARLIC CLOVES, MINCED**
- 1/4 **CUP SNIPPED FRESH PARSLEY OR FRESH BASIL**
- 1/2 **TEASPOON FINELY SHREDDED LEMON ZEST**
- 1/4 **TEASPOON SALT**
- 1/8 **TEASPOON PEPPER**

- 4 **FRESH OR FROZEN DRESSED RAINBOW TROUT (ABOUT 8 OUNCES EACH; ORGANS, SCALES, HEAD, AND TAIL DISCARDED, LEAVING SKIN AND BONES), THAWED IF FROZEN**
- **PEPPER TO TASTE**
- 1 **MEDIUM LEMON, QUARTERED**

To prepare the stuffing, combine the boiling water and bulgur in a medium bowl. Let stand for 20 minutes, or until the water is absorbed.

Preheat the oven to 350°F.

Heat a medium saucepan over medium–low heat. Remove from the heat and lightly spray with vegetable oil spray (being careful not to spray near a gas flame). Return the pan to the heat and cook the onion, celery, and garlic for 5 minutes, or until the onion is tender. Remove from the heat. Stir in the bulgur, parsley, lemon zest, salt, and 1/8 teaspoon pepper.

Rinse the fish and pat dry with paper towels. Spoon one fourth (about 1/4 cup) of the bulgur mixture into each fish cavity. Place the fish in a shallow baking pan.

Bake for 30 minutes, or until the fish flakes easily when tested with a fork and the filling is heated through. Remove the skin from the fish. Season with the pepper. Garnish with the lemon wedges.

PER SERVING

CALORIES 258	CHOLESTEROL 98 mg
TOTAL FAT 8.5 g	SODIUM 243 mg
SATURATED 2.5 g	CARBOHYDRATES 10 g
POLYUNSATURATED 2.5 g	FIBER 2 g
MONOUNSATURATED 2.5 g	PROTEIN 34 g

Microwave Directions

Prepare as above, except after stuffing the fish, place it in a single layer in a 9-inch square microwave-safe baking dish. Cover with vented plastic wrap. Microwave on 100 percent power (high) for 5 minutes. Rotate the dish a half-turn. Cook for 5 minutes, or until the fish flakes easily when tested with a fork and the filling is heated through.

tuna-pasta casserole

serves 6

This heart–healthy version of an old standby will please everyone in your family who loves comfort food.

8	OUNCES DRIED LINGUINE, VERMICELLI, SPAGHETTI, OR OTHER THIN PASTA
1	TEASPOON ACCEPTABLE VEGETABLE OIL
1	SMALL ONION, CHOPPED
1	MEDIUM GARLIC CLOVE, MINCED
2	6-OUNCE CANS TUNA IN SPRING WATER, RINSED, DRAINED, AND FLAKED
1/2	CUP FINELY CHOPPED CARROT
1/3	CUP FINELY CHOPPED GREEN BELL PEPPER
1/4	CUP FINELY SNIPPED FRESH PARSLEY
1/4	TEASPOON PAPRIKA, OR TO TASTE
1	CUP FAT-FREE OR LOW-FAT COTTAGE CHEESE
1/2	CUP FAT-FREE OR LIGHT SOUR CREAM
1/2	CUP FAT-FREE OR LOW-FAT PLAIN YOGURT
	VEGETABLE OIL SPRAY
1/2	CUP PLAIN DRY BREAD CRUMBS, TOASTED
1/4	CUP GRATED OR SHREDDED PARMESAN CHEESE

PER SERVING

CALORIES 349	CHOLESTEROL 32 mg
TOTAL FAT 4.5 g	SODIUM 361 mg
SATURATED 1.5 g	CARBOHYDRATES 46 g
POLYUNSATURATED 1.5 g	FIBER 2 g
MONOUNSATURATED 1.5 g	PROTEIN 29 g

Prepare the pasta using the package directions, omitting the salt and oil. Drain well.

Meanwhile, preheat the oven to 350°F.

Heat a nonstick skillet over medium-high heat. Pour the oil into the skillet and swirl to coat the bottom. Cook the onion and garlic for 2 to 3 minutes, or until the onion is tender, stirring frequently. Transfer the onion and garlic to a large bowl.

Stir the tuna, carrot, bell pepper, parsley, and paprika into the onion-garlic mixture.

In a small bowl, stir together the cottage cheese, sour cream, and yogurt. Stir the cottage cheese mixture and pasta into the tuna mixture.

Lightly spray a 9 x 11 x 2-inch casserole dish with vegetable oil spray. Pour the tuna mixture into the casserole dish.

In a small bowl, combine the bread crumbs and Parmesan. Sprinkle over the casserole.

Bake for 30 to 45 minutes, or until the top is lightly browned.

tuna salad pita sandwiches

serves 6

Take delicious advantage of the freshest produce to make this low-cholesterol update of a classic favorite.

TUNA SALAD

6-OUNCE CAN TUNA IN SPRING WATER, RINSED, DRAINED, AND FLAKED

1 MEDIUM CARROT, SHREDDED

1 SMALL TOMATO, FINELY CHOPPED

3 GREEN ONIONS (GREEN AND WHITE PARTS), FINELY CHOPPED

3 TABLESPOONS FAT-FREE OR LIGHT MAYONNAISE DRESSING

2 TABLESPOONS FINELY CHOPPED CELERY

2 TABLESPOONS FINELY SNIPPED FRESH PARSLEY

2 TABLESPOONS FINELY CHOPPED GREEN PEPPER

2 TABLESPOONS SALSA OR PICANTE SAUCE

PEPPER TO TASTE

3 7-INCH WHOLE-WHEAT PITA BREADS

6 LETTUCE LEAVES, RINSED AND DRIED

1 MEDIUM TOMATO, CUT INTO 6 SLICES

6 FRESH MEDIUM MUSHROOMS, SLICED

6 FRESH PARSLEY SPRIGS (OPTIONAL)

Stir together the tuna salad ingredients. Cover and refrigerate for at least 1 hour.

Cut each pita in half. Line each half with a leaf of lettuce, a slice of tomato, and mushroom slices. Spoon the tuna salad into the pitas. Garnish each pita half with a sprig of parsley if desired.

PER SERVING

CALORIES 150	CHOLESTEROL 12 mg
TOTAL FAT 2.0 g	SODIUM 285 mg
SATURATED 0.5 g	CARBOHYDRATES 24 g
POLYUNSATURATED 1.0 g	FIBER 4 g
MONOUNSATURATED 0.5 g	PROTEIN 11 g

baked crabmeat

This dish is a real treat—light, festive, and healthful.

VEGETABLE OIL SPRAY

1   TEASPOON LIGHT STICK MARGARINE

1/4   CUP FINELY CHOPPED ONION

1   POUND CRABMEAT, SHELLS AND CARTILAGE DISCARDED

2   TABLESPOONS DIJON MUSTARD

1   TEASPOON WORCESTERSHIRE SAUCE

WHITES OF 4 LARGE EGGS, STIFFLY BEATEN

2   TABLESPOONS GRATED OR SHREDDED PARMESAN CHEESE

Preheat the oven to 350°F.

Lightly spray a 9-inch square casserole dish or baking pan with vegetable oil spray.

In a small saucepan, melt the margarine over medium-high heat. Cook the onion for 2 to 3 minutes, or until tender.

Transfer the onion to a medium bowl. Stir in the crabmeat, mustard, and Worcestershire sauce.

PER SERVING

CALORIES 137

TOTAL FAT 2.5 g

  SATURATED 0.5 g

  POLYUNSATURATED 0.5 g

  MONOUNSATURATED 0.5 g

CHOLESTEROL 71 mg

SODIUM 564 mg

CARBOHYDRATES 3 g

FIBER 0 g

PROTEIN 24 g

Gently fold in the beaten egg whites. Pour the mixture into the casserole dish. Sprinkle with the cheese.

Bake for 25 minutes, or until puffed and lightly browned. Remove from the oven and cut into rectangles. Serve immediately.

Cook's Tip on Beating Egg Whites

Even a single drop of egg yolk will prevent egg whites from rising, so separate eggs very carefully.

california bowls

Enjoy the popular California sushi roll without the fuss! Crabmeat and fresh-crisp vegetables top seasoned cooked rice. Add wasabi-spiked sauce and pickled ginger for just the right amount of tingle to your taste buds.

3	CUPS WATER
2	CUPS UNCOOKED MEDIUM-GRAIN RICE
1/4	CUP PLAIN RICE VINEGAR
1/4	CUP DRY WHITE WINE (REGULAR OR NONALCOHOLIC) OR WATER
1	TABLESPOON LIGHT BROWN SUGAR
12	OUNCES IMITATION CRABMEAT
1	MEDIUM CUCUMBER, PEELED IF DESIRED, AND THINLY SLICED CROSSWISE
1 1/2	CUPS SHREDDED CARROT
1 1/2	CUPS THINLY SLICED GREEN ONIONS (GREEN AND WHITE PARTS)
1	SMALL AVOCADO, CHOPPED

SAUCE

1/2	CUP PLUS 2 TABLESPOONS FAT-FREE, LOW-SODIUM CHICKEN BROTH
2	TABLESPOONS LOW-SALT SOY SAUCE
1	TEASPOON PREPARED WASABI, WASABI POWDER, OR PREPARED WHITE HORSERADISH

2	TABLESPOONS PICKLED GINGER SLICES (OPTIONAL)

In a medium nonstick saucepan, stir together the water, rice, rice vinegar, wine, and brown sugar. Bring to a boil over high heat. Reduce the heat and simmer, covered, for 20 minutes (no stirring needed).

Remove the pan from the heat and put on a cooling rack. Let stand, covered, for 5 minutes. Uncover and fluff with a fork. Let cool for 10 minutes.

Spoon about 1 cup rice into each of six soup bowls. Arrange the crabmeat, cucumber, carrot, green onions, and avocado on top of the rice, distributing the ingredients evenly.

In a small bowl, whisk together the sauce ingredients. Spoon about 2 tablespoons sauce over each bowl, or serve the sauce on the side.

Top each bowl with pickled ginger if desired.

Cook's Tip

These California bowls are great to keep handy for a quick meal to go. Store in an airtight container in the refrigerator for up to four days.

PER SERVING	
CALORIES 378	CHOLESTEROL 11 mg
TOTAL FAT 5.0 g	SODIUM 640 mg
SATURATED 1.0 g	CARBOHYDRATES 68 g
POLYUNSATURATED 1.0 g	FIBER 4 g
MONOUNSATURATED 2.5 g	PROTEIN 13 g

Remember to add the avocado just before serving.

Cook's Tip on Wasabi and Pickled Ginger

Japanese horseradish is known as wasabi and has a bright green color and peppery flavor, similar to prepared horseradish. Pickled ginger adds a spicy-sweet flavor to foods and makes a great garnish. Wafer-thin slices of fresh ginger are preserved in sweet vinegar and sold in jars. Find both wasabi and pickled ginger in Asian markets or the Asian section of your grocery store.

mussels with yogurt-caper sauce

serves 6

This elegant recipe is also quick to prepare. Mussels have a sweet flavor and tender texture that is complemented by basil, lemon, and a yogurt sauce seasoned with capers and chives. Serve with crusty whole-wheat bread to soak up the aromatic cooking liquid.

YOGURT SAUCE

- 3/4   CUP FAT-FREE OR LOW-FAT PLAIN YOGURT
- 1   TABLESPOON CAPERS, RINSED AND DRAINED
- 1   TABLESPOON SNIPPED FRESH CHIVES OR CHOPPED GREEN ONIONS (GREEN PART ONLY)
- 1   TEASPOON GRATED LEMON ZEST
- 1/4   TEASPOON SUGAR

◆

- 2   POUNDS RAW MUSSELS IN SHELLS
- 1   CUP DRY WHITE WINE (REGULAR OR NONALCOHOLIC), VERMOUTH, OR WATER
- 1   SMALL LEMON, THINLY SLICED CROSSWISE
- 2   TABLESPOONS COARSELY CHOPPED FRESH BASIL OR 2 TEASPOONS DRIED, CRUMBLED
- 2   MEDIUM GARLIC CLOVES, MINCED

In a small bowl, stir together the yogurt sauce ingredients. Cover and refrigerate until ready to serve. (This sauce will keep in the refrigerator for up to four days.)

Scrub the mussels under cold running water. With fingertips or kitchen scissors, remove any black, stringy beards.

In a large stockpot, bring the wine, lemon, basil, and garlic to a boil over high heat, stirring occasionally. Stir in the mussels. Reduce the heat and simmer, covered, for 6 to 8 minutes, or until the shells open.

Using tongs or a slotted spoon, remove and discard any mussels that have not opened.

Transfer the mussels with the cooking liquid to a serving bowl. Serve the yogurt sauce on the side.

Cook's Tip on Choosing Fresh Mussels

Use these simple rules of thumb when choosing fresh mussels: Be sure the mussels have no offensive odor, select those which have a tightly closed shell, and do not use mussels with broken or

PER SERVING	
CALORIES 195	CHOLESTEROL 48 mg
TOTAL FAT 4.0 g	SODIUM 377 mg
SATURATED 1.0 g	CARBOHYDRATES 10 g
POLYUNSATURATED 1.0 g	FIBER 0 g
MONOUNSATURATED 1.0 g	PROTEIN 22 g

cracked shells. Cook mussels the same day you buy them, or at least by the next day. Do not use any mussels that are not alive. Although a mussel may open and close periodically before being cooked, if still alive its shell should close tightly when tapped. Also be sure to discard any mussels that do not open after cooking.

shrimp rémoulade

serves 4

This hot and spicy Cajun specialty is a perfect light main dish for those sultry summer days.

6	CUPS WATER
1	MEDIUM LEMON, QUARTERED
2	MEDIUM GARLIC CLOVES, HALVED
2	BAY LEAVES
1/4	TEASPOON SALT
1/4	TEASPOON CAYENNE

DRESSING

1/4	CUP FINELY CHOPPED CELERY
1/4	CUP SLICED GREEN ONIONS (GREEN AND WHITE PARTS)
1/4	CUP SNIPPED FRESH PARSLEY
3	TABLESPOONS VINEGAR
2	TABLESPOONS WATER
2	TABLESPOONS CREOLE OR GERMAN MUSTARD
1	TABLESPOON GRATED FRESH OR PREPARED WHITE HORSERADISH
1	TEASPOON PAPRIKA
1/4	TEASPOON RED HOT-PEPPER SAUCE

1 **POUND RAW LARGE SHRIMP, PEELED**

4 **LARGE LETTUCE LEAVES**

In a medium saucepan, stir together the water, lemon, garlic, bay leaves, salt, and cayenne. Bring to a boil over high heat. Reduce the heat and simmer, uncovered, for 10 minutes.

Meanwhile, in a medium bowl, stir together the dressing ingredients.

Increase the heat to high. Add the shrimp and return to a boil. Reduce the heat and simmer for 1 to 3 minutes, or until the shrimp turn pink. Drain. Discard the lemon, bay leaves, and garlic.

Stir the shrimp into the dressing to coat thoroughly. Cover and refrigerate for 4 to 24 hours, stirring occasionally.

To serve, spoon the chilled shrimp mixture onto the lettuce leaves.

PER SERVING

CALORIES 93	CHOLESTEROL 166 mg
TOTAL FAT 1.0 g	SODIUM 476 mg
SATURATED 0.5 g	CARBOHYDRATES 2 g
POLYUNSATURATED 0.5 g	FIBER 1 g
MONOUNSATURATED 0.0 g	PROTEIN 18 g

Cook's Tip on Mustards

Your choice of mustard affects the overall flavor of the dressing. Horseradish contributes to the heat and spiciness of Creole mustard. German mustard, spicy and a little sweet, ranges from mild to hot.

seafood and lemon risotto

Creamy lemon-flavored rice joins scallops and shrimp in this hearty entrée, made colorful by snow peas and red bell pepper. This recipe uses a streamlined preparation method that lets you stir less than in most other risotto recipes.

VEGETABLE OIL SPRAY

1 MEDIUM LEEK, SLICED

2 MEDIUM GARLIC CLOVES, MINCED

1 CUP UNCOOKED ARBORIO RICE

2 CUPS FAT-FREE, LOW-SODIUM CHICKEN BROTH, DIVIDED USE

1 CUP DRY WHITE WINE (REGULAR OR NONALCOHOLIC)

8 OUNCES BAY SCALLOPS, RINSED AND PATTED DRY WITH PAPER TOWELS

8 OUNCES RAW MEDIUM SHRIMP IN SHELLS, RINSED AND PEELED

3 OUNCES FRESH SNOW PEA PODS, TRIMMED AND HALVED CROSSWISE

1/2 MEDIUM RED BELL PEPPER, CHOPPED

3 TABLESPOONS GRATED OR SHREDDED PARMESAN CHEESE

2 TABLESPOONS CHOPPED FRESH BASIL OR 2 TEASPOONS DRIED, CRUMBLED

1 1/2 TO 2 TABLESPOONS FINELY SHREDDED LEMON ZEST

GRATED OR SHREDDED PARMESAN CHEESE (OPTIONAL)

Heat a medium saucepan over medium-low heat. Remove from the heat and lightly spray with vegetable oil spray (being careful not to spray near a gas flame). Return the pan to the heat and cook the leeks and garlic for 5 minutes, or until the leeks are tender.

Stir in the rice. Cook for 5 minutes, stirring often.

Stir in 1 1/2 cups broth. Bring to a boil over high heat, stirring occasionally. Reduce the heat and simmer for 5 minutes, stirring occasionally.

Pour in the remaining 1/2 cup chicken broth and the wine. Increase the heat to medium; cook for 5 to 8 minutes, stirring constantly (a small amount of liquid should remain).

Add the scallops, shrimp, pea pods, and bell pepper. Cook for 5 minutes, or until the liquid is almost absorbed, stirring constantly. (The rice should be just tender and slightly creamy.)

Stir in 3 tablespoons Parmesan, basil, and lemon

PER SERVING

CALORIES 395	CHOLESTEROL 106 mg
TOTAL FAT 2.0 g	SODIUM 297 mg
SATURATED 1.0 g	CARBOHYDRATES 54 g
POLYUNSATURATED 0.5 g	FIBER 3 g
MONOUNSATURATED 0.5 g	PROTEIN 26 g

zest. Heat through. Serve immediately. Serve with additional Parmesan if desired.

Cook's Tip on Risotto

For proper consistency, carefully regulate the cooking temperature so the risotto boils lightly, not vigorously. If the liquid is absorbed before the rice reaches the just-tender stage, add more broth, wine, or water, a little at a time. Arborio rice is usually used in risottos, but you can substitute a medium-grain rice if you prefer. It won't be quite as creamy, however.

cajun red scallops

Scared of scallops? The secret for perfectly cooked and tender scallops is in the timing—as soon as scallops become opaque, pull them off the heat.

6   OUNCES DRIED NO-YOLK EGG NOODLES

1/2 TEASPOON PAPRIKA

1/2 TEASPOON CAJUN SEASONING

1   POUND SEA SCALLOPS, RINSED AND PATTED DRY WITH PAPER TOWELS

3   TABLESPOONS LIGHT TUB MARGARINE

1   TEASPOON DIJON MUSTARD

1   TEASPOON GRATED LEMON ZEST

1/4 TEASPOON SALT

     VEGETABLE OIL SPRAY

2   TABLESPOONS FINELY SNIPPED PARSLEY

1   MEDIUM LEMON, QUARTERED

Prepare the noodles using the package directions, omitting the salt and margarine. Drain in a colander. Transfer to a platter and cover to keep warm.

PER SERVING

CALORIES 291

TOTAL FAT 4.5 g

  SATURATED 0.0 g

  POLYUNSATURATED 1.0 g

  MONOUNSATURATED 2.0 g

CHOLESTEROL 37 mg

SODIUM 507 mg

CARBOHYDRATES 35 g

FIBER 2 g

PROTEIN 24 g

In a small bowl, stir together the paprika and Cajun seasoning. Sprinkle evenly over the scallops to coat.

In the same bowl, stir together the margarine, mustard, lemon zest, and salt.

Heat a large nonstick skillet over medium-high heat. Remove from the heat and lightly spray with vegetable oil spray (being careful not to spray near a gas flame). Return the skillet to the heat and cook the scallops for 3 minutes. Turn and cook for 2 minutes, or until just opaque in the center. Remove from the heat.

Using a rubber spatula, stir the margarine mixture into the scallops until completely blended, scraping the bottom and sides of the skillet.

Spoon the scallops over the noodles. Sprinkle with the parsley. Serve with the lemon wedges.

cioppino

Cioppino, an entrée in a bowl, is great for no-worry entertaining.

- 1 TEASPOON ACCEPTABLE VEGETABLE OIL
- 1 LARGE CARROT, THINLY SLICED
- 1/2 CUP COARSELY CHOPPED CELERY
- 1 MEDIUM GREEN BELL PEPPER, COARSELY CHOPPED
- 1/2 LARGE ONION, COARSELY CHOPPED
- 1 POUND HALIBUT OR SHARK STEAKS, SKIN DISCARDED
- 1 CUP BOTTLED CLAM JUICE
- 1 1/2 CUPS FAT-FREE, LOW-SODIUM CHICKEN BROTH
- 2 CUPS DRY WHITE WINE (REGULAR OR NONALCOHOLIC)
- 6-OUNCE CAN TOMATO PUREE
- 1 BAY LEAF
- 8-OUNCE CAN BABY CLAMS, WITH JUICE
- 1 TABLESPOON CHOPPED FRESH BASIL OR 1 TEASPOON DRIED, CRUMBLED
- 1 1/2 TEASPOONS CHOPPED FRESH OREGANO OR 1/2 TEASPOON DRIED, CRUMBLED
- 1 1/2 TEASPOONS CHOPPED FRESH THYME OR 1/2 TEASPOON DRIED, CRUMBLED
- 1/4 CUP FINELY SNIPPED FRESH PARSLEY
- 6 COOKED CRAB CLAWS

Heat a large nonstick skillet over medium-high heat. Pour the oil into the skillet and swirl to coat the bottom. Cook the carrot, celery, bell pepper, and onion for 5 to 7 minutes, or until tender, stirring occasionally.

Rinse the fish and pat dry with paper towels. Cut into 1-inch pieces.

In a 4-quart saucepan, bring the vegetable mixture, clam juice, broth, wine, tomato puree, and bay leaf to a boil. Stir in the remaining ingredients except the crab claws and return to a boil. Reduce the heat and simmer, partially covered, for 15 minutes. Add the crab claws. Simmer for 2 minutes, or until heated through. Remove the bay leaf. Serve immediately.

PER SERVING

CALORIES 279	CHOLESTEROL 98 mg
TOTAL FAT 4.5 g	SODIUM 683 mg
SATURATED 1.0 g	CARBOHYDRATES 10 g
POLYUNSATURATED 1.0 g	FIBER 2 g
MONOUNSATURATED 1.0 g	PROTEIN 36 g

poultry

Crispy Oven-Fried Chicken

Asian Grilled Chicken

Brunswick Stew

Creamy Chicken Curry

Thai Chicken with Basil and Vegetables

Chicken Fajitas

Hearty Chicken Stew

Chicken with Mustard and Herbs

Chicken-Vegetable Stir-Fry

Cheese-Herb Chicken Medallions

Chicken Breasts Stuffed with Ricotta and Goat Cheese

Chicken Ragout

Quick Curry-Roasted Chicken with Cucumber Raita

Garlic Chicken Fillets in Balsamic Vinegar

Moroccan Chicken

Cajun Chicken Pasta

Greek-Style Stewed Chicken

Asparagus-Chicken à la King with Roasted Peppers

Southwestern Turkey and Chayote Squash

Ziti and Turkey Meatball Casserole

Turkey Tetrazzini

Open-Face Turkey Sandwiches

Roast Cornish Hens

Tandoori Cornish Hens with Nectarine-Plum Chutney

crispy oven-fried chicken

This heart-friendly alternative to traditional fried chicken is spicy and easy to make. The ginger is a pleasant surprise for your taste buds.

VEGETABLE OIL SPRAY

4 CUPS WHEAT-FLAKE OR CORNFLAKE CEREAL, LIGHTLY CRUSHED

1 MEDIUM GARLIC CLOVE, CRUSHED (OPTIONAL)

1 TEASPOON GROUND GINGER, OR TO TASTE

1 TEASPOON PAPRIKA

1/4 TEASPOON SALT (OPTIONAL)

PEPPER TO TASTE

6 PIECES SKINLESS CHICKEN WITH BONE (ABOUT 2 1/4 POUNDS), ALL VISIBLE FAT DISCARDED

VEGETABLE OIL SPRAY, BUTTER-FLAVORED OR ORIGINAL

Preheat the oven to 350°F. Lightly spray a baking sheet with vegetable oil spray.

PER SERVING

CALORIES 224

TOTAL FAT 2.5 g
  SATURATED 0.5 g
  POLYUNSATURATED 0.5 g
  MONOUNSATURATED 0.5 g

CHOLESTEROL 79 mg
SODIUM 234 mg
CARBOHYDRATES 17 g
FIBER 2 g
PROTEIN 34 g

In a pie pan or on a piece of aluminum foil, stir together the cereal and garlic.

In a small bowl, combine the ginger, paprika, salt if desired, and pepper. Sprinkle the seasonings on both sides of each piece of chicken.

Roll the chicken in the cereal crumbs to coat. Lightly spray the chicken on all sides with vegetable oil spray and put on the prepared baking sheet.

Bake for 45 to 60 minutes, or until the chicken is golden brown, tender, and no longer pink in the center. (Timing will vary according to the thickness of the chicken pieces.)

Cook's Tip on Skinning Poultry

You can dramatically reduce the amount of fat and cholesterol in poultry by discarding the skin. Due to its slippery nature, however, poultry skin can be a challenge to remove. Hold the poultry piece on a flat surface (a plastic cutting board is recommended), grasp the skin with a double thickness of paper towels, and pull firmly. Discard the paper towels. Use a knife or kitchen scissors to trim any remaining visible fat.

asian grilled chicken

An oil-free marinade gives this chicken its deliciously different barbecue taste.

MARINADE

1/4	CUP HONEY
3	TABLESPOONS RED WINE VINEGAR
1/4	CUP LOW-SALT SOY SAUCE
1	MEDIUM GARLIC CLOVE, MINCED
2	TABLESPOONS FINELY SNIPPED FRESH PARSLEY
2	TEASPOONS GRATED PEELED GINGERROOT OR 1 TEASPOON GROUND GINGER
1/2	TEASPOON PEPPER

◆

6	SKINLESS CHICKEN BREAST HALVES WITH BONE (ABOUT 6 OUNCES EACH), ALL VISIBLE FAT DISCARDED
	VEGETABLE OIL SPRAY

In a large bowl, stir together the marinade ingredients to mix well.

PER SERVING	
CALORIES 120	CHOLESTEROL 63 mg
TOTAL FAT 1.5 g	SODIUM 331 mg
SATURATED 0.5 g	CARBOHYDRATES 0 g
POLYUNSATURATED 0.5 g	FIBER 0 g
MONOUNSATURATED 0.5 g	PROTEIN 25 g

Add the chicken to the marinade, turning to coat thoroughly. Cover and refrigerate for at least 2 hours, turning occasionally.

Preheat the grill on high. Lightly spray the grill rack with vegetable oil spray.

Grill the chicken for 30 to 45 minutes, or until no longer pink in the center, brushing the pieces with marinade and turning them frequently. Or to broil, preheat the broiler. Lightly spray a broiler-safe baking sheet with vegetable oil spray. Put the chicken on the prepared sheet. Broil about 5 inches from the heat for 25 to 30 minutes, or until the chicken is no longer pink in the center, brushing the pieces with marinade and turning them frequently.

brunswick stew

serves 6

You don't have to live in Brunswick County, Virginia, to enjoy this variation of its famous stew. Chicken chunks accented with vegetables and lima beans will warm you up on a cold day.

VEGETABLE OIL SPRAY

1 TEASPOON OLIVE OIL

1 MEDIUM ONION, CHOPPED

1 POUND BONELESS, SKINLESS CHICKEN BREASTS, ALL VISIBLE FAT DISCARDED

1 1/2 CUPS FRESH OR FROZEN BABY LIMA BEANS

2 CUPS FRESH OR FROZEN WHOLE-KERNEL CORN

3 CUPS FAT-FREE, LOW-SODIUM CHICKEN BROTH

1 1/2 CUPS CHOPPED TOMATOES

6-OUNCE CAN NO-SALT-ADDED TOMATO PASTE

3 TABLESPOONS FRESH LEMON JUICE

1 TABLESPOON VERY LOW SODIUM OR LOW-SODIUM WORCESTERSHIRE SAUCE

Heat a deep skillet or Dutch oven over medium-high heat. Remove the skillet from the heat and

PER SERVING	
CALORIES 234	CHOLESTEROL 44 mg
TOTAL FAT 3.0 g	SODIUM 123 mg
SATURATED 0.5 g	CARBOHYDRATES 29 g
POLYUNSATURATED 1.0 g	FIBER 6 g
MONOUNSATURATED 1.0 g	PROTEIN 25 g

lightly spray with vegetable oil spray (being careful not to spray near a gas flame). Pour the oil into the skillet and swirl to coat the bottom. Return the skillet to the heat and cook the onion for 3 minutes, or until tender.

Meanwhile, cut the chicken breasts into 1-inch cubes.

Stir the chicken and remaining ingredients into the skillet. Reduce the heat and simmer, covered, for 1 hour.

creamy chicken curry

serves 6

This intricately flavored dish brings the warmth and intensity of Indian cuisine to your table. Serve over basmati rice to savor the deep orange sauce flecked with fresh cilantro.

2	TABLESPOONS ACCEPTABLE VEGETABLE OIL
1	MEDIUM ONION, FINELY CHOPPED
2	TEASPOONS GARLIC POWDER
	6-OUNCE CAN NO-SALT-ADDED TOMATO PASTE
2	TEASPOONS GROUND CUMIN
1 1/2	TEASPOONS GROUND CORIANDER
1/2	TEASPOON GROUND TURMERIC
1/2	TEASPOON CAYENNE
8	OUNCES FAT-FREE OR LIGHT SOUR CREAM
1	POUND BONELESS, SKINLESS CHICKEN BREASTS, ALL VISIBLE FAT DISCARDED, CUT INTO BITE-SIZE PIECES
1	TEASPOON SALT
1	TABLESPOON MINCED PEELED GINGERROOT
1	MEDIUM JALAPEÑO PEPPER, SEEDS AND RIBS DISCARDED
1/2	CUP FINELY SNIPPED FRESH CILANTRO
1	TEASPOON GARAM MASALA (OPTIONAL)

Heat a large skillet over medium-high heat. Pour the oil into the skillet and swirl to coat the bottom. Cook the onion for 4 to 5 minutes. Add the garlic powder; cook for 1 minute to brown, stirring constantly.

Stir in the tomato paste, cumin, coriander, turmeric, and cayenne. Cook for 1 minute, stirring occasionally. Stir in the sour cream.

Add the chicken and salt. If the mixture seems dry, add a little water as needed. Stir and bring to a boil. Reduce the heat and simmer, uncovered, for 15 minutes, stirring occasionally.

Stir in the gingerroot and jalapeño. Cook for 10 minutes, or until the chicken is no longer pink in the center.

To serve, sprinkle with the cilantro and garam masala if desired.

Cook's Tip on Garam Masala

Dry-roasted spices are ground together to make this distinctive blend. Garam masala—which may include 10 to 12 different spices such as cumin, coriander, cloves, cardamom, black pepper, mace, and others—is usually added to food just before it is finished cooking or right before the dish is served to enhance the complexity of flavor.

PER SERVING

CALORIES 209	CHOLESTEROL 50 mg
TOTAL FAT 6.0 g	SODIUM 496 mg
SATURATED 0.5 g	CARBOHYDRATES 17 g
POLYUNSATURATED 1.5 g	FIBER 2 g
MONOUNSATURATED 3.0 g	PROTEIN 22 g

Cook's Tip on Turmeric

Ground turmeric is a worthwhile investment for your spice collection. Sometimes known as "poor man's saffron" because it is more affordable, turmeric adds a beautiful reddish-orange color to foods. It also has a pungent flavor, so use it sparingly if you only want to enhance the color of your dish.

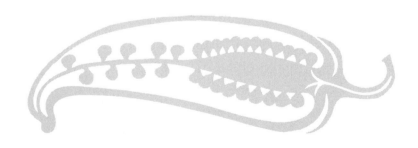

thai chicken with basil and vegetables

serves 4

Tender chicken is stir-fried with colorful vegetables and flavored with fragrant fresh basil. Because this dish cooks quickly, have your ingredients gathered and prepped before you start cooking.

SAUCE

- 2 **TABLESPOONS FAT-FREE, LOW-SODIUM CHICKEN BROTH OR WATER**
- 2 **TEASPOONS FISH SAUCE**
- 2 **TEASPOONS SUGAR**
- 1 **TEASPOON LOW-SALT SOY SAUCE**

◆

- 1 **TEASPOON ACCEPTABLE VEGETABLE OIL**
- 2 **MEDIUM GARLIC CLOVES, MINCED**
- 1 **SERRANO PEPPER, SEEDS AND RIBS DISCARDED, CHOPPED (OPTIONAL)**
- 1 **POUND BONELESS, SKINLESS CHICKEN BREASTS, ALL VISIBLE FAT DISCARDED, CUT INTO THIN SLICES**
- 2 **CUPS BROCCOLI FLORETS**
- 2 **CARROTS, CUT INTO VERY THIN STRIPS**
- 4 **GREEN ONIONS (GREEN AND WHITE PARTS), CUT INTO 1-INCH PIECES**
- 1/4 **CUP FIRMLY PACKED FRESH BASIL**
- 2 **CUPS COOKED RICE (JASMINE PREFERRED)**

In a small bowl, stir together the sauce ingredients. Set aside.

Heat a wok or large skillet on medium-high heat. Pour the oil into the wok and swirl to coat the bottom. Cook the garlic and serrano pepper for 10 to 15 seconds.

Add the chicken; cook for 3 to 4 minutes, or until the chicken is no longer pink in the center, stirring constantly.

Add the broccoli, carrots, and green onions; cook for 2 to 3 minutes, or until the vegetables are tender-crisp, stirring constantly.

Add the reserved sauce mixture and basil leaves. Cook for 1 minute, or until the mixture is warmed through, stirring constantly.

Serve over the cooked rice.

Cook's Tip on Jasmine Rice

Expand your taste horizons by preparing jasmine rice from Thailand to accompany this dish. Jas-

PER SERVING	
CALORIES 280	CHOLESTEROL 66 mg
TOTAL FAT 3.0 g	SODIUM 365 mg
SATURATED 0.5 g	CARBOHYDRATES 32 g
POLYUNSATURATED 1.0 g	FIBER 3 g
MONOUNSATURATED 1.0 g	PROTEIN 30 g

mine rice is classified as an aromatic rice because of its perfumy fragrance and nutlike flavor.

Cook's Tip on Fish Sauce

Pungent and salty, fish sauce imparts a rich flavor to many Asian dishes. A little goes a long way, so you may want to purchase only a small bottle. Store fish sauce in a cool place for up to six months.

chicken fajitas

Before rolling up the tortillas, add shredded lettuce, chopped tomatoes, salsa, and fat-free or low-
fat sour cream if you wish.

- 8 6-INCH CORN TORTILLAS OR FAT-FREE OR LOW-FAT
     FLOUR TORTILLAS
- 1 POUND BONELESS, SKINLESS CHICKEN BREASTS, ALL
     VISIBLE FAT DISCARDED

MARINADE

- 3 TABLESPOONS VERY LOW SODIUM OR LOW-SODIUM
     WORCESTERSHIRE SAUCE
- 1 1/2 TABLESPOONS FRESH LEMON OR LIME JUICE
- 1 TABLESPOON WATER
- 1 TEASPOON ACCEPTABLE VEGETABLE OIL
- 1 MEDIUM GARLIC CLOVE, FINELY MINCED
- 1/8 TEASPOON BLACK PEPPER, OR TO TASTE

◆

- 1 LARGE ONION (ANY COLOR)
- 1 LARGE GREEN BELL PEPPER
- 1 TEASPOON ACCEPTABLE VEGETABLE OIL
     VEGETABLE OIL SPRAY

Preheat the oven to 350°F. Wrap the tortillas in
aluminum foil. Set aside.

Cut the chicken lengthwise into 3/8-inch
strips.

In a large bowl, stir together the marinade ingredients.

Add the chicken to the marinade. Stir to coat evenly. Cover and refrigerate for 10 to 20 minutes, stirring at least once.

Meanwhile, cut the onion and bell pepper into 1/8-inch strips. Put the vegetables in a small bowl. Stir in 1 teaspoon oil.

Heat the tortillas in the oven for 8 to 10 minutes.

Meanwhile, heat a large nonstick skillet over medium-high heat. Remove from the heat and lightly spray with vegetable oil spray (being careful not to spray near a gas flame). Return the skillet to the heat. Put the chicken in the skillet, discarding the marinade. Cook for 4 minutes, stirring occasionally.

Add the onion and pepper slices. Cook for 5 minutes, or until the onion is slightly brown and the chicken is no longer pink in the center, stirring constantly.

To serve, place equal amounts of the chicken-vegetable mixture on each tortilla. Roll the tortilla around the filling jelly-roll style.

PER SERVING

CALORIES 240	CHOLESTEROL 66 mg
TOTAL FAT 3.5 g	SODIUM 166 mg
SATURATED 0.5 g	CARBOHYDRATES 23 g
POLYUNSATURATED 1.0 g	FIBER 7 g
MONOUNSATURATED 1.0 g	PROTEIN 29 g

hearty chicken stew

This is a good recipe to make ahead and refrigerate. Then, at the end of a busy day, come home to
the comfort of a home-cooked meal.

2   POUNDS BONELESS, SKINLESS CHICKEN BREASTS, ALL
    VISIBLE FAT DISCARDED

1   TABLESPOON ACCEPTABLE VEGETABLE OIL

1   MEDIUM ONION, FINELY CHOPPED

1   TABLESPOON MINCED PEELED GINGERROOT OR 1
    TEASPOON GROUND GINGER

3   MEDIUM GARLIC CLOVES, MINCED

2   TABLESPOONS ALL-PURPOSE FLOUR

2   MEDIUM TOMATOES, DICED

8   TO 10 PEPPERCORNS, OR TO TASTE

6   WHOLE CLOVES

1   CINNAMON STICK

2   CUPS WATER

1   TABLESPOON VERY LOW SODIUM OR LOW-SODIUM
    WORCESTERSHIRE SAUCE

8   OUNCES SMALL RED OR WHITE POTATOES, UNPEELED
    AND HALVED

12 OUNCES FRESH OR FROZEN BABY CARROTS

6   OUNCES FRESH OR FROZEN GREEN PEAS

Cut the chicken into 1-inch cubes. Set aside.
    Heat a deep skillet or Dutch oven over
medium-high heat. Pour the oil into the skillet

and swirl to coat the bottom. Cook the onion, gingerroot, and garlic for about 3 minutes, or until the onion is tender. Add the flour. Cook for 1 minute, stirring quickly to prevent sticking. Stir in the tomatoes; cook for 2 minutes.

Meanwhile, tie the peppercorns, cloves, and cinnamon in a piece of cheesecloth. Stir the cheesecloth package, chicken, water, and Worcestershire sauce into the onion mixture. Reduce the heat and simmer, covered, for 20 minutes.

Stir in the potatoes, carrots, and peas. Simmer, covered, for 20 to 25 minutes. Remove the cheesecloth package before serving.

PER SERVING

CALORIES 218	CHOLESTEROL 66 mg
TOTAL FAT 3.5 g	SODIUM 103 mg
SATURATED 0.5 g	CARBOHYDRATES 17 g
POLYUNSATURATED 1.0 g	FIBER 3 g
MONOUNSATURATED 1.5 g	PROTEIN 29 g

chicken with mustard and herbs

Just because you don't have a lot of time to fix dinner doesn't mean you have to sacrifice flavor— or eat high-fat, high-sodium takeout food. With only a few ingredients, you can whip up an elegant entrée in minutes. Make extra to use for special sandwiches.

VEGETABLE OIL SPRAY

4 BONELESS, SKINLESS CHICKEN BREAST HALVES (ABOUT 4 OUNCES EACH), ALL VISIBLE FAT DISCARDED

1 TABLESPOON SALT-FREE HERB SEASONING

1 TEASPOON SALT-FREE LEMON-PEPPER SEASONING

1 TABLESPOON FAT-FREE OR LIGHT MAYONNAISE DRESSING

1/4 CUP SPICY BROWN MUSTARD

Preheat the oven to 350°F. Lightly spray a baking pan with vegetable oil spray.

Put the chicken breasts in the prepared pan.

Stir together the remaining ingredients to make a paste. Spread thickly and evenly over the top of each breast.

Bake for 20 minutes, or until the chicken is no longer pink in the center.

PER SERVING

CALORIES 156	CHOLESTEROL 66 mg
TOTAL FAT 1.5 g	SODIUM 344 mg
SATURATED 0.5 g	CARBOHYDRATES 4 g
POLYUNSATURATED 0.5 g	FIBER 2 g
MONOUNSATURATED 0.5 g	PROTEIN 27 g

chicken-vegetable stir-fry

serves 6

A bed of steamed rice or yolk-free noodles pairs nicely with this stir-fry. Add pizzazz by using a mixture of bell peppers.

1	POUND BONELESS, SKINLESS CHICKEN BREASTS, ALL VISIBLE FAT DISCARDED, CUT INTO 1-INCH CUBES
1 1/2	TABLESPOONS LOW-SALT SOY SAUCE
1	TABLESPOON GRATED PEELED GINGERROOT OR 1 TEASPOON GROUND GINGER
1	TEASPOON ACCEPTABLE VEGETABLE OIL
2	MEDIUM GREEN, RED, OR YELLOW BELL PEPPERS, OR ANY COMBINATION, CUT INTO 1-INCH STRIPS
4	GREEN ONIONS (GREEN AND WHITE PARTS), CUT INTO 1-INCH STRIPS
3/4	CUP PINEAPPLE CHUNKS, FRESH OR CANNED IN THEIR JUICE, 1/4 CUP OF JUICE RESERVED
1 1/2	TABLESPOONS CORNSTARCH
2/3	CUP FAT-FREE, LOW-SODIUM CHICKEN BROTH
1/4	CUP PINEAPPLE JUICE OR JUICE RESERVED FROM CANNED PINEAPPLE
1	TABLESPOON SESAME SEEDS, TOASTED

In an airtight plastic bag or glass baking dish, combine the chicken, soy sauce, and ginger. Seal the bag and turn to coat. Refrigerate for 30 to 45 minutes, turning occasionally.

Heat a large nonstick skillet or wok over high heat. Pour the oil into the skillet and swirl to coat the bottom. Cook the chicken, soy sauce, and ginger for 2 minutes, stirring constantly. Using a slotted spoon, remove the chicken, leaving the juices in the skillet.

Stir in the peppers and green onions; cook for 1 minute, stirring constantly. Stir in the pineapple and chicken; cook for 2 to 3 minutes, or until the vegetables are tender-crisp, stirring constantly.

Put the cornstarch in a small bowl. Add the broth and pineapple juice, stirring to dissolve. Stir the cornstarch mixture into the chicken mixture. Bring to a boil and cook for 1 minute, or until thickened and smooth, stirring occasionally. Remove from the heat.

To serve, transfer the mixture to a serving dish. Sprinkle with the sesame seeds.

PER SERVING

CALORIES 140	CHOLESTEROL 44 mg
TOTAL FAT 3.0 g	SODIUM 157 mg
SATURATED 0.5 g	CARBOHYDRATES 9 g
POLYUNSATURATED 1.0 g	FIBER 1 g
MONOUNSATURATED 1.0 g	PROTEIN 19 g

cheese-herb chicken medallions

serves 6

Although just about any fresh vegetable can be used to garnish this family favorite, carrots add a wonderful splash of color. Chilling the mozzarella beforehand keeps it from oozing when baking.

6   BONELESS, SKINLESS CHICKEN BREAST HALVES (ABOUT 4 OUNCES EACH), ALL VISIBLE FAT DISCARDED

1   TABLESPOON FINELY SNIPPED FRESH CHIVES OR FINELY CHOPPED GREEN ONIONS (GREEN PART ONLY)

1   TABLESPOON FINELY CHOPPED FRESH BASIL OR 1 TEASPOON DRIED, CRUMBLED

1/4   TEASPOON PAPRIKA

PEPPER TO TASTE

3   OUNCES SHREDDED FAT-FREE OR PART-SKIM MOZZARELLA CHEESE, CHILLED

2   CARROTS (OPTIONAL)

Preheat the oven to 400°F.

Put the chicken on a flat surface. Evenly sprinkle each breast with chives, basil, paprika, and pepper.

PER SERVING	
CALORIES 148	CHOLESTEROL 68 mg
TOTAL FAT 1.5 g	SODIUM 246 mg
SATURATED 0.5 g	CARBOHYDRATES 1 g
POLYUNSATURATED 0.5 g	FIBER 1 g
MONOUNSATURATED 0.5 g	PROTEIN 31 g

Form the cheese into six loose balls and place one in the center of each breast. Roll the chicken around the cheese, making sure the ends are tucked in. Tie each breast with twine to hold the cheese. Put the breasts in an ungreased baking dish.

Bake for 15 to 20 minutes, or until the chicken is no longer pink. Let cool for 10 minutes before serving.

Meanwhile, prepare carrot curls. Using a potato peeler, pare the carrots lengthwise into long, thin strips and soak in ice water for at least 10 minutes. Drain well and pat dry with paper towels.

To serve, cut each breast into 1/2-inch medallions. Arrange on a bed of carrot curls if desired.

Cook's Tip on Dried Herbs and Spices

Always store herbs and spices in airtight containers (glass jars recommended) away from heat and light. In general, whole spices and herbs will keep for about one year, though some may retain their flavor for as long as three to four years. Ground spices and herbs will keep for six months to two years. When the aroma becomes faint, use more of the spices and herbs to compensate for flavor loss.

chicken breasts stuffed with ricotta and goat cheese

serves 4

This impressive dish is a snap to make and classy enough to serve for very special occasions. The tomato sauce keeps the chicken breasts moist.

VEGETABLE OIL SPRAY

STUFFING

- 7 OUNCES FAT-FREE OR REDUCED-FAT RICOTTA CHEESE
- 2 OUNCES SOFT GOAT CHEESE
- 2 TABLESPOONS SNIPPED FRESH PARSLEY OR 2 TEASPOONS DRIED, CRUMBLED
- 1 TABLESPOON SNIPPED FRESH CHIVES OR CHOPPED GREEN ONIONS (GREEN PART ONLY)

SAUCE

- 8-OUNCE CAN NO-SALT-ADDED TOMATO SAUCE
- 2 TEASPOONS SALT-FREE ITALIAN HERB SEASONING
- 1 1/2 TEASPOONS CHOPPED FRESH OREGANO OR 1/2 TEASPOON DRIED, CRUMBLED
- 1 MEDIUM GARLIC CLOVE, MINCED
- 1/4 TO 1/2 TEASPOON SALT
- 1/8 TEASPOON PEPPER

◆

- 4 BONELESS, SKINLESS CHICKEN BREAST HALVES (ABOUT 4 OUNCES EACH), ALL VISIBLE FAT DISCARDED

Preheat the oven to 350°F. Lightly spray a 1-quart casserole dish with vegetable oil spray.

In a small bowl, stir together the stuffing ingredients.

In another small bowl, stir together the sauce ingredients.

Put the chicken with the smooth side up between two pieces of plastic wrap. Using a tortilla press, the smooth side of a meat mallet, or a rolling pin, lightly flatten the breasts to a thickness of 1/4 inch, being careful not to tear the meat.

Spoon about one quarter of the stuffing down the middle of each breast. Starting with the short end, roll up the breast jelly-roll style. Place the breast in the prepared casserole dish with the seam side down (no need to secure with toothpicks). Repeat with the other breasts. Spoon the sauce over the breasts.

Bake, covered, for 40 to 45 minutes, or until the chicken is no longer pink in the center.

PER SERVING	
CALORIES 236	CHOLESTEROL 81 mg
TOTAL FAT 5.5 g	SODIUM 481 mg
SATURATED 3.5 g	CARBOHYDRATES 7 g
POLYUNSATURATED 0.5 g	FIBER 1 g
MONOUNSATURATED 1.5 g	PROTEIN 36 g

chicken ragout

serves 6

This easy French stew is delicately flavored with thyme and tarragon. Using fresh instead of dried herbs will make it exceptionally tasty. For guests, serve it in your nicest casserole dish with plenty of crusty French bread on hand to mop up the savory juices.

- 1/3 CUP ALL-PURPOSE FLOUR
- 1/2 TEASPOON PEPPER, OR TO TASTE
- 6 BONELESS, SKINLESS CHICKEN BREAST HALVES (ABOUT 4 OUNCES EACH), ALL VISIBLE FAT DISCARDED

  VEGETABLE OIL SPRAY
- 1 TEASPOON OLIVE OIL
- 1 MEDIUM ONION, SLICED
- 1 POUND FRESH MUSHROOMS, SLICED
- 1 CUP FAT-FREE, LOW-SODIUM CHICKEN BROTH
- 1 CUP DRY WHITE WINE (REGULAR OR NONALCOHOLIC) OR FAT-FREE, LOW-SODIUM CHICKEN BROTH
- 1/4 CUP FRESH THYME OR 1 TABLESPOON PLUS 1 TEASPOON DRIED, CRUMBLED
- 1/4 CUP FRESH TARRAGON OR 1 TABLESPOON PLUS 1 TEASPOON DRIED, CRUMBLED
- 1/4 CUP FINELY SNIPPED FRESH PARSLEY
- 2 MEDIUM GARLIC CLOVES, MINCED
- 1/4 TEASPOON SALT (OPTIONAL)
- 1/4 CUP COLD WATER

2 **TABLESPOONS ALL-PURPOSE FLOUR**

2 **CUPS FROZEN GREEN PEAS**

Preheat the oven to 400°F.

Combine 1/3 cup flour and pepper in a paper or self-sealing plastic bag. Add the chicken and shake well to coat.

Heat a large nonstick skillet over medium-high heat. Remove from the heat and lightly spray with vegetable oil spray (being careful not to spray near a gas flame). Return the skillet to the heat, add a few pieces of chicken, and brown on all sides. Transfer the pieces to an ovenproof casserole dish or Dutch oven. Repeat the process with the remaining chicken.

Pour the oil into the same skillet and swirl to coat the bottom. Cook the onion for 2 to 3 minutes, or until tender. Stir in the mushrooms, broth, wine, thyme, tarragon, parsley, garlic, and salt. Pour over the chicken in the casserole dish.

Bake, covered, for 45 minutes.

PER SERVING

CALORIES 270	CHOLESTEROL 66 mg
TOTAL FAT 3.0 g	SODIUM 192 mg
SATURATED 0.5 g	CARBOHYDRATES 21 g
POLYUNSATURATED 0.5 g	FIBER 4 g
MONOUNSATURATED 1.0 g	PROTEIN 33 g

In a small bowl, whisk together the water and 2 tablespoons flour. Gradually pour into the liquid in the casserole, stirring gently.

Stir the peas into the casserole.

Bake, covered, for 15 to 20 minutes, or until the chicken is no longer pink in the center, the peas are tender, and the sauce has thickened.

quick curry-roasted chicken with cucumber raita

serves 4

In a hurry but tired of the typical? This simple curry-flavored chicken goes nicely with the cool and refreshing cucumber raita, which is an Indian yogurt sauce. Serve this dish over quick-cooking couscous instead of rice. It's much faster to prepare and adds new interest.

VEGETABLE OIL SPRAY

1 TEASPOON CURRY POWDER

1/2 TEASPOON GROUND CUMIN

1/4 TEASPOON ONION OR GARLIC SALT

1/8 TEASPOON CAYENNE

4 BONELESS, SKINLESS CHICKEN BREAST HALVES (ABOUT 4 OUNCES EACH), ALL VISIBLE FAT DISCARDED

QUICK CURRY-ROASTED CHICKEN

PER SERVING
CALORIES 128
TOTAL FAT 1.5 g
  SATURATED 0.5 g
  POLYUNSATURATED 0.5 g
  MONOUNSATURATED 0.5 g

CHOLESTEROL 66 mg
SODIUM 188 mg
CARBOHYDRATES 1 g
FIBER 0 g
PROTEIN 26 g

CUCUMBER RAITA

1   SMALL CUCUMBER, PEELED AND SEEDS DISCARDED

1/8 TEASPOON SALT

8   OUNCES FAT-FREE PLAIN YOGURT

1/4 CUP FINELY DICED RED BELL PEPPER

1/2 TEASPOON GRATED PEELED GINGERROOT

2   TABLESPOONS FINELY SNIPPED FRESH PARSLEY
    OR CILANTRO

1/4 TEASPOON CUMIN SEEDS OR GROUND CUMIN

    PEPPER TO TASTE

Preheat the oven to 350°F. Lightly spray a baking sheet with vegetable oil spray.

In a small bowl, combine the curry powder, cumin, onion salt, and cayenne.

Sprinkle both sides of the chicken with the curry mixture. Place the chicken on the prepared

CUCUMBER RAITA

PER SERVING

CALORIES 40	CHOLESTEROL 1 mg
TOTAL FAT 0.5 g	SODIUM 119 mg
SATURATED 0.0 g	CARBOHYDRATES 6 g
POLYUNSATURATED 0.0 g	FIBER 1 g
MONOUNSATURATED 0.0 g	PROTEIN 4 g

baking sheet with the smooth side up. Lightly spray with vegetable oil spray.

Bake for 20 minutes, or until the chicken is no longer pink in the center.

Meanwhile, for the cucumber raita, grate the cucumber. Put in a colander and sprinkle with the salt. Let drain for at least 5 minutes. Squeeze the cucumber to remove excess liquid.

In a medium bowl, whisk the yogurt until smooth. Stir in the remaining ingredients except the pepper.

Cover and refrigerate until ready to serve. Sprinkle with the pepper before serving as an accompaniment to the chicken.

garlic chicken fillets in balsamic vinegar

This elegant entrée is easy to prepare for unexpected company.

- 8   BONELESS, SKINLESS CHICKEN BREAST HALVES (ABOUT 4 OUNCES EACH), ALL VISIBLE FAT DISCARDED
- 1/2 CUP ALL-PURPOSE FLOUR
- 2   TEASPOONS OLIVE OIL
- 6   TO 8 MEDIUM GARLIC CLOVES, MINCED
-     VEGETABLE OIL SPRAY
- 1   CUP FAT-FREE, LOW-SODIUM CHICKEN BROTH
- 1/3 CUP BALSAMIC VINEGAR
-     PEPPER TO TASTE
- 1   TABLESPOON CORNSTARCH
- 2   TABLESPOONS WATER

Dust the chicken with the flour; shake off the excess.

Heat a large nonstick skillet over medium-high heat. Pour the oil into the skillet and swirl to coat the bottom. Heat the oil. Cook the breasts on one

PER SERVING	
CALORIES 181	CHOLESTEROL 66 mg
TOTAL FAT 2.5 g	SODIUM 85 mg
SATURATED 0.5 g	CARBOHYDRATES 10 g
POLYUNSATURATED 0.5 g	FIBER 0 g
MONOUNSATURATED 1.0 g	PROTEIN 28 g

side for 2 to 3 minutes, or until golden. Add the garlic. Spray the top of the breasts with vegetable oil spray. Turn. Cook for 2 to 3 minutes, or until golden.

Add the broth, balsamic vinegar, and pepper. Reduce the heat to medium-low. Cook, covered, for 5 to 10 minutes, or until the chicken is tender and no longer pink in the center. (The timing depends on the thickness of the chicken breasts.) Remove the chicken from the skillet. Cover to keep warm.

Put the cornstarch in a cup. Add the water, stirring to dissolve. Pour into the skillet. Cook for 1 to 2 minutes, or until thick and smooth, stirring occasionally. Pour over the chicken. Serve immediately.

moroccan chicken

The power of spice is beautifully demonstrated in this classic dish with Moroccan influences. Fluffy couscous absorbs and distributes the flavors.

1 TEASPOON OLIVE OIL

1 POUND BONELESS, SKINLESS CHICKEN BREASTS, ALL VISIBLE FAT DISCARDED, CUT INTO QUARTERS

1 MEDIUM ONION, QUARTERED

4 MEDIUM GARLIC CLOVES, PEELED

3/4 CUP FAT-FREE, LOW-SODIUM CHICKEN BROTH

1/2 CUP DRY WHITE WINE (REGULAR OR NONALCOHOLIC) OR WATER

1/4 CUP KALAMATA OLIVES, DRAINED AND COARSELY CHOPPED

1 MEDIUM LEMON, QUARTERED

1/2 TEASPOON PAPRIKA

1/4 TEASPOON GROUND GINGER

1/4 TEASPOON GROUND TURMERIC

1/8 TEASPOON PEPPER

3/4 CUP UNCOOKED COUSCOUS

PER SERVING	
CALORIES 354	CHOLESTEROL 66 mg
TOTAL FAT 5.5 g	SODIUM 226 mg
SATURATED 1.0 g	CARBOHYDRATES 37 g
POLYUNSATURATED 1.0 g	FIBER 2 g
MONOUNSATURATED 3.0 g	PROTEIN 33 g

Heat a large nonstick skillet over medium–high heat. Pour the oil into the skillet and swirl to coat the bottom. Cook the chicken for 2 minutes on each side.

Stir in the onion and garlic cloves. Cook for 2 to 3 minutes, or until the onion is tender-crisp, stirring occasionally.

Add the broth, wine, olives, lemon, paprika, ginger, turmeric, and pepper to the skillet, and bring to a boil over medium–high heat, stirring occasionally. Reduce the heat and simmer, covered, for 15 to 20 minutes, or until the chicken is no longer pink in the center.

Stir in the couscous. Turn off the heat and let stand, covered, for 5 minutes, or until the liquid is absorbed and the couscous is tender. (Do not stir while the mixture is standing.) Using a fork, fluff the couscous mixture. Remove the lemon before serving the chicken and couscous.

cajun chicken pasta

serves 4

Creamy but moderately spicy sauce, browned chicken, and tender twists of gemelli pasta are hard to resist.

- **8 OUNCES DRIED GEMELLI PASTA**
- **1 TEASPOON ACCEPTABLE VEGETABLE OIL**
- **1 POUND CHICKEN BREAST TENDERS OR TENDERLOINS, ALL VISIBLE FAT DISCARDED**
- **1 1/2 TEASPOONS CAJUN-CREOLE SEASONING**
- **1 MEDIUM GREEN BELL PEPPER, CHOPPED**
- **1 MEDIUM ONION, CHOPPED**
- **2 MEDIUM RIBS OF CELERY, CHOPPED**
- **2 MEDIUM GARLIC CLOVES, MINCED**
- **1 1/2 CUPS FAT-FREE, LOW-SODIUM CHICKEN BROTH**
- **1/2 CUP FAT-FREE HALF-AND-HALF**
- **2 TABLESPOONS ALL-PURPOSE FLOUR**

Prepare the pasta using the package directions, omitting the salt and oil. Drain in a colander. Set aside.

PER SERVING

CALORIES 414	CHOLESTEROL 66 mg
TOTAL FAT 3.5 g	SODIUM 270 mg
SATURATED 0.5 g	CARBOHYDRATES 56 g
POLYUNSATURATED 1.0 g	FIBER 3 g
MONOUNSATURATED 1.0 g	PROTEIN 38 g

Heat a large, nonstick skillet over medium-high heat. Pour the oil into the skillet and swirl to coat the bottom. Stir in the chicken. Sprinkle with the Cajun-Creole seasoning. Brown the chicken for 2 minutes on each side (chicken will be slightly undercooked).

Stir in the bell pepper, onion, celery, and garlic. Cook for 2 to 3 minutes, or until the vegetables are tender-crisp, stirring occasionally.

Pour in the broth. Bring to a simmer. Reduce the heat and simmer, covered, for 8 to 10 minutes, or until the vegetables are tender and the chicken is no longer pink in the center (no stirring needed).

In a small bowl, whisk together the half-and-half and flour until smooth. Pour into the chicken mixture. Cook over medium-high heat for 3 to 4 minutes, or until thickened, stirring occasionally. Add the pasta and warm through.

greek-style stewed chicken

Stock your pantry with the flavors of Greece—
tomatoes, olives, lemons, oregano—and you'll be
ready to prepare this robust dish at any time. Serve
with steamed green beans, roasted potatoes, and
whole-wheat pita bread.

- 1 TEASPOON OLIVE OIL
- 1 POUND CHICKEN BREAST TENDERS OR TENDERLOINS, ALL VISIBLE FAT DISCARDED
- 1 MEDIUM GREEN BELL PEPPER, CUT INTO 1-INCH STRIPS
- 2 MEDIUM SHALLOTS, PEELED AND QUARTERED
- 14.5-OUNCE CAN NO-SALT-ADDED DICED TOMATOES, UNDRAINED
- 1/2 CUP FAT-FREE, LOW-SODIUM CHICKEN BROTH
- 1/4 CUP KALAMATA OLIVES, DRAINED AND COARSELY CHOPPED
- 1 TEASPOON GRATED LEMON ZEST
- 2 TABLESPOONS FRESH LEMON JUICE
- 1 TEASPOON DRIED OREGANO, CRUMBLED
- 1/4 TEASPOON SALT
- 1/4 TEASPOON PEPPER
- 1/8 TEASPOON GROUND CINNAMON

Heat a large nonstick skillet over medium-high heat. Pour the oil into the skillet and swirl to coat the bottom. Cook the chicken for 2 minutes. Turn and cook for 2 minutes.

Add the bell pepper and shallots. Cook for 2 to 3 minutes, or until the vegetables are tender-crisp, stirring occasionally.

Stir in the remaining ingredients. Bring to a simmer. Reduce the heat and simmer, covered, for 25 to 30 minutes, or until the chicken is no longer pink in the center.

PER SERVING

CALORIES 197	CHOLESTEROL 66 mg
TOTAL FAT 5.0 g	SODIUM 404 mg
SATURATED 1.0 g	CARBOHYDRATES 10 g
POLYUNSATURATED 0.5 g	FIBER 3 g
MONOUNSATURATED 3.0 g	PROTEIN 28 g

asparagus-chicken à la king with roasted peppers

serves 4

Although this creamy chicken mixture is typically served over toast points, try it with cooked pasta, rice, couscous, or spaghetti squash strands for a change.

	VEGETABLE OIL SPRAY
2	MEDIUM RED OR GREEN BELL PEPPERS
8	OUNCES FRESH ASPARAGUS, ENDS TRIMMED AND BIAS-SLICED INTO BITE-SIZE PIECES, OR 10-OUNCE PACKAGE FROZEN CUT ASPARAGUS
	10.5-OUNCE CAN FAT-FREE, LOW-SODIUM CHICKEN BROTH
1/4	TEASPOON DRIED TARRAGON OR THYME, CRUMBLED
1/8	TEASPOON SALT
1/8	TEASPOON PEPPER
1/3	CUP ALL-PURPOSE FLOUR
1 1/2	CUPS FAT-FREE EVAPORATED MILK, DIVIDED USE
2	CUPS CHOPPED COOKED CHICKEN OR TURKEY BREAST, COOKED WITHOUT SALT, SKIN AND ALL VISIBLE FAT DISCARDED

Preheat the broiler. Lightly spray a broiler pan or baking sheet with vegetable oil spray.

Cut the peppers into quarters or halves. Remove the stems, seeds, and ribs. Put the peppers cut side down on the prepared pan.

Broil 3 to 4 inches from the heat for 3 to 5 minutes, or until the skin is bubbly and black.

Put the peppers in a plastic bag, a bowl covered with plastic wrap, or a clean paper sack. Seal and let stand for at least 15 minutes, or until cool enough to handle. Using your fingers or paper towels, gently pull the skin off the cooled peppers or trim off with a paring knife. Discard the skin. Rinse and chop the peppers.

In a large saucepan, stir together the asparagus, broth, tarragon, salt, and pepper. Bring to a boil over high heat. Reduce the heat and simmer, covered, for 5 minutes.

In a small bowl, whisk together the flour and 3/4 cup evaporated milk. Stir into the asparagus mixture.

Stir the remaining 3/4 cup evaporated milk into the asparagus mixture. Cook for 10 minutes, or until thickened and bubbly, stirring occasionally. Cook for 2 minutes, stirring constantly.

Stir the peppers and chicken into the asparagus mixture.

PER SERVING	
CALORIES 255	CHOLESTEROL 63 mg
TOTAL FAT 3.0 g	SODIUM 243 mg
SATURATED 1.0 g	CARBOHYDRATES 24 g
POLYUNSATURATED 0.5 g	FIBER 3 g
MONOUNSATURATED 1.0 g	PROTEIN 32 g

southwestern turkey and chayote squash

serves 4

For south-of-the-border flavor, try this dish of turkey cutlets and chayote squash baked with green enchilada sauce. Serve with cooked chickpeas topped with roasted red bell peppers.

- 1 **TEASPOON ACCEPTABLE VEGETABLE OIL**
- 1 **POUND TURKEY CUTLETS, ALL VISIBLE FAT DISCARDED**
- 1 **MEDIUM CHAYOTE SQUASH, PEELED, SEED DISCARDED, AND CUT LENGTHWISE INTO 1/4-INCH SLICES (ABOUT 8 OUNCES), OR 2 MEDIUM ZUCCHINI OR YELLOW SUMMER SQUASH**
- 1 **MEDIUM FRESH ANAHEIM PEPPER, SEEDS AND RIBS DISCARDED, CHOPPED**
- 1/2 **TEASPOON CHILI POWDER**
- **10-OUNCE CAN GREEN ENCHILADA SAUCE**
- 1/2 **CUP SHREDDED LOW-FAT MONTEREY JACK CHEESE**
- 2 **TABLESPOONS SLICED BLACK OLIVES**

Preheat the oven to 375°F.

PER SERVING	
CALORIES 235	CHOLESTEROL 85 mg
TOTAL FAT 7.0 g	SODIUM 564 mg
SATURATED 2.0 g	CARBOHYDRATES 8 g
POLYUNSATURATED —	FIBER 2 g
MONOUNSATURATED —	PROTEIN 33 g

Heat a Dutch oven over medium-high heat. Pour the oil into the Dutch oven and swirl to coat the bottom. Brown the turkey for 2 to 3 minutes on each side (turkey will be slightly undercooked).

Stir in the squash and Anaheim pepper. Sprinkle with the chili powder. Cook for 2 to 3 minutes, or until the squash is tender-crisp, stirring occasionally.

Pour the enchilada sauce over the mixture. Top with the shredded cheese and olives.

Bake for 30 minutes, covered, or until the turkey is no longer pink in the center and the squash is tender.

Cook's Tip on Chayote

Chayote squash looks like a jade green pear with a wrinkled, puckered end. The flavor is mild like that of summer squash, and the single almond-shaped seed is very easy to remove when the squash is cut in half. Also known as mirliton, chayote squash is rich in potassium. You can keep chayote refrigerated in a plastic bag for up to one month.

ziti and turkey meatball casserole

serves 6

Thin tubes of tender pasta in a comforting blend of tomatoes, yellow squash, and plump turkey meatballs—this hearty casserole is sure to please your whole family.

8   OUNCES DRIED ZITI PASTA

1   POUND LEAN GROUND TURKEY BREAST, SKIN REMOVED BEFORE GRINDING

4   OUNCES FAT-FREE OR LOW-FAT PLAIN YOGURT

EGG SUBSTITUTE EQUIVALENT TO 1 EGG, OR 1 EGG, LIGHTLY BEATEN

2   TEASPOONS SALT-FREE ALL-PURPOSE SEASONING

VEGETABLE OIL SPRAY

1   TEASPOON OLIVE OIL

2   MEDIUM GARLIC CLOVES, MINCED

3   MEDIUM YELLOW SUMMER SQUASH, THINLY SLICED CROSSWISE (ABOUT 3 CUPS)

2   14.5-OUNCE CANS NO-SALT-ADDED DICED TOMATOES, UNDRAINED

1   TEASPOON DRIED OREGANO, CRUMBLED

1/4   TEASPOON SALT

1   CUP SHREDDED PART-SKIM MOZZARELLA CHEESE

2   TABLESPOONS GRATED OR SHREDDED PARMESAN CHEESE

Prepare the pasta using the package directions, omitting the salt and oil. Drain in a colander. Set aside.

In a medium bowl, using a spoon or clean hands, stir together the turkey, yogurt, egg substitute, and all-purpose seasoning. Using clean hands, shape the mixture into 24 meatballs.

Heat a Dutch oven or large, deep ovenproof nonstick skillet over medium-high heat. Remove from the heat and lightly spray with vegetable oil spray (being careful not to spray near a gas flame). Return the Dutch oven to the heat and cook the meatballs for 8 to 10 minutes, or until browned on the outside and almost cooked through the center, turning occasionally. Using a slotted spoon, remove the meatballs and set aside. Wipe the skillet with paper towels.

Preheat the oven to 375°F.

Pour the oil into the skillet and swirl to coat the bottom. Cook the garlic over medium-high heat

PER SERVING

CALORIES 354	CHOLESTEROL 64 mg
TOTAL FAT 6.0 g	SODIUM 319 mg
SATURATED 2.5 g	CARBOHYDRATES 41 g
POLYUNSATURATED 0.5 g	FIBER 4 g
MONOUNSATURATED 2.0 g	PROTEIN 33 g

for 5 to 10 seconds, stirring constantly. Stir in the squash; cook for 2 to 3 minutes, or until tender-crisp, stirring occasionally.

Stir in the tomatoes, oregano, and salt. Bring to a simmer, stirring occasionally. Turn off the heat.

Stir in the meatballs and pasta. Sprinkle with the mozzarella and Parmesan.

Bake, covered, for 30 minutes, or until the squash is tender and the meatballs are cooked through.

turkey tetrazzini

serves 8

A great way to use turkey leftovers, this is a tasty twist on an old favorite. Classic tetrazzini is made with spaghetti, but we used rotini because the delicious sauce adheres to it so well.

12	OUNCES DRIED ROTINI OR OTHER PASTA
	VEGETABLE OIL SPRAY
1	MEDIUM ONION, DICED
1/2	MEDIUM GREEN BELL PEPPER, DICED
2	MEDIUM GARLIC CLOVES, MINCED
8	OUNCES FRESH MUSHROOMS, SLICED
12	OUNCES COOKED SKINLESS TURKEY BREAST, CUBED (ABOUT 2 CUPS)
	10.75-OUNCE CAN LOW-FAT, REDUCED-SODIUM CONDENSED CREAM OF CHICKEN SOUP
1/2	CUP FAT-FREE EVAPORATED MILK
2	TABLESPOONS DRY SHERRY OR DRY WHITE WINE (REGULAR OR NONALCOHOLIC) (OPTIONAL)
2	TABLESPOONS GRATED OR SHREDDED PARMESAN CHEESE
2	OUNCES DICED PIMIENTOS, DRAINED
1/8	TEASPOON PEPPER
1/4	CUP PLAIN DRY BREAD CRUMBS

Prepare the pasta using the package directions, omitting the salt and oil. Drain well.

Meanwhile, preheat the oven to 350°F.

Heat a deep skillet over medium heat. Remove from the heat and lightly spray with vegetable oil spray (being careful not to spray near a gas flame). Return the skillet to the heat and cook the onion, bell pepper, and garlic for 2 to 3 minutes, or until soft.

Stir in the mushrooms; cook for 2 minutes, or until soft.

Add the pasta to the skillet. Stir in the remaining ingredients except the bread crumbs.

Spray a 3-quart casserole dish with vegetable oil spray. Pour the pasta mixture into the prepared casserole dish. Sprinkle with the bread crumbs.

Bake, covered, for 35 to 40 minutes.

Cook's Tip on Fresh Mushrooms

Bulk-purchased mushrooms are best stored in a paper sack on your refrigerator shelf, rather than in the vegetable crisper. You can refrigerate prepackaged mushrooms in their original container. Once opened, refrigerate them in a paper sack. Because mushrooms absorb water, clean them by wiping them gently with a damp towel or rinsing them briefly under cold water.

PER SERVING

CALORIES 293	CHOLESTEROL 41 mg
TOTAL FAT 2.5 g	SODIUM 248 mg
SATURATED 1.0 g	CARBOHYDRATES 44 g
POLYUNSATURATED 0.5 g	FIBER 2 g
MONOUNSATURATED 0.5 g	PROTEIN 22 g

open-face turkey sandwiches

A hint of blue cheese is a delightful addition to this untraditional turkey sandwich. Pickled Cucumbers (page 96) add a special kick.

- 4   SLICES RYE-PUMPERNICKEL SWIRL, RYE, OR PUMPERNICKEL BREAD
- 1   TABLESPOON PLUS 1 TEASPOON LIGHT TUB MARGARINE
- 4   LEAVES BIBB LETTUCE
- 8   OUNCES THINLY SLICED COOKED TURKEY BREAST, COOKED WITHOUT SALT, SKIN AND ALL VISIBLE FAT DISCARDED
- 1/2   SMALL GREEN BELL PEPPER, CUT INTO 4 THIN RINGS
- 1/2   CUP PICKLED CUCUMBERS (PAGE 96) (OPTIONAL)
- 1/2   SMALL RED ONION, THINLY SLICED
- 1   MEDIUM ITALIAN PLUM TOMATO, THINLY SLICED
- 4   TEASPOONS CRUMBLED BLUE CHEESE

PER SERVING

CALORIES 196	CHOLESTEROL 51 mg
TOTAL FAT 2.5 g	SODIUM 360 mg
SATURATED 1.0 g	CARBOHYDRATES 21 g
POLYUNSATURATED 0.5 g	FIBER 2 g
MONOUNSATURATED 1.0 g	PROTEIN 22 g

Spread each slice of bread with margarine; put each slice on a separate plate. On each bread slice, decoratively arrange the remaining ingredients in the order listed. Sprinkle 1 teaspoon cheese over each sandwich.

WITHOUT PICKLED CUCUMBERS

PER SERVING	
CALORIES 183	CHOLESTEROL 51 mg
TOTAL FAT 2.5 g	SODIUM 323 mg
SATURATED 1.0 g	CARBOHYDRATES 18 g
POLYUNSATURATED 0.5 g	FIBER 2 g
MONOUNSATURATED 1.0 g	PROTEIN 21 g

roast cornish hens

serves 6

Cornish hens always make an impressive presentation. Add a dash of color to the serving platter with a variety of steamed vegetables.

- 3 CORNISH HENS (ABOUT 1 POUND EACH), THAWED IF FROZEN
- 1 TABLESPOON WHOLE PEPPERCORNS, COARSELY CRUSHED
- 3 TABLESPOONS CHOPPED FRESH TARRAGON OR 1 TABLESPOON DRIED, CRUMBLED
- 1 MEDIUM PEAR, ANY KIND, CUT INTO THIRDS
- 1 CUP FRESH PARSLEY SPRIGS
- 3/4 TO 1 CUP FAT-FREE, LOW-SODIUM CHICKEN BROTH
- 1/4 CUP FAT-FREE, LOW-SODIUM CHICKEN BROTH, IF NEEDED

Preheat the oven to 425°F.

Remove the giblets from the hens and discard. Gently loosen the skin from the meat on the breast and legs by breaking the membrane that

PER SERVING

CALORIES 176	CHOLESTEROL 132 mg
TOTAL FAT 5.0 g	SODIUM 87 mg
SATURATED 1.0 g	CARBOHYDRATES 1 g
POLYUNSATURATED 1.0 g	FIBER 1 g
MONOUNSATURATED 1.5 g	PROTEIN 29 g

holds the skin to the meat and sliding your fingers between the two. Carefully remove all visible fat.

Spread the peppercorns and tarragon under the skin and in the cavity of each hen. Place a piece of pear and about one third of the parsley into each cavity.

Put the hens with breast side up on a rack in a 3-inch-deep roasting pan. Soak 3 pieces of cheesecloth, each large enough to cover the top and sides of a hen, in 1/2 to 3/4 cup chicken broth. Cover the hens with the cloth to keep the meat from drying out. Fill the pan with water to a depth of 1 to 1 1/2 inches to provide moisture.

Put the hens in the oven. Reduce the heat immediately to 325°F.

Bake for 45 to 60 minutes, basting occasionally with the remaining 1/4 cup broth if needed. Hens are done when a meat thermometer inserted between the thigh and breast registers 180°F or when the juice runs clear when the skin of a thigh is cut and the thickest part of the meat near the bone is no longer pink.

Cut each hen in half and remove the skin before serving.

tandoori cornish hens with nectarine-plum chutney

serves 6

A popular Indian dish, tandoori chicken is spicy but not hot. We used Cornish hens, served with a sweet-and-sour nectarine-plum chutney, to make this dinner a cosmopolitan event. The recipe works well with chicken parts or a whole chicken, too.

CHUTNEY

3	SMALL PLUMS, DICED
1	MEDIUM NECTARINE, DICED
1	MEDIUM GRANNY SMITH APPLE, PEELED AND DICED
1/3	CUP SUGAR
1/4	SMALL ONION, DICED
1/4	MEDIUM RED BELL PEPPER, DICED
1/4	CUP CIDER VINEGAR
2	TABLESPOONS GOLDEN RAISINS
1	TEASPOON GRATED ORANGE ZEST

TANDOORI CORNISH HENS

PER SERVING

CALORIES 170	CHOLESTEROL 132 mg
TOTAL FAT 5.0 g	SODIUM 114 mg
SATURATED 1.0 g	CARBOHYDRATES 1 g
POLYUNSATURATED 1.0 g	FIBER 0 g
MONOUNSATURATED 1.5 g	PROTEIN 29 g

1/8 TEASPOON SALT

1/8 TEASPOON GROUND NUTMEG

◆

3 CORNISH HENS (ABOUT 1 POUND EACH),
GIBLETS DISCARDED

3 TABLESPOONS FRESH LIME JUICE

1 TEASPOON CHILI POWDER, OR TO TASTE

1/2 TEASPOON SALT (OPTIONAL)

PEPPER TO TASTE

MARINADE

1 CUP FAT-FREE OR LOW-FAT PLAIN YOGURT

1 SMALL ONION, COARSELY CHOPPED

3 MEDIUM GARLIC CLOVES

1-INCH PIECE GINGERROOT, PEELED AND
COARSELY CHOPPED

NECTARINE-PLUM CHUTNEY

PER SERVING	
CALORIES 101	CHOLESTEROL 0 mg
TOTAL FAT 0.5 g	SODIUM 49 mg
SATURATED 0.0 g	CARBOHYDRATES 26 g
POLYUNSATURATED 0.0 g	FIBER 2 g
MONOUNSATURATED 0.0 g	PROTEIN 1 g

1 TEASPOON CUMIN SEEDS OR GROUND CUMIN

1 TEASPOON SUGAR

1/2 TEASPOON GROUND TURMERIC

1/2 TEASPOON CHILI POWDER, OR TO TASTE

VEGETABLE OIL SPRAY

In a 2-quart stainless steel, enameled steel, or nonstick saucepan, stir together all the chutney ingredients. Cook over medium-high heat for 3 to 4 minutes, or until the sugar dissolves, stirring occasionally. Reduce the heat and simmer, uncovered, for 40 to 45 minutes, or until the fruit is tender, stirring occasionally. Let cool and refrigerate until ready to use.

Using poultry shears or sturdy kitchen scissors, start at the neck of a hen and cut down both sides of the backbone. Discard the backbone. Carefully snip between the breasts, separating the hen into halves. Repeat with the other hens.

In a small bowl, stir together the lime juice, chili powder, salt if desired, and pepper. Rub the mixture over the hens. Let stand for 15 minutes.

Meanwhile, in a food processor or blender, process the marinade ingredients.

In a large bowl, combine the hens and marinade. Turn well to coat the pieces. Cover and refrigerate for at least 8 hours, turning occasionally.

Preheat the oven to 400°F. Lightly spray a shallow roasting pan with wire rack with vegetable oil spray. Put the hens skin side up on the prepared rack in the pan. Spoon all the marinade over the pieces.

Basting frequently with the marinade, bake for 45 to 60 minutes, or until a meat thermometer inserted between the thigh and breast registers 180°F or the juice runs clear. Remove the skin before serving the hens.

meats

Elegant Beef Tenderloin

Braised Eye-of-Round Roast with Brown Gravy

Sirloin Steak with Portobello Mushrooms

Peppery Beef with Blue Cheese Sauce

Marinated Steak

Balsamic Braised Beef with Exotic Mushrooms

Philadelphia-Style Cheese Steak Pizza

Spiced Shish Kebabs with Horseradish Cream

Chili

Swedish Meat Loaf with Dill Sauce

Ground Beef Ragout

Bulgur and Ground Beef Casserole

Mexican Beef and Corn Bread Pie

Pork with Corn-Cilantro Pesto

Pork with Savory Sauce

Skillet Pork Chops with Cinnamon-Apple Salsa

Spicy Baked Pork Chops

Lemon-Mustard Lamb Chops

Lamb and Red Beans

Layered Irish Stew with Lamb

elegant beef tenderloin

Perfect for a grand entrance, this beautiful tenderloin roast is flavored with a variety of aromatic ingredients. Serve it on your most decorative platter, and enjoy the applause.

AROMATIC RUB

- **1/4 CUP DIJON MUSTARD**
- **1/4 CUP PREPARED WHITE HORSERADISH**
- **1/4 CUP CHOPPED FRESH ROSEMARY**
- **4 MEDIUM GARLIC CLOVES, MINCED**
- **2 TABLESPOONS PINK PEPPERCORNS, CRUSHED WITH A MORTAR AND PESTLE, OR 2 TEASPOONS COARSELY GROUND BLACK PEPPER**
- **1 TABLESPOON ONION POWDER**
- **2 TEASPOONS OLIVE OIL**

- **2 POUNDS BEEF TENDERLOIN, ALL VISIBLE FAT DISCARDED**

PER SERVING

CALORIES 203	CHOLESTEROL 71 mg
TOTAL FAT 9.5 g	SODIUM 258 mg
SATURATED 3.0 g	CARBOHYDRATES 3 g
POLYUNSATURATED 0.5 g	FIBER 1 g
MONOUNSATURATED 4.0 g	PROTEIN 24 g

Preheat the oven to 400°F.

In a medium bowl, stir together the rub ingredients. With a pastry brush, spoon, or clean hands, rub the mixture over the entire surface of the beef.

Put the beef in a heavy nonstick roasting pan without a rack.

Bake, uncovered, for 40 to 45 minutes for medium-rare (internal temperature of 135°F to 145°F), 45 to 55 minutes for medium (150°F to 160°F), or 55 to 65 minutes for well done (160°F to 170°F).

Transfer the roast to a carving board. Cover with aluminum foil and let stand for 10 to 15 minutes before carving into thin slices.

Cook's Tip on Meat Thermometers

The best way to know when meat and poultry are properly cooked is to use a meat thermometer to gauge the internal temperature. Insert the thermometer into the thickest part of the meat, making sure it doesn't touch bone or gristle. The regular type of meat thermometer stays in the meat during the cooking process. The popular instant-read thermometer cannot withstand the constant heat of the oven, however, so insert it just when you think the food is done.

Cook's Tip on Peppercorns

Did you know that peppercorns are berries that grow on pepper plant vines? Depending on when they are picked, the berries vary quite a bit in flavor. The green peppercorn is mild and fresh flavored. The common black peppercorn tastes pungent, yet slightly sweet. For a mild-flavored pepper, try the white peppercorn. Pink peppercorns add a colorful and flavorful (similar to black pepper) touch to sauces and other dishes. They aren't true peppercorns; they are the dried berries from a rose plant traditionally cultivated in Madagascar.

braised eye-of-round roast with brown gravy

serves 8

The slow process of braising intensifies the flavor and tenderizes this lean cut of meat stuffed with whole cloves of garlic. Pour the gravy, made from the braising liquid, over the beef and mashed potatoes or rice.

2	POUNDS EYE-OF-ROUND ROAST, ALL VISIBLE FAT DISCARDED
4	MEDIUM GARLIC CLOVES, PEELED
1	TEASPOON DRIED THYME, CRUMBLED
1/4	TEASPOON PEPPER
1/4	TEASPOON DRIED OREGANO, CRUMBLED
	VEGETABLE OIL SPRAY
1	LARGE ONION, FINELY CHOPPED
1	MEDIUM RIB OF CELERY, FINELY CHOPPED
2	CUPS FAT-FREE, NO-SALT-ADDED BEEF BROTH
2	TABLESPOONS NO-SALT-ADDED TOMATO PASTE
1	BAY LEAF
1	TEASPOON SALT
1/2	CUP WATER
1/4	CUP ALL-PURPOSE FLOUR

With a small, sharp knife, make four small cuts, evenly spaced and about 1 1/2 inches deep, in the roast. Push the cloves of garlic into these cuts with your fingers (garlic should not be visible on the surface).

In a small bowl, combine the thyme, pepper, and oregano. With clean hands, sprinkle the mixture evenly over the meat and lightly rub into the entire surface. Lightly spray all surface areas of the roast with vegetable oil spray.

Heat a Dutch oven over medium-high heat. Remove from the heat and lightly spray with vegetable oil spray (being careful not to spray near a gas flame). Return the Dutch oven to the heat and brown the entire roast, including the sides, for about 3 minutes per surface area. Add the onion and celery; cook for 2 to 3 minutes, stirring occasionally.

Stir in the broth, tomato paste, bay leaf, and salt. Bring to a boil over high heat. Reduce the heat to low. Cook, covered, for 2 to 2 1/2 hours,

PER SERVING

CALORIES 177	CHOLESTEROL 58 mg
TOTAL FAT 4.0 g	SODIUM 371 mg
SATURATED 1.5 g	CARBOHYDRATES 7 g
POLYUNSATURATED 0.0 g	FIBER 1 g
MONOUNSATURATED 1.5 g	PROTEIN 27 g

or until the meat is tender. Transfer the roast to a cutting board. Cover with aluminum foil to keep warm.

Bring the braising liquid to a boil over high heat. In a jar with a tight-fitting lid, combine the water and flour. Shake until completely blended. Stir the flour mixture into the liquid. Cook for 2 to 3 minutes, or until thickened, stirring occasionally.

Slice the beef across the grain. Serve with the gravy.

sirloin steak with portobello mushrooms

serves 4

This juicy sirloin with a peppery bite and meaty portobellos is delicious with robust mashed potatoes, perhaps flavored with garlic and horseradish.

1	POUND BONELESS SIRLOIN STEAK, ALL VISIBLE FAT DISCARDED, CUT INTO 4 SERVINGS
1	TEASPOON DRIED THYME, CRUMBLED
1/2	TEASPOON COARSELY GROUND PEPPER
	OLIVE OIL SPRAY
8	OUNCES PORTOBELLO MUSHROOMS, CUT INTO 1-INCH SQUARES (ABOUT 4 CUPS)
1	LARGE RED ONION, SLICED
1/2	CUP FAT-FREE, NO-SALT-ADDED BEEF BROTH
2	TABLESPOONS BRANDY (OPTIONAL)
1	TABLESPOON DIJON MUSTARD
1	TABLESPOON VERY LOW SODIUM OR LOW-SODIUM WORCESTERSHIRE SAUCE

Sprinkle both sides of the meat with the thyme and pepper.

Heat a large nonstick skillet over medium-high heat. Remove from the heat and lightly spray with olive oil spray (being careful not to spray near a gas flame). Return the skillet to the heat and cook the meat for 4 to 6 minutes on each side to desired doneness. Transfer to a platter and cover with aluminum foil to keep warm.

In the same skillet, cook the mushrooms and onion over medium-high heat for 1 to 2 minutes, or until the onion is tender-crisp, stirring occasionally. Stir in the broth, brandy if desired, mustard, and Worcestershire sauce. Cook for 5 to 6 minutes, or until the mushrooms are tender and the liquid has reduced by half, stirring occasionally.

To serve, spoon the mushroom mixture over the steaks.

PER SERVING

CALORIES 178	CHOLESTEROL 68 mg
TOTAL FAT 4.0 g	SODIUM 179 mg
SATURATED 1.5 g	CARBOHYDRATES 8 g
POLYUNSATURATED 0.5 g	FIBER 2 g
MONOUNSATURATED 1.5 g	PROTEIN 27 g

peppery beef with blue cheese sauce

serves 4

A little blue cheese has a big impact on this rich, creamy sauce.

VEGETABLE OIL SPRAY

12 OUNCES FLANK STEAK, ALL VISIBLE FAT AND SILVER SKIN DISCARDED

2 TEASPOONS COARSELY CRACKED PEPPER

SAUCE

1 TEASPOON LIGHT STICK MARGARINE

1 MEDIUM GARLIC CLOVE, MINCED

1 TABLESPOON ALL-PURPOSE FLOUR

2/3 CUP FAT-FREE MILK

2 TABLESPOONS CRUMBLED BLUE CHEESE

2 TABLESPOONS FINELY CHOPPED GREEN ONIONS (GREEN AND WHITE PARTS)

1 TABLESPOON DRY WHITE WINE (REGULAR OR NONALCOHOLIC) (OPTIONAL)

PER SERVING

CALORIES 171	CHOLESTEROL 45 mg
TOTAL FAT 8.0 g	SODIUM 138 mg
SATURATED 3.5 g	CARBOHYDRATES 5 g
POLYUNSATURATED 0.5 g	FIBER 1 g
MONOUNSATURATED 3.0 g	PROTEIN 19 g

Preheat the broiler. Lightly spray the broiler pan and rack with vegetable oil spray.

Make six shallow crisscross slashes on the meat (three slashes in each direction). Rub the meat with half the pepper. Make six slashes on the other side of the meat. Rub with the remaining pepper. Put the meat on the prepared rack.

Broil the meat about 4 inches from the heat for 5 minutes. Turn and broil for 3 to 5 minutes, or until desired doneness. Transfer to a cutting board and let stand for 5 minutes. Thinly slice diagonally across the grain.

Meanwhile, in a small saucepan, melt the margarine over medium heat. Stir in the garlic; cook for 1 minute. Using a wire whisk, stir in the flour. Whisk in the milk all at once. Cook for 5 minutes, or until thickened and bubbly, stirring constantly. Cook for 1 minute more, stirring constantly. Remove from the heat. Stir in the remaining sauce ingredients.

Serve the meat with the sauce.

marinated steak

This simple marinade is a favorite among steak lovers.

1 TO 1 1/2 POUNDS FLANK STEAK, 1 INCH THICK, ALL VISIBLE FAT AND SILVER SKIN DISCARDED

MARINADE

1/2 CUP DRY RED WINE (REGULAR OR NONALCOHOLIC) OR FAT-FREE, NO-SALT-ADDED BEEF BROTH

3 TABLESPOONS FINELY SNIPPED FRESH PARSLEY

3 TABLESPOONS TARRAGON VINEGAR OR WINE VINEGAR

1 TEASPOON ACCEPTABLE VEGETABLE OIL

1 TABLESPOON CHOPPED FRESH OREGANO OR
1 TEASPOON DRIED, CRUMBLED

1 TABLESPOON CHOPPED FRESH TARRAGON OR
1 TEASPOON DRIED, CRUMBLED

3 MEDIUM GARLIC CLOVES, CRUSHED

1 BAY LEAF

1/2 TEASPOON PEPPER

VEGETABLE OIL SPRAY

PEPPER TO TASTE

PER SERVING

CALORIES 140	CHOLESTEROL 45 mg
TOTAL FAT 7.0 g	SODIUM 56 mg
SATURATED 3.0 g	CARBOHYDRATES 0 g
POLYUNSATURATED 0.5 g	FIBER 0 g
MONOUNSATURATED 2.5 g	PROTEIN 18 g

Put the steak in an airtight plastic bag or in a glass baking dish. In a small nonmetallic bowl, stir together the marinade ingredients. Pour over the meat and turn to coat. Seal and refrigerate for at least 8 hours, turning occasionally.

Preheat the broiler. Lightly spray the broiler pan and rack with vegetable oil spray.

Remove the meat from the marinade. Discard the marinade. Sprinkle with the pepper. Put the meat on the prepared rack.

Broil the meat 4 to 6 inches from the heat for 3 to 7 minutes on each side, or to desired doneness (3 to 5 minutes for medium-rare, 4 to 7 for medium). Thinly slice diagonally across the grain.

Cook's Tip

To test the doneness of steaks, make a small slit near the center of the steak and check the color. Medium rare is very pink in the center and slightly brown toward the exterior; medium is light pink in the center. Well done beef is uniformly brown.

Cook's Tip on Beef Cuts

Steak on a cholesterol-lowering diet? Sure. Just select the cut of meat carefully and trim away all visible fat. Besides flank steak, wise beef choices include tenderloin, sirloin, and round steak.

balsamic braised beef with exotic mushrooms

serves 4

What makes a lean cut of meat fork-tender? Slow braising, of course! One of the other benefits is savory gravy, with the bonus of exotic mushrooms. Serve with yolk-free noodles, a perfect accompaniment for this winning recipe.

	OLIVE OIL SPRAY
1	POUND BONELESS EYE-OF-ROUND STEAK, ALL VISIBLE FAT DISCARDED
1	POUND MIXED FRESH MUSHROOMS, SUCH AS WHITE BUTTON, SHIITAKE, CHANTERELLE, AND MOREL
1	CUP FAT-FREE, NO-SALT-ADDED BEEF BROTH
2	TABLESPOONS BALSAMIC VINEGAR
1	TABLESPOON FRESH CHOPPED ROSEMARY OR 1 TEASPOON DRIED, CRUSHED
1	TEASPOON ONION POWDER
1	TEASPOON GARLIC POWDER
1	BAY LEAF
1/4	CUP WATER
2	TABLESPOONS ALL-PURPOSE FLOUR

Heat a large nonstick skillet over medium-high heat. Remove the skillet from the heat and lightly spray with olive oil spray (being careful not to spray near a gas flame). Return the skillet to the heat and cook the meat for 2 minutes on each side.

Add the mushrooms. Cook for 2 to 3 minutes, or until the mushrooms are slightly tender, stirring occasionally.

Stir in the broth, vinegar, rosemary, onion powder, garlic powder, and bay leaf. Bring to a simmer over medium-high heat, stirring occasionally.

Reduce the heat and simmer, covered, for 45 to 50 minutes, or until the meat is tender.

In a small bowl, whisk together the water and flour. Pour into the beef mixture. Cook, uncov-

PER SERVING

CALORIES 209	CHOLESTEROL 61 mg
TOTAL FAT 5.5 g	SODIUM 86 mg
SATURATED 2.0 g	CARBOHYDRATES 10 g
POLYUNSATURATED 0.5 g	FIBER 2 g
MONOUNSATURATED 2.0 g	PROTEIN 30 g

ered, over medium–high heat for 2 to 3 minutes, or until thickened, stirring occasionally.

Remove the bay leaf before serving.

Cook's Tip

If you cannot easily find eye-of-round steak, feel free to substitute boneless top or bottom round or sirloin steaks.

philadelphia-style cheese steak pizza

serves 6

The true Philadelphia cheese steak has three essential components: steak, cheese, and fried onions. This modern spin incorporates more vegetables and is baked until bubbly on a pizza crust.

OLIVE OIL SPRAY

1/4 TEASPOON PEPPER

12 OUNCES BONELESS EYE-OF-ROUND ROUND STEAK, ALL VISIBLE FAT DISCARDED, CUT INTO THIN STRIPS

1 LARGE ONION, THINLY SLICED

1 LARGE GREEN BELL PEPPER, THINLY SLICED

1 CUP FRESH MUSHROOMS, THINLY SLICED

2 MEDIUM GARLIC CLOVES, MINCED

2 TEASPOONS VERY LOW SODIUM OR LOW-SODIUM WORCESTERSHIRE SAUCE

14-OUNCE PREPARED PIZZA CRUST

1 CUP SHREDDED PART-SKIM MOZZARELLA CHEESE

8-OUNCE CAN NO-SALT-ADDED TOMATO SAUCE

2 TABLESPOONS GRATED OR SHREDDED PARMESAN CHEESE

1/2 TEASPOON DRIED OREGANO, CRUMBLED

Preheat the oven to 450°F.

Heat a large nonstick skillet over medium-high heat. Remove from the heat and lightly spray with olive oil spray (being careful not to spray near a gas flame). Sprinkle the meat with pepper. Return the skillet to the heat and cook the meat for 5 to 6 minutes, or until almost cooked through, stirring occasionally.

Stir in the onion, bell pepper, mushrooms, garlic, and Worcestershire sauce. Cook for 3 to 4 minutes, or until the vegetables are tender, stirring occasionally.

Put the pizza crust on a nonstick baking sheet. Spread the beef mixture evenly over the crust. Sprinkle with the mozzarella.

In a small bowl, stir together the tomato sauce, Parmesan, and oregano. Spoon over the pizza.

Bake for 8 to 10 minutes, or until the cheese is melted and the pizza is warmed through.

PER SERVING

CALORIES 343	CHOLESTEROL 46 mg
TOTAL FAT 9.5 g	SODIUM 502 mg
SATURATED 4.0 g	CARBOHYDRATES 38 g
POLYUNSATURATED —	FIBER 2 g
MONOUNSATURATED —	PROTEIN 27 g

spiced shish kebabs with horseradish cream

serves 4

These colorful and quick kebabs combine the earthy flavor of chili powder with the bite of a creamy horseradish sauce.

- 1 **POUND BONELESS TOP SIRLOIN STEAK, ALL VISIBLE FAT DISCARDED, CUT INTO 1-INCH CUBES**
- 2 **TEASPOONS CHILI POWDER**
- 2 **TEASPOONS DRIED OREGANO, CRUMBLED**
- 1 **TEASPOON GROUND CUMIN**
- 3/4 **TEASPOON GARLIC SALT**
  VEGETABLE OIL SPRAY

HORSERADISH CREAM

- 1/3 **CUP FAT-FREE SOUR CREAM**
- 2 **TABLESPOONS FAT-FREE OR LIGHT MAYONNAISE DRESSING**
- 1 **TABLESPOON PREPARED WHITE HORSERADISH**
- 1/2 **TEASPOON GARLIC SALT**
  CHILI POWDER TO TASTE

◆

- 1 **LARGE RED ONION (ABOUT 6 OUNCES), QUARTERED AND LAYERS SEPARATED**
- 1 **MEDIUM YELLOW BELL PEPPER, CUT INTO 1-INCH PIECES**
- 16 **CHERRY TOMATOES**

Put the steak in a shallow bowl. Sprinkle with the chili powder, oregano, cumin, and 3/4 teaspoon garlic salt. Toss gently yet thoroughly to coat completely. Let stand for 15 minutes to absorb flavors.

Meanwhile, preheat the broiler. Lightly spray the broiler pan and rack with vegetable oil spray.

In a small bowl, stir together the horseradish cream ingredients except the chili powder. Sprinkle the chili powder on top.

Thread the vegetables and meat onto four 12-inch metal skewers in alternating order: onion, bell pepper, tomato, and steak. Put the kebabs on the prepared rack.

Broil the kebabs about 4 inches from the heat for 4 minutes. Turn the kebabs and broil for 3 minutes, or until desired doneness.

Serve with the horseradish cream.

PER SERVING

CALORIES 223	CHOLESTEROL 67 mg
TOTAL FAT 6.0 g	SODIUM 461 mg
SATURATED 2.0 g	CARBOHYDRATES 17 g
POLYUNSATURATED 0.5 g	FIBER 3 g
MONOUNSATURATED 2.5 g	PROTEIN 25 g

chili

serves 6

Every cook has a favorite chili recipe—we think this one will be yours. Like many other soups and stews, it tastes best when made the day before, allowing the flavors to mingle.

VEGETABLE OIL SPRAY

1 POUND LEAN GROUND BEEF

VEGETABLE OIL SPRAY

2 LARGE ONIONS, CHOPPED

2 8-OUNCE CANS NO-SALT-ADDED TOMATO SAUCE

1 1/2 CUPS WATER

2 TO 4 MEDIUM GARLIC CLOVES, MINCED

2 15-OUNCE CANS NO-SALT-ADDED PINTO BEANS, RINSED IF DESIRED AND DRAINED

3 TABLESPOONS CHILI POWDER

1 TABLESPOON CHOPPED FRESH OREGANO OR 1 TEASPOON DRIED, CRUMBLED

1 TEASPOON GROUND CUMIN

1/2 TEASPOON SALT (OPTIONAL)

1/8 TEASPOON CAYENNE, OR TO TASTE

PEPPER TO TASTE

2 TABLESPOONS CORNSTARCH

1/4 CUP COLD WATER

Heat a large, heavy saucepan or Dutch oven over medium-high heat. Remove from the heat and lightly spray with vegetable oil spray (being careful not to spray near a gas flame). Return the pan to the heat and cook the beef for 4 to 5 minutes, or until no longer pink, stirring occasionally. Pour into a colander and rinse under hot water to remove excess fat. Drain well. Set aside. Wipe the skillet with a paper towel.

Heat the saucepan over medium-high heat. Remove from the heat and lightly spray with vegetable oil spray. Return the pan to the heat and cook the onions for 2 to 3 minutes, or until tender.

Stir in the beef, tomato sauce, 1 1/2 cups water, and garlic. Reduce the heat and simmer, partially covered, for 20 minutes.

Stir in the beans, chili powder, oregano, cumin, salt if desired, cayenne, and pepper. Simmer, partially covered, for 30 to 40 minutes.

Put the cornstarch in a cup. Add 1/4 cup water, stirring to dissolve. Stir into the chili mixture. Cook for 3 to 4 minutes, or until desired consistency.

Cook's Tip

For that four-alarm taste, add one or two chopped jalapeño peppers.

PER SERVING

CALORIES 282	CHOLESTEROL 34 mg
TOTAL FAT 3.5 g	SODIUM 100 mg
SATURATED 1.0 g	CARBOHYDRATES 38 g
POLYUNSATURATED 0.5 g	FIBER 9 g
MONOUNSATURATED 1.5 g	PROTEIN 23 g

swedish meat loaf with dill sauce

If you like Swedish meatballs, you'll love this moist and flavorful meat loaf, made with both chicken and beef.

VEGETABLE OIL SPRAY

3/4	CUP RYE BREAD CRUMBS
1/3	CUP LOW-FAT BUTTERMILK
1	TEASPOON ACCEPTABLE VEGETABLE OIL
1/2	MEDIUM ONION, FINELY MINCED
2	MEDIUM GARLIC CLOVES, FINELY MINCED
	WHITE OF 1 LARGE EGG, LIGHTLY BEATEN
1/8	TEASPOON PEPPER
1/4	TEASPOON GROUND NUTMEG
1/4	TEASPOON GROUND GINGER
1/8	TEASPOON GROUND ALLSPICE
1	TABLESPOON CHOPPED FRESH DILLWEED OR 1 TEASPOON DRIED, CRUMBLED
12	OUNCES LEAN GROUND CHICKEN BREASTS, SKIN REMOVED BEFORE GRINDING
8	OUNCES LEAN GROUND BEEF

SAUCE

1	TABLESPOON LIGHT STICK MARGARINE
2	TABLESPOONS ALL-PURPOSE FLOUR
1	CUP FAT-FREE, NO-SALT-ADDED BEEF BROTH

3/4 CUP FAT-FREE EVAPORATED MILK

3 TABLESPOONS DRY SHERRY OR FAT-FREE,
NO-SALT-ADDED BEEF BROTH

3 TABLESPOONS CHOPPED FRESH DILLWEED OR
1 TABLESPOON DRIED, CRUMBLED

1/4 TEASPOON GROUND NUTMEG

1/4 TEASPOON GROUND ALLSPICE

1/4 TEASPOON GROUND GINGER

1/8 TEASPOON PEPPER

Preheat the oven to 425°F. Lightly spray a 9 x 5 x 3-inch loaf pan with vegetable oil spray.

In a large bowl, stir together the bread crumbs and buttermilk. Let soak for 5 minutes.

Meanwhile, heat a large nonstick skillet over medium heat. Pour the oil into the skillet and swirl to coat the bottom. Cook the onion for 4 minutes, stirring frequently. Stir in the garlic. Cook for 1 minute, or until the onion is tender, stirring constantly.

PER SERVING

CALORIES 256	CHOLESTEROL 58 mg
TOTAL FAT 7.0 g	SODIUM 288 mg
SATURATED 2.0 g	CARBOHYDRATES 19 g
POLYUNSATURATED 1.0 g	FIBER 2 g
MONOUNSATURATED 2.5 g	PROTEIN 27 g

Add the onion and garlic to the bread crumb mixture. Add the egg white, pepper, nutmeg, ginger, allspice, and dillweed. Using clean hands, mix lightly. Add the ground chicken and beef. Mix well. Lightly pat into the prepared loaf pan.

Reduce the oven temperature to 350°F. Bake for 30 minutes.

Meanwhile, in a medium saucepan, melt the margarine over medium heat. Remove from the heat. Using a wire whisk, stir in the flour. Return to the heat and gradually whisk in the broth, milk, and sherry. Cook for 6 to 8 minutes, or until thickened, whisking constantly.

Remove the saucepan from the heat. Stir in the remaining ingredients.

Remove the meat loaf from the oven and pour off any fat. Pour the sauce over the meat loaf. Cover with aluminum foil.

Bake for 15 minutes, or until meat loaf reaches an internal temperature of 165°F. Let stand 5 to 10 minutes before slicing.

ground beef ragout

serves 6

These ingredients may seem like those for chili, but this dish is true to its name. A ragout is a rich, well-seasoned stew. For economy in cost but not in taste, you can stretch the original recipe without increasing the amount of meat. Prepare about 2 ounces of dried spaghetti or yolk-free noodles per person to make a bed for the ragout.

1 1/2	POUNDS LEAN GROUND BEEF
1	LARGE ONION, CHOPPED
2	LARGE TOMATOES, CHOPPED
	8-OUNCE CAN NO-SALT-ADDED TOMATO SAUCE
3/4	CUP DRY RED WINE (REGULAR OR NONALCOHOLIC) OR WATER
1/2	CUP WATER
1	RED CHILE PEPPER, SEEDS AND RIBS DISCARDED, CHOPPED (OPTIONAL)
1	TABLESPOON FRESH OREGANO OR 1 TEASPOON DRIED, CRUMBLED
3	MEDIUM GARLIC CLOVES, MINCED
1	TEASPOON CHILI POWDER, OR TO TASTE
1	TEASPOON GROUND CUMIN
1/2	TEASPOON SALT (OPTIONAL)
	PEPPER TO TASTE
	15-OUNCE CAN NO-SALT-ADDED KIDNEY BEANS, RINSED IF DESIRED AND DRAINED

15-OUNCE CAN GREAT NORTHERN OR LIMA BEANS, RINSED AND DRAINED

1/4 CUP SNIPPED FRESH PARSLEY

Heat a 3-quart Dutch oven over medium-high heat. Cook the beef for 4 to 5 minutes, or until no longer pink, stirring occasionally. Pour into a colander and rinse under hot water to remove excess fat. Drain well. Wipe the skillet with a paper towel. Return the beef to the skillet.

Stir the onion into the beef. Cook for 4 to 5 minutes, or until the onion is tender.

Stir in the remaining ingredients except the beans and parsley. Bring to a boil. Reduce the heat and simmer, partially covered, for 45 minutes, stirring occasionally.

Stir in the beans. Simmer for 10 to 15 minutes, or until the beans are thoroughly heated.

Sprinkle with the parsley before serving.

PER SERVING	
CALORIES 300	CHOLESTEROL 51 mg
TOTAL FAT 4.5 g	SODIUM 146 mg
SATURATED 1.5 g	CARBOHYDRATES 30 g
POLYUNSATURATED 0.5 g	FIBER 7 g
MONOUNSATURATED 2.0 g	PROTEIN 29 g

Cook's Tip

Sometimes a small change makes a big difference. To see what we mean, substitute 1 cup of pearl onions (about 4 ounces) for the chopped onion in this recipe. Add the pearl onions with the wine, water, and other ingredients just after rinsing the cooked beef.

bulgur and ground beef casserole

Bulgur, or cracked wheat, is available in most supermarkets and health food stores. It has a delicious, nutty flavor and is an excellent substitute for rice.

1	CUP UNCOOKED BULGUR (5 TO 6 OUNCES)
1 1/2	CUPS COLD WATER
1	POUND LEAN GROUND BEEF
2	MEDIUM ONIONS, CHOPPED
1/2	CUP FINELY SNIPPED FRESH CILANTRO OR PARSLEY
1	TABLESPOON CHOPPED FRESH DILLWEED OR 1 TEASPOON DRIED, CRUMBLED
1/4	TEASPOON SALT
	PEPPER TO TASTE
4	MEDIUM TOMATOES, CHOPPED
1/2	CUP CANNED LOW-SODIUM VEGETABLE JUICE
2	TABLESPOONS FRESH LEMON JUICE
2	TOMATOES, CUT INTO WEDGES (OPTIONAL)
1	MEDIUM LEMON, THINLY SLICED (OPTIONAL)

PER SERVING

CALORIES 207	CHOLESTEROL 34 mg
TOTAL FAT 3.0 g	SODIUM 156 mg
SATURATED 1.0 g	CARBOHYDRATES 28 g
POLYUNSATURATED 0.5 g	FIBER 7 g
MONOUNSATURATED 1.0 g	PROTEIN 18 g

In a medium bowl, soak the bulgur in cold water for 15 to 30 minutes, or until soft. Set aside.

Meanwhile, heat a heavy nonstick skillet over medium-high heat. Cook the beef for 4 to 5 minutes, or until no longer pink, stirring occasionally. Pour into a colander and rinse under hot water to remove excess fat. Drain well. Wipe the skillet with a paper towel. Return the beef to the skillet.

Preheat the oven to 350°F.

Stir the onions into the beef. Cook for 3 to 4 minutes, or until the onions are tender.

Drain the bulgur. Gently stir into the beef mixture with the cilantro, dillweed, salt, pepper, tomatoes, vegetable juice, and lemon juice.

Spoon the mixture into a 10-inch square or 9 x 11 x 2-inch baking pan or ovenproof casserole dish.

Bake, uncovered, for 15 to 20 minutes, or until thoroughly heated. Garnish with tomato wedges and lemon slices if desired.

mexican beef and corn bread pie

A blend of the Old South and south of the border, this family favorite is a winner. Complete your meal with a fresh green salad.

MEAT MIXTURE

- 1   POUND LEAN GROUND BEEF
- 1   LARGE ONION, CHOPPED
- 2   LARGE TOMATOES, CHOPPED
- 1   LARGE GREEN BELL PEPPER, CHOPPED
-     10-OUNCE PACKAGE FROZEN WHOLE-KERNEL CORN
- 1   CUP FAT-FREE, LOW-SODIUM CHICKEN BROTH OR FAT-FREE, NO-SALT-ADDED BEEF BROTH
- 1   TABLESPOON VERY LOW SODIUM OR LOW-SODIUM WORCESTERSHIRE SAUCE
- 1   TEASPOON GROUND CUMIN
- 1   TEASPOON CHILI POWDER, OR TO TASTE
- 1/2   TEASPOON SALT (OPTIONAL)

CORN BREAD MIXTURE

- 1 1/2   CUPS YELLOW CORNMEAL
- 1/4   CUP ALL-PURPOSE FLOUR
- 2   TEASPOONS BAKING POWDER
- 1   TEASPOON SUGAR (OPTIONAL)

1/4 TEASPOON SALT (OPTIONAL)

    WHITES OF 3 LARGE EGGS, LIGHTLY BEATEN

1/2 CUP FAT-FREE MILK

  1 TABLESPOON ACCEPTABLE VEGETABLE OIL

Preheat the oven to 400°F.

Heat a large heavy nonstick skillet over medium-high heat. Cook the beef for 4 to 5 minutes, or until no longer pink, stirring occasionally. Pour into a colander and rinse under hot water to remove excess fat. Drain well. Wipe the skillet with a paper towel. Return the beef to the skillet.

Add the onion to the beef. Cook for 3 minutes, or until the onion is tender. Stir in the remaining meat mixture ingredients. Reduce the heat and simmer, uncovered, for 20 to 25 minutes.

In a medium bowl, stir together the cornmeal, flour, and baking powder, and sugar and salt if desired. In a small bowl, stir together the egg whites, milk, and oil. Pour into the dry mixture. Mix lightly to avoid overbeating.

PER SERVING

CALORIES 346	CHOLESTEROL 34 mg
TOTAL FAT 6.5 g	SODIUM 259 mg
SATURATED 1.5 g	CARBOHYDRATES 51 g
POLYUNSATURATED 1.5 g	FIBER 6 g
MONOUNSATURATED 3.0 g	PROTEIN 23 g

Spoon the meat mixture into a 10-inch square baking pan. Spoon the corn bread mixture over the meat; spread lightly to cover the surface.

Bake, uncovered, for 30 to 40 minutes, or until the corn bread is golden brown.

pork with corn-cilantro pesto

serves 4

The delicious pesto inside these pork pinwheels is a Southwestern rendition of an Italian favorite. The recipe makes more pesto than you need for the pork, so try some with pasta or spaghetti squash strands, or stir a dollop into vegetable soup for a fresh flavor boost.

VEGETABLE OIL SPRAY

CORN-CILANTRO PESTO (ABOUT 3/4 CUP)

- 1 CUP FIRMLY PACKED FRESH CILANTRO
- 1/4 CUP FIRMLY PACKED FRESH PARSLEY
- 1/4 CUP GRATED OR SHREDDED PARMESAN OR ROMANO CHEESE
- 1/3 CUP CANNED NO-SALT-ADDED WHOLE-KERNEL CORN, DRAINED
- 2 TABLESPOONS CHOPPED PECANS
- 1 TABLESPOON CHOPPED SHALLOT
- 1 TABLESPOON FRESH LIME JUICE
- 2 MEDIUM GARLIC CLOVES, QUARTERED
- 1/4 TEASPOON SALT
- 4 TEASPOONS OLIVE OIL

  FRESH LIME JUICE OR WATER (OPTIONAL)

◆

1 POUND PORK TENDERLOIN, ALL VISIBLE
   FAT DISCARDED

TOMATO SAUCE (ABOUT 1 CUP)

      VEGETABLE OIL SPRAY
1/2 CUP CHOPPED ONION
  1 MEDIUM GARLIC CLOVE, MINCED
     8-OUNCE CAN NO-SALT-ADDED TOMATO SAUCE
1/4 TEASPOON SUGAR
1/4 TEASPOON SALT
1/8 TEASPOON PEPPER

Lightly spray a shallow roasting pan with a wire
rack or a broiler pan with rack with vegetable oil
spray.

In a food processor or blender, process the
cilantro, parsley, Parmesan, corn, pecans, shallots,
1 tablespoon lime juice, garlic, and salt until well

PER SERVING	
CALORIES 202	CHOLESTEROL 75 mg
TOTAL FAT 7.0 g	SODIUM 304 mg
SATURATED 2.0 g	CARBOHYDRATES 8 g
POLYUNSATURATED 1.0 g	FIBER 1 g
MONOUNSATURATED 3.5 g	PROTEIN 25 g

combined, stopping and scraping the sides occasionally.

With the machine running, gradually pour in the oil. Process until well combined. If the pesto is thicker than you like, add lime juice as needed.

Preheat the oven to 425°F.

Cut the tenderloin lengthwise almost in half. Lay the meat flat between two pieces of plastic wrap. Using the smooth side of a meat mallet or a rolling pin, lightly pound the pork to a thickness of 1/4 inch, being careful not to tear the meat.

Spread 1/4 cup of pesto over the cut surface of the tenderloin. (Reserve the remaining pesto for later uses.) Roll up the tenderloin from one of the short ends; tie in several places with string to secure the roll. (Pork can be wrapped in plastic wrap at this point and refrigerated for 4 to 6 hours before cooking.) Put the tenderloin on the prepared rack in the pan.

Bake, uncovered, for 20 minutes. Turn the tenderloin over. Bake for 10 to 20 minutes, or until a meat thermometer registers an internal temperature of 160°F. Remove from the oven; let stand for 5 minutes.

Meanwhile, heat a medium saucepan over medium-low heat. Remove from the heat and lightly spray with vegetable oil spray (being careful not to spray near a gas flame). Return the pan to the heat and cook the onion and garlic for 5 minutes, or until tender.

Stir in the remaining sauce ingredients. Bring to a boil over high heat. Reduce the heat and simmer, uncovered, for 5 minutes, or until the sauce reaches the desired consistency.

Slice the pork into medallions. Serve with the sauce.

pork with savory sauce

serves 4

The raspberry or balsamic vinegar and port give this dish a dash of elegance.

SAUCE

- 3/4 CUP FAT-FREE, LOW-SODIUM CHICKEN BROTH
- 1/4 CUP RASPBERRY OR BALSAMIC VINEGAR
- 2 TABLESPOONS PORT
- 1 TEASPOON OLIVE OIL
- 1/2 TEASPOON COARSELY GROUND PEPPER
- 1/2 TEASPOON DRIED OREGANO, CRUMBLED
- 1 MEDIUM GARLIC CLOVE, MINCED
- 1 TEASPOON CORNSTARCH
- 2 TABLESPOONS WATER

- VEGETABLE OIL SPRAY
- 1 POUND PORK TENDERLOIN, ALL VISIBLE FAT DISCARDED, CUT INTO 1/4-INCH MEDALLIONS

In a small saucepan, stir together the broth, vinegar, port, oil, pepper, oregano, and garlic. Cook,

PER SERVING	
CALORIES 178	CHOLESTEROL 74 mg
TOTAL FAT 5.0 g	SODIUM 73 mg
SATURATED 1.5 g	CARBOHYDRATES 5 g
POLYUNSATURATED 0.5 g	FIBER 0 g
MONOUNSATURATED 2.5 g	PROTEIN 24 g

uncovered, over medium-high heat for 20 minutes, or until reduced to 1/2 cup.

Meanwhile, put the cornstarch in a cup. Add the water, stirring to dissolve.

Stir the cornstarch mixture into the sauce. Cook over medium heat for 1 minute, or until thickened, stirring constantly. Cover, remove from the heat, and set aside.

Heat a large nonstick skillet over medium-high heat. Remove from the heat and lightly spray with vegetable oil spray (being careful not to spray near a gas flame). Return the skillet to the heat and cook the meat for 3 to 4 minutes on each side, or until no longer pink in the center.

Serve the pork medallions with the sauce.

skillet pork chops with cinnamon-apple salsa

serves 4

This easy-to-prepare dish will appeal to "kids" of all ages. What a delicious way to incorporate more fruit into your diet!

CINNAMON-APPLE SALSA

8 OUNCES GRANNY SMITH APPLES, FINELY CHOPPED (ABOUT 2 CUPS)

4 DRIED PLUMS WITH ORANGE ESSENCE, FINELY CHOPPED

1 TABLESPOON FIRMLY PACKED DARK BROWN SUGAR

1/2 TEASPOON GRATED ORANGE ZEST

2 TABLESPOONS FRESH ORANGE JUICE

1/4 TEASPOON GROUND CINNAMON

◆

4 PORK CHOPS WITH BONE IN (ABOUT 5 OUNCES EACH), ALL VISIBLE FAT DISCARDED

1/2 TEASPOON DRIED THYME, CRUMBLED

1/4 TEASPOON GARLIC SALT

VEGETABLE OIL SPRAY

PER SERVING	
CALORIES 286	CHOLESTEROL 61 mg
TOTAL FAT 6.0 g	SODIUM 107 mg
SATURATED 2.5 g	CARBOHYDRATES 38 g
POLYUNSATURATED 0.5 g	FIBER 7 g
MONOUNSATURATED 2.5 g	PROTEIN 22 g

In a medium bowl, combine the salsa ingredients. Toss gently yet thoroughly to blend. Set aside.

Sprinkle both sides of the pork chops with the thyme and garlic salt.

Heat a large nonstick skillet over medium heat. Remove from the heat and lightly spray with vegetable oil spray (being careful not to spray near a gas flame). Return the skillet to the heat and cook the meat for 5 minutes on each side, or until no longer pink in the center.

Serve the pork chops with the cinnamon-apple salsa.

spicy baked pork chops

serves 4

Fixing dinner is as easy as 1–2–3! Simplify preparation with an assembly line: Place the bowl with the milk mixture at the left, the plate of crumb mixture in the center, and the baking pan at the right.

VEGETABLE OIL SPRAY

EGG SUBSTITUTE EQUIVALENT TO 1 EGG, OR 1 EGG

2 TABLESPOONS FAT-FREE MILK

1/3 CUP CORNFLAKE CRUMBS

2 TABLESPOONS CORNMEAL

1/2 TEASPOON DRIED MARJORAM, CRUMBLED

1/8 TEASPOON PEPPER

1/8 TEASPOON DRY MUSTARD

1/8 TEASPOON GROUND GINGER

1/8 TEASPOON CAYENNE

1 POUND BONELESS PORK LOIN CHOPS, ALL VISIBLE FAT DISCARDED, CUT INTO 4 PORTIONS

PER SERVING

CALORIES 216	CHOLESTEROL 67 mg
TOTAL FAT 6.5 g	SODIUM 148 mg
SATURATED 2.0 g	CARBOHYDRATES 10 g
POLYUNSATURATED 0.5 g	FIBER 0 g
MONOUNSATURATED 3.0 g	PROTEIN 27 g

Preheat the oven to 375°F. Using vegetable oil spray, lightly spray a shallow baking pan large enough to hold the pork chops in a single layer.

In a small, shallow bowl, stir together the egg substitute and milk.

In a shallow dish such as a pie pan, combine the crumbs, cornmeal, marjoram, pepper, mustard, ginger, and cayenne. Using tongs, dip the pork chops in the milk mixture, letting excess liquid drip off. Coat both sides of the pork chops with the crumb mixture. Put the chops in the prepared pan.

Bake, uncovered, for 15 minutes. Turn the chops. Bake for 10 minutes, or until the chops are tender and just slightly pink in the center.

lemon-mustard lamb chops

serves 4

This impressive yet extra-easy entrée is perfect for entertaining.

- 2 TABLESPOONS FINELY SNIPPED FRESH PARSLEY
- 2 TABLESPOONS DIJON MUSTARD
- 1 MEDIUM GARLIC CLOVE, MINCED
- 1 TEASPOON GRATED LEMON ZEST
- 1/2 TEASPOON DRIED ROSEMARY, CRUSHED
- 4 LOIN OR SHOULDER ARM LAMB CHOPS, 1 1/2 INCHES THICK (ABOUT 4 OUNCES EACH), ALL VISIBLE FAT DISCARDED
- 2 TABLESPOONS FRESH LEMON JUICE
  VEGETABLE OIL SPRAY
- 1 MEDIUM LEMON, QUARTERED

In a small bowl, stir together the parsley, mustard, garlic, lemon zest, and rosemary.

Put the lamb chops in a shallow pan, such as a pie pan or 9-inch baking pan. Spoon the lemon juice over the chops. Let stand for 15 minutes.

PER SERVING	
CALORIES 155	CHOLESTEROL 64 mg
TOTAL FAT 6.5 g	SODIUM 238 mg
SATURATED 2.5 g	CARBOHYDRATES 1 g
POLYUNSATURATED 0.5 g	FIBER 0 g
MONOUNSATURATED 3.0 g	PROTEIN 20 g

Meanwhile, preheat the broiler. Spray the broiler pan and rack with vegetable oil spray. Put the lamb chops on the prepared rack. Spoon half of the mustard mixture evenly over the chops.

Broil the chops about 4 inches from the heat for 4 minutes; turn. Spoon the remaining mustard mixture evenly over the chops. Broil for 4 to 5 minutes, or until slightly pink in the center. Serve with the lemon wedges.

lamb and red beans

serves 8

When you're in the mood for something a little exotic, try this tasty stew incorporating the flavors of the Middle East.

VEGETABLE OIL SPRAY

2 POUNDS LEAN LAMB, ALL VISIBLE FAT DISCARDED, CUT INTO BITE-SIZE PIECES

2 MEDIUM ONIONS, CHOPPED

3 MEDIUM GARLIC CLOVES, MINCED

2 15-OUNCE CANS NO-SALT-ADDED KIDNEY BEANS, RINSED IF DESIRED AND DRAINED

6 MEDIUM TOMATOES, CHOPPED

3/4 CUP FAT-FREE, LOW-SODIUM CHICKEN BROTH

1/4 CUP FINELY SNIPPED FRESH PARSLEY

1 TABLESPOON FRESH LEMON JUICE

1 TABLESPOON FINELY CHOPPED FRESH MINT OR 1 TEASPOON DRIED, CRUMBLED

1 TEASPOON GROUND TURMERIC

1 TEASPOON PEPPER, OR TO TASTE

1 TEASPOON SALT (OPTIONAL)

1/2 CUP FAT-FREE OR LOW-FAT PLAIN YOGURT, LIGHTLY BEATEN

2 TABLESPOONS SNIPPED FRESH PARSLEY

Preheat the oven to 350°F.

Heat a Dutch oven over medium–high heat. Remove from the heat and lightly spray with vegetable oil spray (being careful not to spray near a gas flame). Return the Dutch oven to the heat and cook the lamb on all sides for 5 to 7 minutes, or until browned, stirring occasionally.

Stir in the onions and garlic. Cook for 3 to 4 minutes, or until the onions are tender. Stir in the beans, tomatoes, broth, 1/4 cup parsley, lemon juice, mint, turmeric, and pepper and salt if desired. Bring to a boil over high heat.

Place the Dutch oven in the oven. Bake, covered, for 1 to 1 1/2 hours, or until the lamb is tender. Remove from the oven. Stir in the yogurt. Sprinkle with 2 tablespoons parsley.

PER SERVING

CALORIES 291	CHOLESTEROL 74 mg
TOTAL FAT 6.5 g	SODIUM 108 mg
SATURATED 2.0 g	CARBOHYDRATES 27 g
POLYUNSATURATED 0.5 g	FIBER 6 g
MONOUNSATURATED 2.5 g	PROTEIN 32 g

layered irish stew with lamb

serves 4

Don't wait until St. Patrick's day to prepare this succulent layered stew. This richly flavored lamb will satisfy your most ardent meat and potato fans.

OLIVE OIL SPRAY

1   POUND LEAN BONELESS LAMB STEW MEAT (FROM LEG, LOIN, OR SHOULDER), ALL VISIBLE FAT DISCARDED, CUT INTO 3/4-INCH CUBES

2   TABLESPOONS ALL-PURPOSE FLOUR

2   CUPS FAT-FREE, NO-SALT-ADDED BEEF BROTH

2   TABLESPOONS IMITATION BACON BITS

1   TEASPOON DRIED THYME, CRUMBLED

1   BAY LEAF

1   LARGE SWEET POTATO, CUT INTO 1/4-INCH SLICES

1   LARGE RUSSET POTATO, CUT INTO 1/4-INCH SLICES

2   CUPS BABY CARROTS

1   CUP FROZEN PEARL ONIONS, THAWED

8   OUNCES FROZEN GREEN PEAS

Preheat the oven to 350°F.

PER SERVING	
CALORIES 378	CHOLESTEROL 74 mg
TOTAL FAT 7.0 g	SODIUM 265 mg
SATURATED 2.0 g	CARBOHYDRATES 47 g
POLYUNSATURATED 1.0 g	FIBER 7 g
MONOUNSATURATED 2.5 g	PROTEIN 33

Heat a Dutch oven over medium-high heat. Remove from the heat and lightly spray with olive oil spray (being careful not to spray near a gas flame). Return the Dutch oven to the heat and cook the lamb on all sides for 5 to 6 minutes, or until browned, stirring occasionally Sprinkle with the flour, stirring to coat.

Stir in the broth, bacon bits, thyme, and bay leaf. Remove from the heat.

Layer the following ingredients on top of the beef in order: sweet potato, russet potato, carrots, and onions.

Bake, covered, for 1 hour. Do not stir. Add the green peas. Do not stir. Bake, covered, for 30 minutes, or until the lamb and vegetables are tender. Remove the bay leaf before serving.

vegetarian
entrées

Spinach-Stuffed Pizza

Pasta Primavera

Whole-Wheat Pasta with Vegetable Sauce

Penne and Cannellini Bean Casserole with Sun-Dried Tomatoes

Soba Lo Mein with Bok Choy and Sugar Snap Peas

Grilled Portobello Mushrooms with Couscous and Greens

Spinach and Black Bean Enchiladas

Spinach, Chick-Pea, and Olive Pasta

Pepper and White Bean Soup with Rotini

Kidney Bean, Barley, and Sweet Potato Stew

Spicy Lentil Curry

Roasted Vegetables, White Beans, and Tomatoes with Feta

Thai Coconut Curry with Vegetables

Polenta with Tofu and Greens

Pan-Fried Pasta Pancake with Vegetables

Rosemary-Artichoke Frittata

Grilled Vegetable Quesadillas

Eggplant Parmigiana

Edamame Stir-Fry

Quinoa in Vegetable Nests

spinach-stuffed pizza

Enlist your family in preparing the dough and assembling the ingredients for this super–fresh pizza. The spinach tucked into the crust gives it a delightful taste. Don't expect leftovers!

DOUGH

3/4	CUP VERY WARM WATER (105°F TO 115°F)
1	TEASPOON SUGAR
1	PACKAGE RAPID-RISE YEAST (1/4 OUNCE)
1 1/2	CUPS WHOLE-WHEAT FLOUR
3/4	CUP ALL-PURPOSE FLOUR
	ALL-PURPOSE FLOUR

FILLING

6	OUNCES FRESH SPINACH
1 1/2	CUPS SHREDDED FAT-FREE OR PART-SKIM MOZZARELLA CHEESE
1/3	CUP GRATED OR SHREDDED PARMESAN CHEESE

VEGETABLE OIL SPRAY

TOPPING

1	TEASPOON OLIVE OIL
4	OUNCES FRESH MUSHROOMS, THINLY SLICED
1	CUP NO-SALT-ADDED MEATLESS SPAGHETTI SAUCE

For the dough, stir together the water and sugar. Add the yeast and stir to dissolve. Let sit for 5 minutes, or until the yeast is bubbly and develops a frothy head.

In a large bowl, combine the whole-wheat flour and 3/4 cup all-purpose flour. Make a well in the center. While stirring, slowly pour in the yeast mixture.

Knead the dough for 6 to 8 minutes, or until a ball of smooth but elastic dough forms. If the dough is sticky, gradually add a little more all-purpose flour while kneading. Lightly dust the ball of dough with all-purpose flour, put it back into the bowl, and cover loosely with a tea towel. Set the bowl in a warm, draft-free place and allow to rise for 30 minutes, or until doubled in bulk.

Meanwhile, for the filling, thoroughly rinse, stem, dry, and chop the spinach.

In a large bowl, stir together the spinach, mozzarella, and Parmesan.

Preheat the oven to 475°F.

Punch the dough, then divide it into two balls. Keep one in the bowl, covered loosely with a tea

PER SERVING	
CALORIES 293	CHOLESTEROL 9 mg
TOTAL FAT 5.0 g	SODIUM 462 mg
SATURATED 1.5 g	CARBOHYDRATES 45 g
POLYUNSATURATED 0.5 g	FIBER 8 g
MONOUNSATURATED 2.5 g	PROTEIN 19 g

towel, and place the other on a lightly floured surface. Using a lightly floured rolling pin, roll the ball into an 11-inch circle.

Spray the bottom and sides of a 9-inch glass pie pan with vegetable oil spray. Place the rolled dough in the plate so that it covers the bottom and sides. With a fork, prick the dough at about 1-inch intervals on the bottom.

Bake the crust for 4 minutes. Transfer to a cooling rack and let cool.

Spread the spinach filling over the crust.

Roll the second dough ball into an 11-inch circle, place over the filling, and tuck the edges of the dough around the bottom crust layer. Compress the filling by applying light pressure on the dough with the palms of your hands. Cut a 1-inch slit in the center of the top crust.

For the topping, heat a small nonstick skillet over medium-high heat. Pour the oil into the skillet and swirl to coat the bottom. Cook the mushrooms for 3 to 4 minutes, or until soft, stirring occasionally.

Evenly spread the mushrooms over the crust. Top with the spaghetti sauce.

Reduce the temperature to 450°F. Put the pizza on the middle oven rack.

Bake for 15 minutes.

Reduce the temperature to 400°F. Bake for 5 to 10 minutes, or until the edges are deep golden-brown.

pasta primavera

serves 4

You can make the sauce for this recipe as much as a day ahead and prepare the vegetables a few hours before mealtime. For full flavor, use freshly grated Parmesan cheese.

3 CUPS BROCCOLI FLORETS, CUT INTO BITE-SIZE PIECES

8 OUNCES FRESH MUSHROOMS, QUARTERED

2 SMALL ZUCCHINI, CUT INTO 1/4-INCH ROUNDS

1 TEASPOON OLIVE OIL

3 MEDIUM GARLIC CLOVES, MINCED

1 PINT CHERRY TOMATOES, HALVED

8 OUNCES DRIED NO-YOLK PASTA

SAUCE

3/4 CUP FAT-FREE MILK

2/3 CUP FAT-FREE OR LOW-FAT RICOTTA CHEESE

1/4 CUP GRATED OR SHREDDED PARMESAN CHEESE

2 TABLESPOONS CHOPPED FRESH BASIL OR 2 TEASPOONS DRIED, CRUMBLED

2 TEASPOONS DRY SHERRY (OPTIONAL)

◆

2 TABLESPOONS GRATED OR SHREDDED PARMESAN CHEESE

PEPPER TO TASTE

Set a steamer basket in a small amount of simmering water in a large saucepan. Layer the broccoli, then the mushrooms, then the zucchini in the basket. Cook, covered, for 3 to 4 minutes, or until just tender–crisp. Set aside.

Heat a large nonstick skillet or nonstick wok over medium–high heat. Pour the oil into the skillet and swirl to coat the bottom. Cook the garlic for 1 minute, stirring frequently.

Add the cherry tomatoes; cook for 2 minutes, or until the tomatoes are slightly cooked but not wilted, stirring frequently. Set aside.

Prepare the pasta using the package directions, omitting the salt and oil. Drain in a colander.

In a food processor or blender, process the sauce ingredients until smooth.

In a small saucepan, cook the sauce over low heat for 2 to 3 minutes, or until warm, stirring occasionally.

In a large serving bowl, toss together the pasta, vegetables, and sauce to coat well. Sprinkle with 2 tablespoons Parmesan and pepper.

PER SERVING

CALORIES 366	CHOLESTEROL 10 mg
TOTAL FAT 5.0 g	SODIUM 301 mg
SATURATED 2.0 g	CARBOHYDRATES 59 g
POLYUNSATURATED 0.5 g	FIBER 7 g
MONOUNSATURATED 1.5 g	PROTEIN 22 g

whole-wheat pasta with vegetable sauce

serves 6

Whole-wheat pasta gives this dish a wonderful, nutty flavor. You can make the sauce in advance and reheat it at serving time for extra flavor.

SAUCE

VEGETABLE OIL SPRAY

1 TEASPOON OLIVE OIL

6 GREEN ONIONS (GREEN AND WHITE PARTS), CHOPPED

1 LARGE RED OR WHITE ONION, CHOPPED

4 MEDIUM GARLIC CLOVES, MINCED

16-OUNCE CAN NO-SALT-ADDED KIDNEY BEANS, RINSED IF DESIRED AND DRAINED

16-OUNCE CAN NO-SALT-ADDED TOMATOES, UNDRAINED

8 OUNCES FRESH MUSHROOMS, SLICED

2 MEDIUM RED, GREEN, OR YELLOW BELL PEPPERS, OR ANY COMBINATION, CHOPPED

2 MEDIUM RIBS OF CELERY WITH LEAVES, CHOPPED

1 CUP WATER

1/2 CUP DRY RED WINE (REGULAR OR NONALCOHOLIC) (OPTIONAL)

1/4 CUP FINELY SNIPPED FRESH PARSLEY

1 TABLESPOON CHOPPED FRESH OREGANO OR 1 TEASPOON DRIED, CRUMBLED

1 TABLESPOON CHOPPED FRESH BASIL OR 1/2 TEASPOON DRIED, CRUMBLED

1   BAY LEAF

    PEPPER TO TASTE

12 OUNCES DRIED WHOLE-WHEAT PASTA

4   OUNCES SHREDDED FAT-FREE OR PART-SKIM
    MOZZARELLA CHEESE

Heat a large saucepan or Dutch oven over medium-high heat. Remove from the heat and lightly spray with vegetable oil spray (being careful not to spray near a gas flame). Pour the oil into the saucepan and swirl to coat the bottom. Return the pan to the heat and cook the onions and garlic for 2 to 3 minutes, or until the onions are tender.

Stir in the remaining sauce ingredients. Bring to a boil over high heat. Reduce the heat and simmer, covered, for 1 hour, stirring frequently. Remove the bay leaf.

Meanwhile, prepare the pasta using the package directions, omitting the salt and oil. Drain in a colander.

Serve the sauce over the hot pasta. Sprinkle with the mozzarella.

PER SERVING

CALORIES 357	CHOLESTEROL 3 mg
TOTAL FAT 2.0 g	SODIUM 264 mg
SATURATED 0.5 g	CARBOHYDRATES 69 g
POLYUNSATURATED 0.5 g	FIBER 12 g
MONOUNSATURATED 0.5 g	PROTEIN 22 g

penne and cannellini bean casserole with sun-dried tomatoes

serves 8

Penne (tube-shaped pasta cut diagonally) and vegetables team up with creamy cannellini beans (white kidney beans) for a winning casserole combination.

8	OUNCES DRIED PENNE PASTA
8	DRY-PACKED SUN-DRIED TOMATOES (ABOUT 1 OUNCE)
	VEGETABLE OIL SPRAY
1	TABLESPOON LOW-SODIUM VEGETABLE BROTH
2	MEDIUM SHALLOTS, FINELY CHOPPED
4	OUNCES FRESH ASPARAGUS, CUT DIAGONALLY INTO 1/2-INCH PIECES (ABOUT 1 CUP)
1/2	MEDIUM RED BELL PEPPER, DICED
1	TEASPOON DRIED OREGANO, CRUMBLED
1/8	TEASPOON PEPPER
	15-OUNCE CAN CANNELLINI BEANS, RINSED AND DRAINED
1/2	CUP LOW-SODIUM VEGETABLE BROTH
1/4	CUP FAT-FREE MILK
4	OUNCES SHREDDED PART-SKIM MOZZARELLA CHEESE
1	TABLESPOON LIGHT TUB MARGARINE

Prepare the pasta using the package directions, omitting the salt and oil. With a large slotted spoon, transfer the pasta to a medium bowl. Set aside.

Add the tomatoes to the cooking water. Turn off the heat. Let the tomatoes soak for 15 to 20 minutes.

Halfway through the soaking time, preheat the oven to 350°F. Lightly spray a shallow 2 1/2-quart casserole dish with vegetable oil spray. Set aside.

Heat a nonstick skillet over medium heat. Cook 1 tablespoon vegetable broth and the shallots for 1 minute, stirring occasionally.

Stir in the asparagus, bell pepper, oregano, and pepper. Cook for 1 to 2 minutes, or until the vegetables are tender–crisp, stirring occasionally. Turn off the heat.

Remove the tomatoes from the soaking liquid and squeeze out any excess liquid. Dice the tomatoes and stir into the vegetables in the skillet.

PER SERVING	
CALORIES 212	CHOLESTEROL 8 mg
TOTAL FAT 3.5 g	SODIUM 190 mg
SATURATED 1.5 g	CARBOHYDRATES 33 g
POLYUNSATURATED 0.5 g	FIBER 4 g
MONOUNSATURATED 1.0 g	PROTEIN 11 g

In the prepared casserole dish, layer half the cannellini beans, half the pasta, and half the vegetables. Repeat the layers.

Pour 1/2 cup vegetable broth and the milk over all. Sprinkle with the mozzarella. Dot with the margarine. Cover with aluminum foil.

Bake for 20 minutes. Uncover and bake for 5 minutes.

soba lo mein with bok choy and sugar snap peas

serves 4

The secret to success in this dish is to not over-cook the soba, which are thin Japanese noodles made from buckwheat and wheat flour. They have a slightly nutty flavor that is quite different from that of other noodles.

4   OUNCES DRIED SOBA NOODLES

SAUCE

1/4   CUP LOW-SODIUM VEGETABLE BROTH

2   TABLESPOONS HOISIN SAUCE

1   TABLESPOON LOW-SALT SOY SAUCE

1   TEASPOON SUGAR (OPTIONAL)

◆

1   TEASPOON ACCEPTABLE VEGETABLE OIL

2   MEDIUM GARLIC CLOVES, MINCED

2   MEDIUM CARROTS, THINLY SLICED

4   OUNCES SUGAR SNAP PEAS, TRIMMED (ABOUT 1 CUP)

2   STALKS BOK CHOY, STEMS AND LEAVES THINLY SLICED

1/2   MEDIUM ONION, THINLY SLICED

In a large saucepan, bring about 8 cups water to a boil over high heat. Stir in the noodles. Reduce the heat to medium-high. Cook for 2 to 3 minutes, or until tender, stirring occasionally. Drain in a colander. Set aside.

In a small bowl, stir together the sauce ingredients.

Heat a large nonstick skillet or wok over medium-high heat. Pour the oil into the skillet and swirl to coat the bottom. Cook the garlic for 15 seconds.

Add the carrots and peas; cook for 1 minute, stirring constantly. Add the bok choy and onion; cook for 1 to 2 minutes, or until the vegetables are tender-crisp, stirring constantly.

Add the sauce and noodles; cook for 1 minute, or until the mixture is heated through, stirring constantly.

Cook's Tip on Bok Choy

Both the crunchy white stems and the leafy green part of bok choy are edible. Cook the stems or eat

PER SERVING	
CALORIES 158	CHOLESTEROL 0 mg
TOTAL FAT 1.5 g	SODIUM 195 mg
SATURATED 0.0 g	CARBOHYDRATES 33 g
POLYUNSATURATED 0.5 g	FIBER 4 g
MONOUNSATURATED 0.5 g	PROTEIN 6 g

them raw like celery. Cook the delicate leafy green parts as you would spinach. Both stems and greens are good stir-fried or added to soups (the greens cook quickly, so add them near the end of cooking time). Tofu, bok choy, and broth are a great combination in either soup or a stir-fry.

grilled portobello mushrooms with couscous and greens

The grand size and meaty texture of the portobello mushroom make it a perfect base for fluffy couscous and vibrant greens. This is an eye-catching recipe that you can really sink your teeth into!

4	WHOLE PORTOBELLO MUSHROOMS
4	TABLESPOONS BALSAMIC VINEGAR
	VEGETABLE OIL SPRAY
1/2	CUP LOW-SODIUM VEGETABLE BROTH
1/2	CUP WATER
1/4	TEASPOON GROUND TURMERIC
2/3	CUP UNCOOKED COUSCOUS
1/4	CUP DRIED CRANBERRIES
1/2	TEASPOON GRATED LEMON ZEST
1/4	TEASPOON SALT
1	TEASPOON OLIVE OIL
2	MEDIUM GARLIC CLOVES
6	OUNCES FRESH COLLARD GREENS OR KALE OR 8 OUNCES FRESH SPINACH, CHOPPED
2	TABLESPOONS WATER
1	TABLESPOON LIGHT TUB MARGARINE
1/2	MEDIUM RED BELL PEPPER, FINELY CHOPPED

In the top of each mushroom, cut four slits, each 2 to 3 inches long and about 1/2 inch deep. Remove the stems. Place the mushrooms with top side up in a shallow casserole dish.

Sprinkle the mushrooms with half the balsamic vinegar. Lightly spray the top sides of the mushrooms with vegetable oil spray. Turn the mushrooms over and sprinkle with the remaining vinegar. Lightly spray the bottom sides with vegetable oil spray. Cover with plastic wrap. Set aside. (Mushrooms will keep in the refrigerator for up to 1 hour.)

In a medium saucepan, bring the broth, 1/2 cup water, and turmeric to a boil over high heat. Stir in the couscous, cranberries, lemon zest, and salt. Remove from the heat. Let stand, covered, for at least 5 minutes.

Meanwhile, preheat the grill on medium-high. Lightly spray the grill rack with vegetable oil spray.

PER SERVING

CALORIES 232	CHOLESTEROL 0 mg
TOTAL FAT 3.5 g	SODIUM 193 mg
SATURATED 0.5 g	CARBOHYDRATES 44 g
POLYUNSATURATED 1.0 g	FIBER 4 g
MONOUNSATURATED 1.5 g	PROTEIN 8 g

Heat a medium saucepan over medium heat. Pour the oil into the saucepan and swirl to coat the bottom. Cook the garlic for 1 minute.

Stir in the collard greens and 2 tablespoons water. Cook, covered, for 2 to 3 minutes, or until the greens are tender.

Add the margarine; stir for 30 seconds, or until melted. Remove from the heat and cover to keep warm.

Grill the mushrooms for 2 to 3 minutes on each side.

Place one mushroom with stem side up on each of four plates. Spoon a quarter of the couscous on top of each mushroom. Spoon a quarter of the greens on top of the couscous. Sprinkle each with the bell pepper. Serve warm.

Cook's Tip

The couscous mixture and cooked greens can be refrigerated separately for up to five days. Reheat each part in a microwave-safe container at 100 percent power (high) for one to two minutes.

spinach and black bean enchiladas

Dress up these hearty enchiladas with a side of seasoned rice or corn on the cob and sliced watermelon or other seasonal fruit.

1	POUND FRESH SPINACH
	VEGETABLE OIL SPRAY, IF NEEDED
	15-OUNCE CAN NO-SALT-ADDED BLACK BEANS, RINSED IF DESIRED AND DRAINED
1/2	CUP SALSA
1/4	TEASPOON GROUND CUMIN
1/4	TEASPOON CHILI POWDER
6	6-INCH CORN TORTILLAS OR FAT-FREE FLOUR TORTILLAS
1/2	CUP FAT-FREE OR LIGHT SOUR CREAM
1 1/2	TO 2 TEASPOONS FRESH LIME JUICE
4	OUNCES SHREDDED REDUCED-FAT MONTEREY JACK CHEESE
2	MEDIUM ITALIAN PLUM TOMATOES, DICED
2	GREEN ONIONS (GREEN AND WHITE PARTS), THINLY SLICED

PER SERVING

CALORIES 149	CHOLESTEROL 10 mg
TOTAL FAT 3.0 g	SODIUM 236 mg
SATURATED 1.5 g	CARBOHYDRATES 20 g
POLYUNSATURATED 0.5 g	FIBER 4 g
MONOUNSATURATED 0.5 g	PROTEIN 10 g

Thoroughly rinse the spinach and remove the stems.

In a large pot, bring several quarts of water to a boil over high heat. Cook the spinach in the boiling water for 1 minute. With a slotted spoon, remove the spinach. Drain well in a colander. Using the back of a spoon, squeeze out as much liquid as possible.

Preheat the oven to 350°F. Lightly spray a shallow nonstick baking pan or casserole dish with vegetable oil spray.

In a medium bowl, stir together the spinach, black beans, salsa, cumin, and chili powder. Spoon one fourth of the mixture down the middle of one tortilla. Roll the tortilla around the filling, jelly-roll style. Place the tortilla with seam side down in the prepared baking pan or casserole dish. Repeat the process with the remaining tortillas.

Bake, uncovered, for 15 minutes.

Meanwhile, stir together the sour cream and lime juice. Remove the enchiladas from the oven. Spread the sour cream mixture evenly over the top. Sprinkle with the cheese, tomatoes, and green onions.

Bake for 5 minutes.

Cook's Tip

This dish freezes so well that you might want to make a batch to keep on hand for unexpected guests or evenings when you just don't want to cook. After rolling the enchiladas, place them in a container and cover tightly with aluminum foil or put them in an airtight plastic freezer bag. Increase baking time to 35 to 40 minutes. You can substitute a 10-ounce package of frozen spinach for the fresh spinach. Prepare according to the package directions, omitting the salt and oil, then continue with the recipe.

Cook's Tip on Flour Tortillas

Whenever you choose to use flour tortillas, remember that the fat-free and low-fat versions can be high in sodium. When shopping, select those with the lowest sodium value or use corn tortillas.

spinach, chick-pea, and olive pasta

serves 4

This one-dish meal is an eye-pleasing and satisfying combination of texture and flavor. It's also a great way to enjoy the many benefits of iron- and calcium-rich spinach.

- 4 OUNCES DRIED RADIATORE OR ROTINI PASTA
- 2 CUPS COARSELY CHOPPED FRESH SPINACH (ABOUT 2 OUNCES)
- 15-OUNCE CAN NO-SALT-ADDED CHICK-PEAS, RINSED IF DESIRED AND DRAINED
- 1 CUP COARSELY CHOPPED BOTTLED ROASTED RED BELL PEPPERS, RINSED AND DRAINED (ABOUT 6 1/2 OUNCES)
- 12 KALAMATA OLIVES, DRAINED AND CHOPPED
- 2 TABLESPOONS CIDER VINEGAR
- 1 TABLESPOON DRIED BASIL, CRUMBLED
- 2 OUNCES FETA CHEESE, CRUMBLED (ABOUT 1/2 CUP)

Prepare the pasta using the package directions, omitting the salt and oil. Drain in a colander and

PER SERVING	
CALORIES 390	CHOLESTEROL 13 mg
TOTAL FAT 10.0 g	SODIUM 427 mg
SATURATED 2.5 g	CARBOHYDRATES 59 g
POLYUNSATURATED 2.0 g	FIBER 11 g
MONOUNSATURATED 4.5 g	PROTEIN 17 g

run under cold water until completely cooled. Drain well.

Meanwhile, in a medium bowl, stir together the remaining ingredients except the feta. Add the pasta to the spinach mixture, tossing gently yet thoroughly to coat. Add the feta and toss gently.

pepper and white bean soup with rotini

serves 4

When it's cold or rainy, this complete meal in a bowl will nourish and soothe you without a lot of effort. Serve with a green salad on the side.

- 2 CUPS LOW-SODIUM VEGETABLE BROTH
- 8 OUNCES FROZEN BELL PEPPER AND ONION STIR-FRY
- 1 MEDIUM ZUCCHINI, HALVED LENGTHWISE, THEN SLICED CROSSWISE
- 1 CUP QUARTERED CHERRY TOMATOES
- 1 TABLESPOON DRIED BASIL, CRUMBLED
- 1/8 TEASPOON CRUSHED RED PEPPER FLAKES
- 6 OUNCES DRIED ROTINI PASTA

    15-OUNCE CAN NO-SALT-ADDED NAVY BEANS, RINSED IF DESIRED AND DRAINED
- 1 TABLESPOON OLIVE OIL (EXTRA-VIRGIN PREFERRED)
- 1/4 TEASPOON SALT

In a Dutch oven, bring the broth to a boil over high heat. Stir in the bell pepper and onion stir-fry, zucchini, tomatoes, basil, and red pepper

PER SERVING	
CALORIES 322	CHOLESTEROL 0 mg
TOTAL FAT 4.5 g	SODIUM 183 mg
SATURATED 0.5 g	CARBOHYDRATES 58 g
POLYUNSATURATED 0.5 g	FIBER 7 g
MONOUNSATURATED 2.5 g	PROTEIN 13 g

flakes. Return to a boil. Reduce the heat and simmer, covered, for 20 minutes.

Meanwhile, prepare the pasta using the package directions, omitting the salt and oil. Drain in a colander.

Stir the beans into the bell pepper stir-fry mixture. Cook for 5 minutes, or until heated through. Remove from the heat. Stir in the olive oil and salt.

Put the pasta into soup bowls. Ladle the soup over the pasta.

kidney bean, barley, and sweet potato stew

serves 8

Heart-healthy sweet potato imparts a subtly different flavor to this unusual and satisfying stew. For maximum flavor, use fresh sage . . . it adds special pizzazz.

4 CUPS LOW-SODIUM VEGETABLE BROTH

1/2 CUP PEARL BARLEY

2 15-OUNCE CANS NO-SALT-ADDED KIDNEY BEANS, RINSED IF DESIRED AND DRAINED

1 LARGE ONION, DICED

1 MEDIUM SWEET POTATO, PEELED AND DICED

3 MEDIUM RIBS OF CELERY, DICED

1/2 TEASPOON SALT

1/8 TEASPOON PEPPER

1/2 TEASPOON DRIED THYME, CRUMBLED

1 TABLESPOON FRESH SAGE LEAVES, CHOPPED (ABOUT 8 MEDIUM LEAVES), OR 1 TEASPOON DRIED

In a large pot or skillet, bring the broth to a boil over high heat. Stir in the barley. Reduce the heat

---

PER SERVING

CALORIES 172	CHOLESTEROL 0 mg
TOTAL FAT 0.0 g	SODIUM 194 mg
SATURATED 0.0 g	CARBOHYDRATES 35 g
POLYUNSATURATED 0.0 g	FIBER 7 g
MONOUNSATURATED 0.0 g	PROTEIN 10 g

and simmer, covered, for 30 minutes, stirring occasionally.

Stir in the kidney beans and onion. Simmer, covered, for 30 minutes, stirring occasionally.

Add the remaining ingredients except the fresh sage. (If using dried sage, add it at this point). Simmer, covered, for 20 minutes, or until the vegetables are tender, stirring occasionally. Stir in the fresh sage; simmer for 5 minutes.

spicy lentil curry

Serve this curry over rice and add a dollop of fat-free or low-fat yogurt. For a delicious way to use leftovers, spoon the curry into pita pockets.

- 1 1/2 CUPS DRIED LENTILS, SORTED FOR STONES AND SHRIVELED LENTILS AND RINSED
- 6 CUPS WATER
- 1 TEASPOON CUMIN SEEDS OR GROUND CUMIN
- 1 TEASPOON ACCEPTABLE VEGETABLE OIL
- 1 LARGE ONION, CHOPPED
- 1 MEDIUM TOMATO, CHOPPED
- 1 RED CHILE PEPPER (OPTIONAL)
- 1 TABLESPOON GRATED PEELED GINGERROOT OR 1 TEASPOON POWDERED GINGER
- 1 MEDIUM GARLIC CLOVE, MINCED
- 1/2 TEASPOON GROUND TURMERIC
- 1/2 TEASPOON SALT
- 2 TABLESPOONS SNIPPED FRESH CILANTRO OR PARSLEY

In a heavy saucepan, bring the lentils and water to a boil over medium-high heat. Reduce the heat

PER SERVING	
CALORIES 191	CHOLESTEROL 0 mg
TOTAL FAT 1.5 g	SODIUM 210 mg
SATURATED 0.0 g	CARBOHYDRATES 32 g
POLYUNSATURATED 0.5 g	FIBER 16 g
MONOUNSATURATED 0.5 g	PROTEIN 14 g

and simmer, partially covered, for 45 to 50 minutes, or until the lentils are tender, skimming off the foam and stirring occasionally.

Meanwhile, heat a nonstick skillet over medium-high heat. Cook the cumin seeds for 1 minute, being careful not to burn them. Stir in the oil and onion; cook for 4 to 5 minutes, or until the onion is light brown.

Add the tomato and chile pepper; cook for 5 minutes, or until the tomato is reduced to pulp, stirring frequently. Remove the chile pepper.

When the lentils are tender, stir in the tomato mixture and all the remaining ingredients except the cilantro. Simmer for 10 to 15 minutes.

To serve, garnish with the cilantro.

roasted vegetables, white beans, and tomatoes with feta

serves 4

The rich flavor of quick-roasted vegetables combined with the freshness of tomatoes and herbs make this easy one-dish meal a perfect choice after a stress-filled day.

VEGETABLE OIL SPRAY

2 MEDIUM ZUCCHINI, COARSELY CHOPPED

1 MEDIUM RED BELL PEPPER, COARSELY CHOPPED

1 MEDIUM YELLOW BELL PEPPER, COARSELY CHOPPED

1 MEDIUM ONION (YELLOW PREFERRED), COARSELY CHOPPED

12 OUNCES SWEET GRAPE OR CHERRY TOMATOES, QUARTERED

2 TABLESPOONS CAPERS, RINSED AND DRAINED

2 TEASPOONS DRIED BASIL, CRUMBLED

15-OUNCE CAN NO-SALT-ADDED NAVY OR CANNELLINI BEANS

4 OUNCES FETA CHEESE, CRUMBLED (ABOUT 1 CUP)

Preheat the broiler. Lightly spray a large baking sheet with vegetable oil spray. Put the zucchini, peppers, and onion on the baking sheet in a single layer. Lightly spray with vegetable oil spray.

Broil the vegetables for 5 minutes. Stir. Broil for 5 minutes, or until the vegetables are a rich brown.

Meanwhile, in a medium bowl, stir together the tomatoes, capers, and basil.

Rinse the beans in a colander under very hot water until heated through. Drain well. Transfer to a platter or shallow bowl. Top with the vegetables. Spoon the tomato mixture evenly over all. Sprinkle with the feta.

Variation

You can substitute 4 ounces dried orzo for the beans. While the vegetables are roasting, prepare the orzo according to the package directions, omitting the oil and salt.

WITH WHITE BEANS

PER SERVING

CALORIES 230	CHOLESTEROL 25 mg
TOTAL FAT 6.5 g	SODIUM 451 mg
SATURATED 4.5 g	CARBOHYDRATES 32 g
POLYUNSATURATED 0.5 g	FIBER 8 g
MONOUNSATURATED 1.5 g	PROTEIN 13 g

Cook's Tip on Tomatoes

When you see a recipe that calls for fresh diced tomatoes, try the sweet-grape variety of cherry tomatoes instead. Those little round morsels are packed with flavor and sweetness year-round.

WITH ORZO

PER SERVING	
CALORIES 246	CHOLESTEROL 25 mg
TOTAL FAT 7.0 g	SODIUM 449 mg
SATURATED 4.5 g	CARBOHYDRATES 37 g
POLYUNSATURATED 0.5 g	FIBER 5 g
MONOUNSATURATED 1.5 g	PROTEIN 11 g

thai coconut curry with vegetables

serves 4

This light yet filling stir-fry boasts colorful vegetables, baby corn, and a spicy coconut-flavored sauce. Fresh lime zest and juice add a final burst of flavor. Serve over steaming jasmine rice.

- 2 TEASPOONS ACCEPTABLE VEGETABLE OIL
- 1/2 MEDIUM ONION, CHOPPED
- 2 CUPS BROCCOLI FLORETS
- 2 MEDIUM CARROTS, THINLY SLICED CROSSWISE
- 1 CUP CANNED BABY CORN, RINSED AND DRAINED
- 14 OUNCES FIRM TOFU, DRAINED AND CUT INTO 1/2-INCH CUBES
- 1 CUP LOW-SODIUM VEGETABLE BROTH
- 2/3 CUP LIGHT COCONUT MILK
- 1/3 FAT-FREE EVAPORATED MILK
- 2 TEASPOONS RED CURRY PASTE (THAI- OR INDIAN-STYLE)
- 1/2 TEASPOON COCONUT EXTRACT
- 2 TABLESPOONS CORNSTARCH
- 3 TABLESPOONS WATER
- 2 TEASPOONS GRATED LIME ZEST
- 1 TABLESPOON FRESH LIME JUICE

Heat a large nonstick skillet over medium–high heat. Pour the oil into the skillet and swirl to coat the bottom. Cook the onion for 1 to 2 minutes, or until tender-crisp.

Stir in the broccoli, carrots, corn, and tofu; cook for 2 to 3 minutes, or until the broccoli and carrots are tender-crisp.

Stir in the broth, coconut milk, evaporated milk, curry paste, and coconut extract. Reduce the heat and simmer, covered, for 2 to 3 minutes, or until the vegetables are tender.

Put the cornstarch in a cup. Add the water, stirring to dissolve. Pour into the skillet. Cook the mixture over medium-high heat for 1 to 2 minutes, or until thickened, stirring occasionally.

Stir in the lime zest and juice. Remove from the heat.

Cook's Tip on Curry Paste

A richly flavored blend of clarified butter, spices, and vinegar, this paste is used instead of curry powder in many Indian dishes. Thai curry pastes feature a blend of several ingredients, including

PER SERVING

CALORIES 202	CHOLESTEROL 0 mg
TOTAL FAT 7.0 g	SODIUM 314 mg
SATURATED 2.0 g	CARBOHYDRATES 23 g
POLYUNSATURATED 2.5 g	FIBER 6 g
MONOUNSATURATED 2.0 g	PROTEIN 12 g

dried chiles, pepper, coriander, cumin, lemongrass, galanga (peppery Thai ginger), lime, garlic, and shrimp paste. Thai curry pastes are preferred in this recipe, but you may substitute Indian-style curry paste. You can find both red and green curry pastes in many supermarkets or in Asian markets.

polenta with tofu and greens

Comfort food at its finest, this creamy one-dish meal has a hint of smoky flavor. A salad of mixed field greens and icy-cold pear slices would be an elegant addition.

- **2 TEASPOONS OLIVE OIL**
- **1 MEDIUM ONION, CHOPPED**
- **1 MEDIUM RED BELL PEPPER, CHOPPED**
- **2 CUPS LOW-SODIUM VEGETABLE BROTH**
- **2 CUPS WATER**
- **2 TABLESPOONS IMITATION BACON BITS**
- **1 CUP CORNMEAL**
- **14 OUNCES FIRM TOFU, DRAINED AND CUT INTO 1/2-INCH CUBES**
- **8 OUNCES FROZEN TURNIP, MUSTARD, OR COLLARD GREENS**
- **1/4 CUP GRATED OR SHREDDED PARMESAN CHEESE**
- **1 TABLESPOON LIGHT TUB MARGARINE**

PER SERVING

CALORIES 294	CHOLESTEROL 4 mg
TOTAL FAT 9.0 g	SODIUM 228 mg
SATURATED 2.0 g	CARBOHYDRATES 39 g
POLYUNSATURATED 2.5 g	FIBER 5 g
MONOUNSATURATED 3.5 g	PROTEIN 16 g

Heat a large nonstick saucepan over medium heat. Pour the oil into the saucepan and swirl to coat the bottom. Cook the onion and bell pepper for 3 to 4 minutes, or until tender-crisp, stirring occasionally.

Stir in the broth, water, and bacon bits. Bring to a boil over high heat, stirring occasionally.

Gradually add the cornmeal to the pan, stirring constantly. Reduce the heat and simmer for 15 to 20 minutes, or until the vegetables are tender and the cornmeal mixture is soft and creamy, stirring occasionally.

Stir in the tofu and greens; cook over medium-high heat for 6 to 8 minutes, or until the greens are tender, stirring occasionally.

Stir in the Parmesan and margarine; cook for 1 to 2 minutes, or until the cheese is melted, stirring occasionally.

pan-fried pasta pancake with vegetables

serves 4

Try this tasty alternative to plain pasta. It's fun to make, it reheats well, and thanks to the egg substitute, it contains no cholesterol.

- 8 OUNCES DRIED PASTA, SUCH AS LINGUINE, VERMICELLI, OR SPAGHETTI
- 1 MEDIUM CARROT, SHREDDED
- 2 GREEN ONIONS (GREEN AND WHITE PARTS), THINLY SLICED
- 1/2 CUP FRESH SNOW PEAS, TRIMMED AND CUT INTO 1/2-INCH PIECES
- 1 TEASPOON TOASTED SESAME OIL
- 1 TEASPOON ACCEPTABLE VEGETABLE OIL
  EGG SUBSTITUTE EQUIVALENT TO 4 EGGS
- 1/8 TEASPOON PEPPER
- 1/4 TEASPOON SALT (OPTIONAL)

Prepare the pasta using the package directions, omitting the salt and oil. Drain in a colander and

PER SERVING

CALORIES 274	CHOLESTEROL 0 mg
TOTAL FAT 3.5 g	SODIUM 137 mg
SATURATED 0.5 g	CARBOHYDRATES 46 g
POLYUNSATURATED 1.0 g	FIBER 2 g
MONOUNSATURATED 1.5 g	PROTEIN 14 g

transfer to a large bowl. Refrigerate for at least 10 minutes.

Stir the carrot, green onions, snow peas, and sesame oil into the pasta.

Heat a 10-inch nonstick omelet pan over medium heat. Pour the oils into the pan and swirl to coat the bottom. Heat for 30 seconds. Carefully spread the pasta mixture evenly in the pan; cook for 1 minute without stirring.

In a small bowl, stir together the egg substitute and pepper and salt if desired. Pour over the pasta, tilting the pan to distribute the egg mixture evenly (do not stir).

Cook, covered, over low heat for 10 to 12 minutes, or until the eggs are thoroughly cooked. To brown the other side, invert the pancake onto a plate, slide it back into the pan, and cook for 1 to 2 minutes.

rosemary-artichoke frittata

serves 4

With its layers of flavor and rich aromas, this Italian omelet is a comforting but elegant dish.

VEGETABLE OIL SPRAY

4 OUNCES FRESH MUSHROOMS, SLICED

14-OUNCE CAN ARTICHOKE HEARTS, DRAINED AND COARSELY CHOPPED

EGG SUBSTITUTE EQUIVALENT TO 4 EGGS

1/4 CUP FAT-FREE MILK

1/4 CUP FINELY CHOPPED GREEN ONIONS (GREEN AND WHITE PARTS)

1/4 CUP FINELY SNIPPED FRESH PARSLEY

1/2 TEASPOON DRIED OREGANO, CRUMBLED

1/4 TEASPOON DRIED ROSEMARY, CRUSHED

3 MEDIUM ITALIAN PLUM TOMATOES, THINLY SLICED CROSSWISE

1/4 TEASPOON SALT

1/4 TEASPOON DRIED OREGANO, CRUMBLED

1/8 TEASPOON DRIED ROSEMARY, CRUSHED

2/3 CUP SHREDDED PART-SKIM MOZZARELLA CHEESE

Heat a 12-inch nonstick ovenproof skillet over medium heat. Remove from the heat and lightly spray with vegetable oil spray (being careful not to spray near a gas flame). Return the skillet to the heat and cook the mushrooms for 3 to 4 minutes, or until slightly limp, stirring occasionally.

In a medium bowl, stir together the artichoke hearts, egg substitute, milk, green onions, parsley, 1/2 teaspoon oregano, and 1/4 teaspoon rosemary. Pour the artichoke mixture evenly over the mushrooms. Cook, covered, over medium-low heat for 10 minutes, or until almost set. Do not stir. (The mixture will appear to be very moist at this point.)

Meanwhile, preheat the broiler.

Remove the skillet from the heat. Arrange the tomato slices over the top. Sprinkle with the salt, 1/4 teaspoon oregano, and 1/8 teaspoon rosemary. Top with the mozzarella.

Broil for 2 minutes, or until the cheese is just beginning to turn golden. Let stand for about 5 minutes to allow flavors to blend and for easier slicing. Cut into four wedges.

PER SERVING

CALORIES 127	CHOLESTEROL 11 mg
TOTAL FAT 3.5 g	SODIUM 551 mg
SATURATED 2.0 g	CARBOHYDRATES 11 g
POLYUNSATURATED 0.0 g	FIBER 2 g
MONOUNSATURATED 1.0 g	

Cook's Tip

Because of the generous amount of moisture in the artichokes, it may appear that the frittata is not cooked at the recommended time. After the frittata stands for a few minutes and the cheese has melted, the liquid will absorb properly.

grilled
vegetable quesadillas

Quesadillas are the answer if you need a last-minute appetizer or lunch. Our version includes grilled vegetables—a great way to add healthful variety to your meals.

VEGETABLE OIL SPRAY

1 MEDIUM EAR OF CORN, SHUCKED AND DESILKED

1 MEDIUM RED BELL PEPPER, HALVED

1 MEDIUM YELLOW SUMMER SQUASH, ENDS TRIMMED, HALVED LENGTHWISE

1/2 SMALL ONION

4 OUNCES SHREDDED LOW-FAT MONTEREY JACK CHEESE

1 MEDIUM ITALIAN PLUM TOMATO, DICED

2 TEASPOONS FRESH LIME JUICE

1/4 TEASPOON CHILI POWDER

1/8 TEASPOON PEPPER

4 6-INCH CORN TORTILLAS

1/2 CUP SALSA

1/2 CUP FAT-FREE OR LIGHT SOUR CREAM

Preheat the grill on medium–high. Lightly spray the grill rack with vegetable oil spray.

Lightly spray all surface areas of the corn, bell pepper, squash, and onion with vegetable oil spray.

Grill the corn on all sides for 2 minutes per side. Grill the bell pepper, squash, and onion for 1 to 2 minutes. Transfer the vegetables to a cutting board. Let cool for 10 minutes.

Dice the cooled bell pepper, squash, and onion. Transfer to a medium bowl. Using a sharp knife, slice the corn kernels off the cob. Stir the corn, cheese, tomato, lime juice, chili powder, and pepper into the vegetable mixture.

Heat a nonstick griddle or cast-iron skillet over medium heat. Lightly spray one side of a tortilla with vegetable oil spray. Put the tortilla on the griddle with sprayed side down. Spread a heaping 1/3 cup of the vegetable-cheese mixture on half of the tortilla. Fold the other half of the tortilla over the filling. Cook for 1 to 2 minutes on each side, or until the tortilla is golden-brown and the cheese has melted. Transfer to a cutting board and keep warm. Repeat with the remaining tortillas and filling.

To serve, cut the quesadillas in half and place on a platter. Top each quesadilla with 1 tablespoon each of salsa and sour cream.

PER SERVING	
CALORIES 205	
TOTAL FAT 6.0 g	CHOLESTEROL 20 mg
SATURATED 3.0 g	SODIUM 372 mg
POLYUNSATURATED 1.0 g	CARBOHYDRATES 24 g
MONOUNSATURATED 1.0 g	FIBER 4 g
	PROTEIN 13 g

eggplant parmigiana

serves 6

Broiling the eggplant instead of frying it is the key to reducing the fat in this recipe. To complete the meal, add a garden salad and whole-wheat French bread.

SAUCE

- 2 8-OUNCE CANS NO-SALT-ADDED TOMATO SAUCE

  14-OUNCE CAN ARTICHOKE HEARTS, RINSED AND DRAINED

  6-OUNCE CAN NO-SALT-ADDED TOMATO PASTE

- 1 TABLESPOON SALT-FREE ITALIAN SEASONING
- 2 MEDIUM GARLIC CLOVES, FINELY MINCED
- 1 TEASPOON OLIVE OIL
- 1/8 TEASPOON PEPPER

  DASH RED HOT-PEPPER SAUCE
- 1/4 TEASPOON FENNEL SEEDS, CRUSHED (OPTIONAL)

  ◆

- 1 MEDIUM EGGPLANT, CUT INTO 3/8-INCH-THICK ROUNDS (ABOUT 1 POUND)
- 10 OUNCES LIGHT FIRM TOFU, DRAINED AND PATTED DRY WITH PAPER TOWELS

  WHITE OF 1 LARGE EGG
- 1 CUP SHREDDED FAT-FREE OR PART-SKIM MOZZARELLA CHEESE

1 TABLESPOON ALL-PURPOSE FLOUR

1/3 CUP GRATED OR SHREDDED PARMESAN CHEESE

1/3 CUP CRUMBS FROM FRENCH OR SOURDOUGH BREAD

In a food processor or blender, process the sauce ingredients for 30 seconds, or until no lumps remain. Set aside.

Preheat the broiler.

Place the eggplant slices on a baking sheet; do not overlap. Broil 4 inches from the heat for 3 to 4 minutes per side, being careful not to burn the eggplant. Remove from the broiler. Set aside to cool.

Preheat the oven to 350°F.

In a food processor or blender, process the tofu and egg white until smooth.

In a small bowl, toss the mozzarella with the flour to keep the cheese from clumping.

In an 11 x 7 x 2-inch glass baking dish, layer the ingredients as follows: one third of the sauce, one half of the eggplant slices, one third of the

PER SERVING	
CALORIES 181	CHOLESTEROL 7 mg
TOTAL FAT 3.0 g	SODIUM 447 mg
SATURATED 1.0 g	CARBOHYDRATES 25 g
POLYUNSATURATED 0.5 g	FIBER 5 g
MONOUNSATURATED 1.0 g	PROTEIN 15 g

sauce, all the mozzarella, all the tofu–egg mixture, remaining eggplant slices, remaining sauce, Parmesan, and bread crumbs.

Bake, uncovered, for 35 minutes. Let stand for 5 minutes before serving.

Cook's Tip

Salt-free herb seasonings, such as the Italian herb variety used here, are handy for adding a dash of flavor in your cooking and at the table.

edamame stir-fry

High in nutrition and mild in flavor, edamame (green soybeans) are enhanced with aromatic vegetables and assertive spices. Serve this very colorful dish warm or chilled. If you are pressed for time, you can substitute no–salt-added canned pinto beans or kidney beans.

- 2 CUPS FROZEN SHELLED GREEN SOYBEANS (EDAMAME)
- 4 CUPS LOW-SODIUM VEGETABLE BROTH OR WATER
  VEGETABLE OIL SPRAY
- 4 MEDIUM GARLIC CLOVES, MINCED
- 2 MEDIUM YELLOW SUMMER SQUASH, DICED
- 1 MEDIUM RED BELL PEPPER, DICED
- 1 LARGE ONION, DICED
- 1 CUP FROZEN WHOLE-KERNEL CORN
  4-OUNCE CAN DICED GREEN CHILE PEPPERS, DRAINED
- 3 TABLESPOONS FRESH LEMON JUICE
- 1 1/2 TEASPOONS GROUND CORIANDER
- 1/2 TEASPOON GROUND GINGER
- 1/2 TEASPOON SALT
- 1/8 TEASPOON PEPPER
- 1/4 MEDIUM HEAD RED CABBAGE, CORED AND THINLY SLICED

In a large saucepan, combine the edamame and vegetable broth. Bring to a boil over high heat. Reduce the heat and simmer, partially covered, for 6 to 7 minutes, or until the soybeans are tender. Drain well.

Heat a medium skillet over medium-low heat. Remove from the heat and lightly spray with vegetable oil spray (being careful not to spray near a gas flame). Return the skillet to the heat and cook the garlic for 30 seconds. Stir in the squash, bell pepper, onion, and corn. Cook for 5 to 7 minutes, or until the vegetables are tender–crisp, stirring occasionally.

Stir in the edamame and remaining ingredients except the cabbage. Cook for 1 to 2 minutes, or until the mixture is warmed through.

To serve, spoon the mixture into serving bowls and garnish with the cabbage.

Cook's Tip on Fresh Soybeans

Fresh soybeans are sometimes available in Asian markets and specialty stores in late summer and early fall. Rinse fresh soybeans in cold water, combine them with vegetable broth or water, and bring to a boil over high heat. Reduce heat to medium-low and cook for 3 to 5 minutes. Drain well.

PER SERVING	
CALORIES 123	CHOLESTEROL 0 mg
TOTAL FAT 3.0 g	SODIUM 233 mg
SATURATED 0.5 g	CARBOHYDRATES 18 g
POLYUNSATURATED 1.5 g	FIBER 6 g
MONOUNSATURATED 0.5 g	PROTEIN 8 g

quinoa in vegetable nests

Quinoa *(keen'-wah)* cooks quickly and is very nutritious—although a grain, it's a complete protein. Rinsing before cooking is important to remove the coating, which can impart a bitter flavor. If you don't find quinoa at your supermarket, try health food stores.

3/4	CUP UNCOOKED QUINOA
1 1/2	CUPS WATER
2	MEDIUM CARROTS, CUT INTO VERY THIN STRIPS
1/2	MEDIUM YELLOW BELL PEPPER, CUT INTO VERY THIN STRIPS
1	CUP THINLY SLICED RED CABBAGE
1 1/2	CUP SHREDDED NAPA CABBAGE
2	TEASPOONS FRESH LIME JUICE
2	TEASPOONS PLAIN RICE VINEGAR
2	TEASPOONS LOW-SALT SOY SAUCE
1	MEDIUM GARLIC CLOVE, MINCED
1/8	TEASPOON PEPPER
2	GREEN ONIONS (GREEN AND WHITE PARTS), CUT INTO VERY THIN STRIPS

Rinse the quinoa in a fine strainer under cold running water for 1 to 2 minutes. Shake off excess water.

In a dry medium saucepan, toast the quinoa for about 5 minutes over medium heat, stirring occasionally.

Stir in water. Bring to a boil over high heat. Reduce the heat and simmer, covered, for 15 minutes.

Remove from the heat. Let stand, covered, for 5 minutes. Refrigerate, covered, for at least 30 minutes.

Meanwhile, in a medium bowl, combine the carrots, bell pepper, and cabbages.

In a large bowl, stir together the lime juice, rice vinegar, soy sauce, garlic, pepper, and cooled quinoa.

For each serving, place one fourth of the vegetable mixture in a shallow bowl. Make an indentation in the middle of the vegetables and place one fourth of the quinoa mixture in the "nest." Garnish with the green onions.

PER SERVING

CALORIES 154	CHOLESTEROL 0 mg
TOTAL FAT 2.0 g	SODIUM 95 mg
SATURATED 0 g	CARBOHYDRATES 29 g
POLYUNSATURATED 1.0 g	FIBER 4 g
MONOUNSATURATED 0.5 g	PROTEIN 6 g

Cook's Tip

You can prepare this recipe up to four days in advance, keeping the vegetable and quinoa mixtures separate. Warm both mixtures, combine as described above, and garnish with green onions.

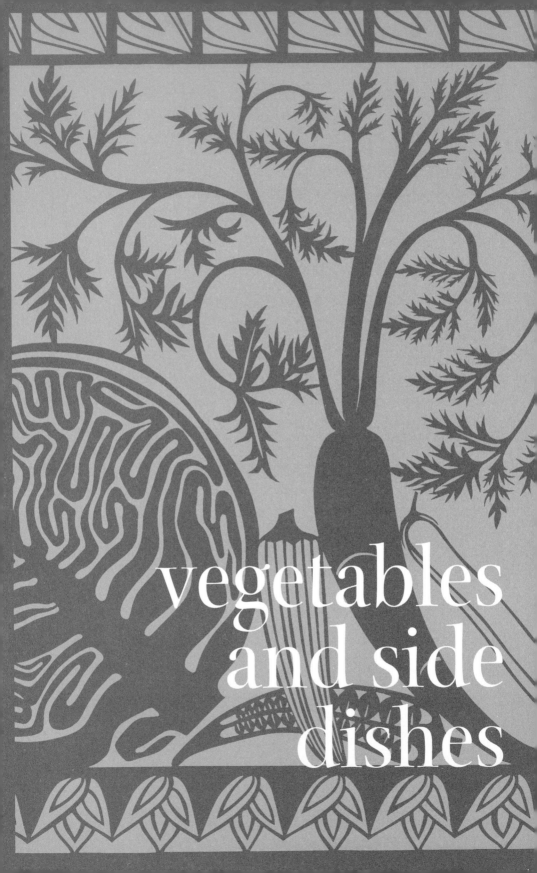

vegetables
and side
dishes

Asparagus with Dill and Pine Nuts

Baked Beans with Chipotle Peppers

Beets in Orange Sauce

Sweet-and-Sour Broccoli and Red Bell Pepper

Braised Brussels Sprouts with Pimiento and Water Chestnuts

Apple-Lemon Carrots

Corn Bread Dressing

Green Beans Amandine

Sautéed Greens and Cabbage

Twice-Baked Potatoes and Herbs

Herbed Baby Potatoes

Home-Fried Potatoes

Scalloped Potatoes

Red and Green Pilaf

Golden Rice

Spinach Parmesan

Wilted Spinach

Praline Butternut Squash

Yellow Squash Sauté

Sweet Potatoes in Creamy Cinnamon Sauce

Swiss Chard with Hot-Pepper Sauce

Oven-Fried Green Tomatoes with Poppy Seeds

Italian-Style Zucchini Slices

Ratatouille

asparagus with dill and pine nuts

serves 4

Take advantage of fresh asparagus during its peak season, February through June, by preparing this quick side dish. Pair these tasty spears with grilled fish, poached chicken, or sizzling lean sirloin steaks.

- 2 **TABLESPOONS PINE NUTS**
- 1 **TEASPOON OLIVE OIL**
- 2 **MEDIUM SHALLOTS, FINELY CHOPPED**
- 1 **POUND FRESH ASPARAGUS, ENDS TRIMMED**
- 2 **TABLESPOONS GRATED PARMESAN CHEESE**
- 1 **TABLESPOON FRESH SNIPPED DILLWEED OR 1 TEASPOON DRIED, CRUMBLED**
- 1 **TEASPOON GRATED LEMON ZEST**
- 1/8 **TEASPOON PEPPER**

In a nonstick skillet, dry-roast the pine nuts over medium heat for 4 to 5 minutes, or until light golden brown, stirring occasionally. Remove the nuts from the skillet and set aside.

PER SERVING

CALORIES 75	CHOLESTEROL 2 mg
TOTAL FAT 4.0 g	SODIUM 48 mg
SATURATED 1.0 g	CARBOHYDRATES 7 g
POLYUNSATURATED 1.0 g	FIBER 3 g
MONOUNSATURATED 2.0 g	PROTEIN 4 g

Pour the oil into the same skillet and swirl to coat the bottom. Cook the shallots for 1 to 2 minutes, or until tender-crisp, stirring occasionally.

Add the asparagus; cook for 3 to 4 minutes, or until the asparagus is tender-crisp, stirring occasionally.

Stir in the Parmesan, dillweed, lemon zest, and pepper; cook for 1 minute, or until the cheese is melted, stirring occasionally.

baked beans with chipotle peppers

serves 10

High-flavor chipotle peppers—dried, smoked jalapeños—are a great substitute for high-fat bacon or salt pork in this classic bean recipe. Use more or less chipotle depending on how spicy you like your beans!

2 TO 3 CANNED CHIPOTLE PEPPERS PACKED IN ADOBO SAUCE

3 15-OUNCE CANS NO-SALT-ADDED NAVY OR GREAT NORTHERN BEANS, RINSED IF DESIRED

1 LARGE ONION, CHOPPED

1/2 CUP WATER

1/4 CUP FIRMLY PACKED DARK BROWN SUGAR

1/4 CUP MOLASSES

1/4 CUP REDUCED-CALORIE MAPLE-FLAVORED SYRUP

2 TABLESPOONS VERY LOW SODIUM OR LOW-SODIUM WORCESTERSHIRE SAUCE

1 TEASPOON DRY MUSTARD

1 TEASPOON SALT

1/4 TEASPOON BLACK PEPPER

PER SERVING

CALORIES 178	CHOLESTEROL 0 mg
TOTAL FAT 0.0 g	SODIUM 300 mg
SATURATED 0.0 g	CARBOHYDRATES 37 g
POLYUNSATURATED 0.0 g	FIBER 6 g
MONOUNSATURATED 0.0 g	PROTEIN 7 g

Preheat the oven to 300°F.

Finely chop the chipotles.

In a 2-quart casserole dish or Dutch oven, stir together the chipotles and the remaining ingredients.

Bake, uncovered, for 1 hour. Stir the mixture. Bake for 30 to 60 minutes, or until desired consistency, stirring occasionally. If the mixture becomes dry, stir in water as needed.

beets in orange sauce

serves 6

Fresh orange sauce adds zest and flair to brightly colored beets.

2 POUNDS FRESH BEETS

SAUCE

1 TABLESPOON SUGAR

1 TABLESPOON CORNSTARCH

1/4 TEASPOON SALT (OPTIONAL)

2 TEASPOONS GRATED ORANGE ZEST, OR TO TASTE

2/3 CUP FRESH ORANGE JUICE

1 TEASPOON LIGHT STICK MARGARINE

◆

1 ORANGE, PEELED AND DIVIDED INTO SECTIONS (OPTIONAL)

Cut off all but about 1 to 2 inches of stems from the beets.

In a large saucepan, bring about 2 quarts water to a boil over high heat. Add the beets. Reduce the heat and simmer, covered, for 40 to 50 minutes, or until tender.

PER SERVING

CALORIES 94	CHOLESTEROL 0 mg
TOTAL FAT 0.5 g	SODIUM 123 mg
SATURATED 0.0 g	CARBOHYDRATES 21 g
POLYUNSATURATED 0.0 g	FIBER 4 g
MONOUNSATURATED 0.0 g	PROTEIN 3 g

Drain the beets; let cool enough to handle. Slip the skins off. Slice the beets into wedges. Cover to keep warm.

Meanwhile, in a small saucepan, stir together the sugar, cornstarch, and salt. Slowly add the orange zest and orange juice, stirring until smooth. Cook over medium heat for 5 to 8 minutes, or until thickened, stirring constantly.

Add the margarine and stir until melted. Pour the sauce over the warm beets. Garnish with the orange sections if desired.

Cook's Tip

You can substitute two 16- or 17-ounce cans of beets for the fresh beets. Heat them in a medium saucepan over medium heat until warmed through. Drain. Sauce and garnish as described.

sweet-and-sour broccoli and red bell pepper

serves 6

This Asian-inspired dish is a great alternative to the usual picnic fare. Served at room temperature, it doesn't need space in the cooler, and the tangy dressing will perk up all kinds of grilled chicken and meats.

1   POUND FRESH BROCCOLI FLORETS

1   MEDIUM RED BELL PEPPER

DRESSING

1/2   CUP PLAIN RICE VINEGAR

3   TABLESPOONS LIGHT BROWN SUGAR

2   TABLESPOONS THINLY SLICED GREEN ONIONS (GREEN PART ONLY)

1   TABLESPOON PLUS 1 TEASPOON LOW-SALT SOY SAUCE

1   TABLESPOON SESAME OIL

1   TABLESPOON GRATED PEELED GINGERROOT

2   MEDIUM GARLIC CLOVES, MINCED

◆

2   TABLESPOONS SLICED ALMONDS, DRY-ROASTED (OPTIONAL)

Set a steamer basket in a small amount of simmering water in a medium saucepan. Put the broccoli and bell pepper in the basket. Cook, covered, for 5 to 7 minutes, or until tender-crisp. Plunge into cold water to stop the cooking process. Drain well and dry on paper towels.

Stir together the dressing ingredients. Pour over the vegetables. Toss gently to coat thoroughly.

Cover and refrigerate for at least 1 hour to allow flavors to blend.

To serve, remove from the refrigerator and bring to room temperature. Sprinkle with the almonds if desired.

PER SERVING

CALORIES 78	CHOLESTEROL 0 mg
TOTAL FAT 2.5 g	SODIUM 112 mg
SATURATED 0.5 g	CARBOHYDRATES 13 g
POLYUNSATURATED 1.0 g	FIBER 3 g
MONOUNSATURATED 1.0 g	PROTEIN 3 g

braised brussels sprouts with pimiento and water chestnuts

serves 4

Serve this quick and colorful side dish to lend a classy touch to lean roast beef or pork.

- 8 OUNCES FRESH BRUSSELS SPROUTS (ABOUT 2 CUPS)
- 1 CUP FAT-FREE, LOW-SODIUM CHICKEN BROTH
- 2 OUNCES DICED PIMIENTOS, DRAINED (ABOUT 1/4 CUP)
- 1/4 TEASPOON SALT
- 1/8 TEASPOON PEPPER
- 2 TABLESPOONS SLICED WATER CHESTNUTS
- 1 TEASPOON LIGHT STICK MARGARINE
- 1 TEASPOON ALL-PURPOSE FLOUR
- 1 TABLESPOON WATER
- 2 TABLESPOONS SLICED ALMONDS, DRY-ROASTED

Remove any yellow outer leaves from the brussels sprouts. With a small knife, trim a small amount from the bottom of the stems. Slice a shallow X

PER SERVING	
CALORIES 60	CHOLESTEROL 0 mg
TOTAL FAT 2.5 g	SODIUM 184 mg
SATURATED 0.5 g	CARBOHYDRATES 8 g
POLYUNSATURATED 0.5 g	FIBER 3 g
MONOUNSATURATED 1.0 g	PROTEIN 3 g

into the stems to help the brussels sprouts cook evenly. Rinse the sprouts in cool water.

In a medium saucepan, bring the broth, pimientos, salt, and pepper to a boil over high heat. Add the sprouts. Cook, covered, over medium-low heat for 9 to 12 minutes, or until tender.

Remove the sprouts, leaving the liquid in the pan. Cover the sprouts to keep warm. Cook the liquid over high heat for 5 minutes, or until reduced to about 1/2 cup.

Stir in the water chestnuts and margarine. Cook over medium heat for 1 minute, stirring occasionally.

Put the flour in a cup. Stir in the water. Pour into the broth mixture. Cook for 1 to 2 minutes, or until sauce is thick, stirring occasionally.

Pour the sauce over the brussels sprouts. Sprinkle with the sliced almonds.

Cook's Tip on Brussels Sprouts

When sprouts have simmered for 1 to 2 minutes, remove the lid for 15 to 20 seconds, replace the lid, and continue cooking as usual. This allows the discharge of the sulfurous compounds that can give sprouts a bitter flavor.

apple-lemon carrots

Tired of plain carrots? Try this distinctive dish for a change. The apple and lemon juices make the difference.

- 1 **POUND CARROTS, GRATED (ABOUT 4 CUPS)**
- 2 **TABLESPOONS FROZEN UNSWEETENED APPLE JUICE CONCENTRATE, THAWED**
- 1 **TABLESPOON FRESH LEMON JUICE**
- 1 **TEASPOON LIGHT TUB MARGARINE**
- 1 **TEASPOON POPPY SEEDS**

In a nonstick skillet, cook the carrots, apple juice, and lemon juice over medium–high heat for 3 minutes, or until the carrots are tender, stirring constantly.

Stir in the margarine to coat thoroughly.

Sprinkle with poppy seeds.

PER SERVING

CALORIES 48	CHOLESTEROL 0 mg
TOTAL FAT 0.5 g	SODIUM 33 mg
SATURATED 0.0 g	CARBOHYDRATES 10 g
POLYUNSATURATED 0.5 g	FIBER 2 g
MONOUNSATURATED 0.0 g	PROTEIN 1 g

corn bread dressing

When it comes to dressing, everyone seems to have a favorite recipe. This winning version uses our own corn bread for real Southern flavor that is good for your heart.

1/4	CUP WATER
1 1/2	CUPS CHOPPED CELERY
1	CUP CHOPPED ONION
3	CUPS CORN BREAD CRUMBS (ABOUT HALF THE SOUTHERN-STYLE CORN BREAD RECIPE, PAGE 403)
4	SLICES STALE OR TOASTED WHOLE-GRAIN BREAD, CUT INTO CUBES
1/4	CUP SNIPPED FRESH PARSLEY
1	TEASPOON DRIED SAGE
1	TEASPOON POULTRY SEASONING
1 1/2	CUPS FAT-FREE, LOW-SODIUM CHICKEN BROTH
	WHITES OF 2 LARGE EGGS, LIGHTLY BEATEN
	VEGETABLE OIL SPRAY
1	TABLESPOON LIGHT TUB MARGARINE

Preheat the oven to 350°F.

PER SERVING

CALORIES 135	CHOLESTEROL 1 mg
TOTAL FAT 2.0 g	SODIUM 306 mg
SATURATED 0.0 g	CARBOHYDRATES 24 g
POLYUNSATURATED 0.5 g	FIBER 3 g
MONOUNSATURATED 1.0 g	PROTEIN 7 g

In a small saucepan, bring the water to a boil over high heat. Stir in the celery and onion; cook for 2 to 3 minutes, or until tender.

In a medium bowl, stir together the corn bread crumbs, bread cubes, parsley, sage, and poultry seasoning.

Stir the broth, egg whites, celery, onion, and cooking liquid into the bowl.

Spray a 2-quart casserole dish with vegetable oil spray. Pour the mixture into the prepared dish. Dot with the margarine.

Bake, uncovered, for 30 minutes.

green beans amandine

Cook fresh green beans quickly to preserve their color and texture, then add oregano for flavor and almonds for crunch. This is an ideal side dish for roast turkey or grilled chicken or fish.

- 1 **TEASPOON LIGHT TUB MARGARINE**
- 1 **POUND FRESH GREEN BEANS, TRIMMED AND CUT INTO 2-INCH PIECES**
- 1/4 **CUP LOW-SODIUM VEGETABLE BROTH OR FAT-FREE, LOW-SODIUM CHICKEN BROTH**
- 1 **TABLESPOON CHOPPED FRESH OREGANO OR 1 TEASPOON DRIED, CRUMBLED**
- **PEPPER TO TASTE**
- 1 **CUP FROZEN PEARL ONIONS (ABOUT 4 OUNCES)**
- 2 **TABLESPOONS SLICED ALMONDS**
- 1/4 **CUP PLAIN DRY BREAD CRUMBS**

Heat a large nonstick skillet over medium-high heat. Add the margarine and swirl to coat the bottom. Cook the green beans for 1 to 2 minutes, stirring constantly.

PER SERVING	
CALORIES 80	CHOLESTEROL 0 mg
TOTAL FAT 2.0 g	SODIUM 54 mg
SATURATED 0.0 g	CARBOHYDRATES 14 g
POLYUNSATURATED 0.5 g	FIBER 3 g
MONOUNSATURATED 1.0 g	PROTEIN 3 g

Stir in the broth, oregano, and pepper. Cook for 20 to 30 seconds.

Stir in the onions. Cook, covered, over medium-low heat for 6 to 8 minutes, or until the beans are tender-crisp.

Meanwhile, in a small nonstick pan, dry-roast the almonds over medium heat for 2 to 3 minutes, stirring occasionally.

Sprinkle the cooked beans with the almonds and bread crumbs.

Cook's Tip on Fresh Green Beans

When green beans are in season, buy extra to freeze. Trim and slice the beans. Blanch them in boiling water to cover by 1 inch for 1 minute. Remove them from the hot water and run them under cold water. Cool the beans, then freeze them for up to six months. Thaw and use in this recipe as directed.

sautéed greens and cabbage

serves 6

Cabbage and rice vinegar enhance the flavor of the greens used in this simple dish.

- 3 QUARTS WATER
- 1 BUNCH COLLARD GREENS, KALE, TURNIP GREENS, OR SPINACH, STEMS REMOVED, RINSED, AND FINELY CHOPPED (12 TO 16 OUNCES)
- 1/3 MEDIUM HEAD CABBAGE, COARSELY SHREDDED (2 1/2 TO 3 CUPS)

  OLIVE OIL SPRAY
- 1 TEASPOON OLIVE OIL
- 1 MEDIUM ONION, QUARTERED AND SLICED
- 1 MEDIUM GARLIC CLOVE, MINCED
- 2 TEASPOONS PLAIN RICE VINEGAR OR WHITE WINE VINEGAR
- 1/4 TEASPOON SALT

  RED HOT-PEPPER SAUCE TO TASTE

In a large saucepan, bring the water to a boil over high heat. Stir in the greens. Return to a boil.

PER SERVING	
CALORIES 50	CHOLESTEROL 0 mg
TOTAL FAT 1.0 g	SODIUM 120 mg
SATURATED 0.0 g	CARBOHYDRATES 9 g
POLYUNSATURATED 0.5 g	FIBER 4 g
MONOUNSATURATED 0.5 g	PROTEIN 3 g

Cook for 3 to 4 minutes, or until tender-crisp.

With a slotted spoon, transfer the greens to a colander, leaving the water in the pan. Drain well.

Return the water to a boil. Stir in the cabbage; cook for 1 minute. Put into the colander with the greens to drain. Set aside.

Heat a large skillet over medium-low heat. Remove from the heat and lightly spray with olive oil spray (being careful not to spray near a gas flame). Pour the oil into the skillet and swirl to coat the bottom. Return the skillet to the heat and cook the onion and garlic for 2 to 3 minutes, or until tender-crisp.

Stir in the greens and cabbage; cook for 2 to 3 minutes, stirring occasionally.

Stir in the vinegar. Season with the salt and hot-pepper sauce as desired.

twice-baked potatoes and herbs

serves 4

Idaho is famous for its potatoes, and for good reason. That state produces about one third of the U.S. potato crop. Most Idaho potatoes are russets, your best choice for this dish.

- 4 **MEDIUM BAKING POTATOES (RUSSETS PREFERRED)**
- 1/3 **CUP FAT-FREE OR LIGHT SOUR CREAM OR FAT-FREE PLAIN YOGURT**
- 2 **TABLESPOONS CHOPPED FRESH HERBS (BASIL, CHIVES, THYME, MARJORAM, OREGANO, PARSLEY, OR ANY COMBINATION)**
- 2 **TABLESPOONS GRATED OR SHREDDED PARMESAN CHEESE**

  FAT-FREE MILK (OPTIONAL)
- 1/4 **CUP SHREDDED FAT-FREE OR PART-SKIM MOZZARELLA CHEESE**

Preheat the oven to 425°F.

Scrub the potatoes and pat dry. Prick in several places. Put on a baking sheet.

PER SERVING	
CALORIES 146	CHOLESTEROL 7 mg
TOTAL FAT 1.0 g	SODIUM 148 mg
SATURATED 0.5 g	CARBOHYDRATES 31 g
POLYUNSATURATED 0.0 g	FIBER 3 g
MONOUNSATURATED 0.0 g	PROTEIN 9 g

Bake for 40 to 60 minutes, or until tender.

Cut a 1-inch slice from the side of each potato. Discard the skin from the slices and put the pulp in a bowl. Using a spoon, carefully scoop out the pulp from each potato, leaving a thin shell. Add the pulp to the bowl.

Using an electric mixer on low speed or a potato masher, beat or mash the potato pulp. Stir in the sour cream, herbs, and Parmesan. Beat or mash until smooth. Stir in 1 to 2 tablespoons milk as needed to reach the desired consistency.

Spoon the potato mixture into the shells. Sprinkle each with 1 tablespoon mozzarella. Place in a shallow baking dish.

Bake for 15 to 20 minutes, or until lightly browned.

Microwave Directions

On a microwave-safe plate, arrange the prepared potatoes in spoke fashion. Microwave, uncovered, on 100 percent power (high) for 11 to 15 minutes, or until tender, rearranging and turning the potatoes over once. Remove the potatoes from the microwave. Wrap in aluminum foil; let stand for 5 to 10 minutes. Continue as directed in the recipe (bake the stuffed potatoes in a conventional oven for best results).

Cook's Tip on Leftover Fresh Herbs

Small amounts of fresh herbs, such as basil, oregano, cilantro, or a mixture, are the basis of easy herb cream cheese or herb margarine spread. Mix 2 tablespoons of chopped fresh herbs with 1 minced garlic clove and 8 ounces of fat-free or low-fat cream cheese or light margarine. Try a little herb cream cheese on a bagel or a dollop of herb margarine on a baked potato.

herbed baby potatoes

Take red potatoes, add simple kitchen staples, and you have a tasty side dish that goes well with almost any main course.

1 1/2	POUNDS UNPEELED SMALL RED POTATOES, QUARTERED
2	TABLESPOONS LIGHT STICK MARGARINE, MELTED
	VEGETABLE OIL SPRAY
2	TABLESPOONS SNIPPED FRESH PARSLEY
1	TABLESPOON CHOPPED FRESH OREGANO OR 1 TEASPOON DRIED, CRUMBLED
1/2	TEASPOON PAPRIKA
1/2	TEASPOON GARLIC POWDER
	PEPPER TO TASTE
2	TABLESPOONS SNIPPED FRESH PARSLEY FOR GARNISH (OPTIONAL)

Preheat the oven to 350°F.

PER SERVING

CALORIES 96	CHOLESTEROL 0 mg
TOTAL FAT 2.0 g	SODIUM 26 mg
SATURATED 0.5 g	CARBOHYDRATES 21 g
POLYUNSATURATED 0.5 g	FIBER 2 g
MONOUNSATURATED 0.5 g	PROTEIN 3 g

In a 2-quart casserole dish, toss the potatoes with the margarine to coat. Lightly spray with vegetable oil spray.

Stir in the remaining ingredients except the parsley for garnish.

Bake, uncovered, for 30 to 40 minutes, or until lightly browned. Sprinkle with the remaining parsley if desired.

home-fried potatoes

These potatoes are delicious with Chicken with Mustard and Herbs (page 204) or with Crispy Oven–Fried Chicken (page 188).

- 1 **TABLESPOON ACCEPTABLE VEGETABLE OIL**
- 1 1/2 **POUNDS SMALL UNPEELED RED POTATOES, COOKED AND QUARTERED**
- 2 **MEDIUM SHALLOTS, CHOPPED**
- 1 **TEASPOON PAPRIKA**
- 1/2 **TEASPOON DRIED ROSEMARY, CRUSHED**
- 1/2 **TEASPOON DRY MUSTARD**
- 1/4 **TEASPOON SALT (OPTIONAL)**
- **PEPPER TO TASTE**

Heat a large, heavy nonstick skillet over medium-high heat. Pour the oil into the skillet and swirl to coat the bottom. Cook the potatoes on one side for 3 to 4 minutes. Turn the potatoes. Add the shallots; cook for 3 to 4 minutes.

Stir in the remaining ingredients. Cook for 1 to 2 minutes to blend flavors.

PER SERVING	
CALORIES 104	CHOLESTEROL 0 mg
TOTAL FAT 2.5 g	SODIUM 1 mg
SATURATED 0.0 g	CARBOHYDRATES 21 g
POLYUNSATURATED 0.5 g	FIBER 3 g
MONOUNSATURATED 1.5 g	PROTEIN 3 g

scalloped potatoes

serves 6

The fat-free and low-fat dairy products available today make it a snap to prepare low-fat scalloped potatoes. Your heart—and your taste buds—will love you for it.

VEGETABLE OIL SPRAY

1 3/4 CUPS FAT-FREE MILK

1 CUP FAT-FREE OR LIGHT SOUR CREAM

3 TABLESPOONS LIGHT STICK MARGARINE, SOFTENED

1 TABLESPOON CORNSTARCH

1/8 TEASPOON PEPPER

4 MEDIUM POTATOES (ABOUT 1 1/2 POUNDS), UNPEELED AND CUT INTO 1/8- TO 1/4-INCH-THICK SLICES

1/2 MEDIUM ONION, DICED

PAPRIKA TO TASTE

Preheat the oven to 350°F. Lightly spray an 11 x 7 x 2-inch baking pan with vegetable oil spray.

In a medium bowl, whisk together the milk, sour cream, margarine, cornstarch, and pepper.

PER SERVING	
CALORIES 174	CHOLESTEROL 8 mg
TOTAL FAT 3.0 g	SODIUM 109 mg
SATURATED 0.5 g	CARBOHYDRATES 32 g
POLYUNSATURATED 1.0 g	FIBER 2 g
MONOUNSATURATED 1.0 g	PROTEIN 8 g

Line the pan bottom with one third of the potatoes. Pour one third of the sour cream mixture over the potatoes. Sprinkle with half the onion. Repeat the layers. Top with the remaining potatoes, then with the remaining sour cream mixture. Cover with aluminum foil.

Bake for 1 hour. Uncover and bake for 20 minutes. Sprinkle with the paprika. Let stand 5 minutes before serving.

red and green pilaf

This pretty rice dish is speckled with sliced okra or green peas and bits of red and green bell pepper, then seasoned with a touch of cayenne.

VEGETABLE OIL SPRAY

1/2 CUP CHOPPED ONION

1/3 CUP CHOPPED GREEN BELL PEPPER

1/3 CUP CHOPPED RED BELL PEPPER

1/2 CUP UNCOOKED BROWN RICE

2 MEDIUM GARLIC CLOVES, MINCED

1 1/2 CUPS FAT-FREE, LOW-SODIUM CHICKEN BROTH

1/4 TEASPOON SALT

1/8 TEASPOON CAYENNE

1 CUP SLICED FRESH OR FROZEN OKRA OR 2/3 CUP FRESH OR FROZEN GREEN PEAS, THAWED IF FROZEN

1 MEDIUM ITALIAN PLUM TOMATO, SEEDS DISCARDED, CHOPPED

Heat a medium saucepan over medium-high heat. Remove from the heat and lightly spray with vegetable oil spray (being careful not to spray near a

PER SERVING	
CALORIES 118	CHOLESTEROL 0 mg
TOTAL FAT 1.0 g	SODIUM 174 mg
SATURATED 0.0 g	CARBOHYDRATES 24 g
POLYUNSATURATED 0.5 g	FIBER 3 g
MONOUNSATURATED 0.5 g	PROTEIN 4 g

gas flame). Return the pan to the heat and cook the onion and bell peppers for 5 minutes, stirring occasionally.

Stir in the rice and garlic; cook for 1 minute.

Stir in the broth, salt, and cayenne. Bring to a boil over high heat. Reduce the heat and simmer, covered, for 30 minutes.

Stir in the okra. Cook, covered, for 5 to 10 minutes, or until the rice is tender and the liquid is absorbed.

Stir in the tomato. Let stand for 5 minutes before serving.

golden rice

serves 6

This dish is known as "pilau" in Indian cuisine and as "pilaf" in Middle Eastern and Greek cuisine.

- 1 **CUP UNCOOKED BASMATI OR OTHER LONG-GRAIN RICE**
- 1 **CUP FAT-FREE, LOW-SODIUM CHICKEN BROTH**
- 1 **CUP WATER**
- 1 **CINNAMON STICK**
- 1 **BAY LEAF**
- 1/4 **TEASPOON SALT (OPTIONAL)**
- 1/4 **TEASPOON GROUND TURMERIC OR SAFFRON**
- 2 **TABLESPOONS SLIVERED ALMONDS, DRY-ROASTED**

Rinse the rice in several changes of water before cooking. Drain well.

In a 2-quart saucepan, bring the broth and water to a boil over medium-high heat. Stir in the rice, cinnamon stick, bay leaf, and salt. Reduce the heat and simmer, covered, for 20 minutes.

Using a fork, lightly stir in the turmeric. Cook, covered, over low heat for 10 minutes, or until the rice is tender and the liquid is absorbed.

PER SERVING

CALORIES 135	CHOLESTEROL 0 mg
TOTAL FAT 1.0 g	SODIUM 11 mg
SATURATED 0.0 g	CARBOHYDRATES 31 g
POLYUNSATURATED 0.5 g	FIBER 1 g
MONOUNSATURATED 0.5 g	PROTEIN 3 g

Remove the cinnamon stick and bay leaf. Sprinkle with the almonds just before serving.

Cook's Tip on Basmati Rice

Basmati means "fragrant" in Hindi, which aptly describes the nutlike taste and aroma of this delicious long-grain rice. Basmati rice is aged after harvest, which lessens its moisture content and intensifies its distinctive flavor. Used in India and Pakistan for thousands of years, several varieties are now grown in the United States, such as Texmati and Kasmati. Store rice in a cool, dry area in a sealed container away from the open air and moisture.

spinach parmesan

serves 4

If you have company coming, this dish can be easily doubled or even tripled. Make it ahead, and then just microwave it to quickly reheat.

VEGETABLE OIL SPRAY

2   **10-OUNCE PACKAGES FROZEN CHOPPED SPINACH, THAWED AND SQUEEZED DRY**

3/4   **CUP FINELY CHOPPED ONION (YELLOW PREFERRED)**

1/2   **CUP FAT-FREE SOUR CREAM**

3   **TABLESPOONS GRATED PARMESAN CHEESE**

1/3   **CUP FAT-FREE MILK**

1/4   **TEASPOON GARLIC POWDER**

1   **TABLESPOON GRATED PARMESAN CHEESE**

Preheat the oven to 350°F.

Lightly spray a pie pan with vegetable oil spray. In the pan, stir together all the ingredients except 1 tablespoon Parmesan. Cover with aluminum foil.

PER SERVING	
CALORIES 111	CHOLESTEROL 9 mg
TOTAL FAT 2.0 g	SODIUM 235 mg
SATURATED 1.0 g	CARBOHYDRATES 16 g
POLYUNSATURATED 0.0 g	FIBER 5 g
MONOUNSATURATED 0.5 g	PROTEIN 9 g

Bake for 25 minutes, or until the onion is just tender. Sprinkle with 1 tablespoon Parmesan.

Cook's Tip

If you decide to triple this recipe, use a shallow 13 x 9 x 2-inch baking dish so the onion will cook through completely.

wilted spinach

If you like wilted spinach salad, you'll love this tender cooked version. The warm sweet-and-sour dressing is accented with capers and lemon zest.

- 1 TEASPOON OLIVE OIL
- 1/4 CUP THINLY SLICED GREEN ONIONS (GREEN AND WHITE PARTS)
- 2 MEDIUM GARLIC CLOVES, MINCED
- 1 POUND FRESH SPINACH, RINSED AND DRAINED WELL
- 2 TABLESPOONS IMITATION BACON BITS
- 1 TABLESPOON WHITE WINE VINEGAR
- 2 TEASPOONS CAPERS, RINSED AND DRAINED
- 1 TEASPOON GRATED LEMON ZEST
- 1 TEASPOON LIGHT BROWN SUGAR
- 1/8 TEASPOON PEPPER
- 1/2 CUP CHOPPED HARD-COOKED EGG WHITES (WHITES OF 2 EGGS) (OPTIONAL)

Heat a large nonstick skillet over medium heat. Pour the oil into the skillet and swirl to coat the bottom. Cook the green onions and garlic for

PER SERVING	
CALORIES 43	CHOLESTEROL 0 mg
TOTAL FAT 2.0 g	SODIUM 126 mg
SATURATED 0.0 g	CARBOHYDRATES 5 g
POLYUNSATURATED 0.0 g	FIBER 2 g
MONOUNSATURATED 1.0 g	PROTEIN 3 g

1 to 2 minutes, or until the green onions are tender–crisp, stirring occasionally.

Stir in the spinach. Cook, covered, over medium-low heat for 3 to 4 minutes, or until the spinach is wilted and soft.

Stir in the bacon bits, vinegar, capers, lemon zest, brown sugar, and pepper. Cook, covered, for 1 to 2 minutes, or until the mixture is warmed through.

Transfer to a serving bowl. Sprinkle with chopped egg whites if desired.

praline butternut squash

Pureed butternut squash topped with sweet, maple-flavored fruit—this is a perfect dish for fall entertaining, especially during the holidays.

2- TO 2 1/2-POUND BUTTERNUT SQUASH

1 CUP WATER

15.25-OUNCE CAN PINEAPPLE CHUNKS, PACKED IN THEIR OWN JUICE, DRAINED

1/2 CUP DRIED FRUIT (APRICOTS, PEACHES, APPLES, OR ANY COMBINATION), DICED

2 TABLESPOONS CHOPPED PECANS, DRY-ROASTED

2 TABLESPOONS MAPLE SYRUP

1 TABLESPOON DARK BROWN SUGAR

1 TEASPOON GRATED LEMON ZEST

Preheat the oven to 350°F.

Cut the squash in half. Scoop out the seeds with a spoon. Lay the squash with cut side down in a shallow baking pan. Pour in the water.

PER SERVING	
CALORIES 127	
TOTAL FAT 1.5 g	CHOLESTEROL 0 mg
SATURATED 0.0 g	SODIUM 11 mg
POLYUNSATURATED 0.5 g	CARBOHYDRATES 30 g
MONOUNSATURATED 1.0 g	FIBER 5 g
	PROTEIN 2 g

Bake for 45 to 50 minutes, or until the squash is tender. Let cool for at least 15 minutes.

Remove the squash pulp from the rind with a spoon. In a food processor, process the pulp for 1 minute, or until smooth. (You may also use a potato masher.) Spoon into an ungreased 1-quart casserole dish.

In a medium bowl, stir together the remaining ingredients. Spoon the mixture over the squash.

Bake, uncovered, for 30 minutes, or until the mixture is warmed through.

yellow squash sauté

serves 4

The light dusting of bread crumbs adds a touch of substance to this satisfying and pretty side dish.

- 2 TEASPOONS OLIVE OIL
- 1 MEDIUM GARLIC CLOVE, MINCED
- 2 CUPS THINLY SLICED YELLOW SUMMER SQUASH
- 3 TABLESPOONS FINELY SNIPPED FRESH PARSLEY
- 1/4 CUP PLAIN DRY BREAD CRUMBS
- 1/8 TEASPOON PEPPER, OR TO TASTE

Heat a medium nonstick skillet over medium-high heat. Pour the oil into the skillet and swirl to coat the bottom. Cook the garlic for 30 seconds.

Add the squash and parsley; cook for 5 to 7 minutes, or until the squash is tender-crisp, stirring occasionally.

Stir in the bread crumbs and pepper. Cook for 1 minute over high heat, tossing to coat. Serve immediately.

PER SERVING

CALORIES 60

TOTAL FAT 3.0 g

   SATURATED 0.5 g

   POLYUNSATURATED 0.5 g

   MONOUNSATURATED 2.0 g

CHOLESTEROL 0 mg

SODIUM 61 mg

CARBOHYDRATES 8 g

FIBER 1 g

PROTEIN 2 g

sweet potatoes in creamy cinnamon sauce

serves 6

Warm and fragrant aromas of spice fill the air as this dish bakes. It's perfect for the holiday season or anytime you want a boost from vitamin-rich sweet potatoes. Serve with tender braised pork chops or lean ham.

1	POUND SWEET POTATOES (ABOUT 2 LARGE), PEELED AND CUT CROSSWISE INTO 1/4-INCH SLICES
1/2	CUP FAT-FREE HALF-AND-HALF
2	TABLESPOONS LIGHT BROWN SUGAR
1	TEASPOON GRATED ORANGE ZEST
1/2	TEASPOON GROUND CINNAMON
1/4	TEASPOON GROUND NUTMEG
1	TABLESPOON LIGHT TUB MARGARINE

Preheat the oven to 400°F.

Arrange the sweet potato slices in even layers on the bottom of a nonstick 8-inch round or square baking pan.

PER SERVING	
CALORIES 114	CHOLESTEROL 0 mg
TOTAL FAT 1.0 g	SODIUM 63 mg
SATURATED 0.0 g	CARBOHYDRATES 27 g
POLYUNSATURATED 0.0 g	FIBER 3 g
MONOUNSATURATED 0.5 g	PROTEIN 3 g

In a small bowl, whisk together the half-and-half, brown sugar, orange zest, cinnamon, and nutmeg. Pour the mixture over the sweet potatoes. Dot with the margarine.

Bake, uncovered, for 35 to 40 minutes, or until the potatoes are tender, stirring once halfway through the baking time.

swiss chard with hot-pepper sauce

serves 4

Cooking greens the old-fashioned Southern way takes time, but this recipe for Swiss chard, a close cousin, takes just a matter of minutes—with delicious results.

8	OUNCES SWISS CHARD, RINSED AND DRAINED
1/2	CUP FAT-FREE, LOW-SODIUM CHICKEN BROTH
1/2	MEDIUM ONION, FINELY CHOPPED
1	MEDIUM GARLIC CLOVE, MINCED
1/2	CUP FAT-FREE, LOW-SODIUM CHICKEN BROTH
2	TEASPOONS OLIVE OIL (EXTRA-VIRGIN PREFERRED)
	RED HOT-PEPPER SAUCE TO TASTE

Remove the stems from the Swiss chard and thinly slice them. Coarsely chop the leaves.

In a large skillet, bring 1/2 cup broth to a boil over high heat. Stir in the chard stems, onion, and garlic. Cook for 3 to 4 minutes, or until the liquid has evaporated and the vegetables are beginning to lightly brown, stirring frequently.

PER SERVING	
CALORIES 42	CHOLESTEROL 0 mg
TOTAL FAT 2.5 g	SODIUM 137 mg
SATURATED 0.5 g	CARBOHYDRATES 4 g
POLYUNSATURATED 0.0 g	FIBER 1 g
MONOUNSATURATED 1.5 g	PROTEIN 2 g

Stir the remaining 1/2 cup broth into the vegetables. Bring to a boil. Stir in the chard leaves. Return to a boil and cook for 3 minutes, or until the liquid has evaporated.

Remove from the heat. Drizzle with the oil. Sprinkle lightly with the hot-pepper sauce to taste.

oven-fried green tomatoes with poppy seeds

serves 6

A typical end-of-summer tradition in the South is to pick the last of the garden tomatoes while they are still green, slice them, coat them with cornmeal, and fry them up. This dish captures that same tradition and flavor, without the fat.

VEGETABLE OIL SPRAY

1 POUND GREEN TOMATOES OR FIRM RED TOMATOES (ABOUT 3 MEDIUM)

EGG SUBSTITUTE EQUIVALENT TO 1 EGG, OR 1 EGG

2 TABLESPOONS FAT-FREE MILK

1/2 CUP CORNMEAL

1/4 CUP ALL-PURPOSE FLOUR

1 TEASPOON POPPY SEEDS

1/4 TEASPOON SALT

1/8 TEASPOON PEPPER

PER SERVING

CALORIES 89

TOTAL FAT 0.5 g

  SATURATED 0.0 g

  POLYUNSATURATED 0.5 g

  MONOUNSATURATED 0.0 g

CHOLESTEROL 0 mg

SODIUM 131 mg

CARBOHYDRATES 17 g

FIBER 2 g

PROTEIN 4 g

Preheat the oven to 450°F. Lightly spray a baking sheet with vegetable oil spray.

Cut the tomatoes into 1/4-inch-thick slices.

In a small bowl, stir together the egg substitute and milk.

In a pic pan or shallow baking pan, combine the cornmeal, flour, poppy seeds, salt, and pepper.

In order, place the tomato slices, egg mixture, cornmeal mixture, and baking sheet in a line.

Using tongs, dip the tomato slices in the egg mixture, letting any excess drip off. Lightly coat both sides of the tomatoes with the cornmeal mixture. Place the tomatoes in a single layer on the baking sheet.

Bake for 10 minutes. Turn. Bake for 5 minutes, or until golden-brown.

italian-style zucchini slices

Bring some Italian flair to your meal. Herbs and spices blend with Parmesan cheese and crunchy almonds to make this side dish special.

1 TEASPOON ACCEPTABLE VEGETABLE OIL

2 POUNDS ZUCCHINI (ABOUT 8 SMALL), CUT INTO 1/2-INCH-THICK SLICES

1/2 CUP WHOLE-WHEAT BREAD CRUMBS, TOASTED

1/4 CUP FINELY SNIPPED FRESH PARSLEY

2 TABLESPOONS MINCED ALMONDS, DRY-ROASTED

1 TABLESPOON GRATED OR SHREDDED PARMESAN CHEESE

1 TABLESPOON CHOPPED FRESH OREGANO OR 1 TEASPOON DRIED, CRUMBLED

1 MEDIUM GARLIC CLOVE, MINCED

PEPPER TO TASTE

Heat a large nonstick skillet over medium–high heat. Pour the oil into the skillet and swirl to coat the bottom. Cook the zucchini for 8 to 10 min–

PER SERVING	
CALORIES 61	CHOLESTEROL 1 mg
TOTAL FAT 3.0 g	SODIUM 46 mg
SATURATED 0.5 g	CARBOHYDRATES 8 g
POLYUNSATURATED 0.5 g	FIBER 3 g
MONOUNSATURATED 1.5 g	PROTEIN 3 g

utes, or until just tender and lightly browned, stirring frequently.

Meanwhile, in a medium bowl, stir together the remaining ingredients.

Gently stir the mixture into the zucchini to coat thoroughly. Serve immediately.

ratatouille

serves 6

Excellent with chicken or fish, this French stew of vegetables is also wonderful served hot on a baked potato or cold with crusty bread.

1	LARGE EGGPLANT, CUT INTO 1-INCH CUBES
1	TEASPOON OLIVE OIL
2	MEDIUM ONIONS, SLICED
4	MEDIUM ZUCCHINI, CUT INTO 1/2-INCH-THICK SLICES
2	MEDIUM RED, GREEN, OR YELLOW BELL PEPPERS, OR ANY COMBINATION, CHOPPED
2	LARGE TOMATOES, CHOPPED
1	TABLESPOON CHOPPED FRESH THYME OR 1 TEASPOON DRIED, CRUMBLED
1	TABLESPOON CHOPPED FRESH OREGANO OR 1 TEASPOON DRIED, CRUMBLED
1	TABLESPOON CHOPPED FRESH BASIL OR 1 TEASPOON DRIED, CRUMBLED
2	MEDIUM GARLIC CLOVES, MINCED
1/2	TEASPOON SALT
	PEPPER TO TASTE

PER SERVING

CALORIES 101

TOTAL FAT 1.5 g

  SATURATED 0.0 g

  POLYUNSATURATED 0.5 g

  MONOUNSATURATED 0.5 g

CHOLESTEROL 0 mg

SODIUM 209 mg

CARBOHYDRATES 21 g

FIBER 7 g

PROTEIN 4 g

Unless the eggplant is very young, remove the peel.

Heat a large, heavy nonstick skillet over medium-high heat. Pour the oil into the skillet and swirl to coat the bottom. Cook the onions for 2 to 3 minutes, or until tender.

Stir in the eggplant and remaining ingredients. Reduce the heat and simmer, covered, for 30 to 45 minutes, or until the vegetables are thoroughly cooked, stirring occasionally to prevent sticking. Cook, uncovered, for 5 minutes to reduce the liquid.

Ratatouille is best made a day ahead to allow the flavors to blend. Serve warm or cold.

breads and
breakfast
dishes

Savory Dill Bread

Honey-Nut Bread

Zucchini Bread

Speckled Spoon Bread

Southern-Style Corn Bread

Buttermilk Biscuits

Oat Bran Muffins

Oatmeal-Fruit Muffins

Cardamom-Lemon Muffins

Spanish-Style Scrambled Eggs

Gingerbread Pancakes with Apple-Berry Topping

Breakfast Tortilla Wrap

savory dill bread

serves 16; 1 slice per serving

The aroma that fills the air when this bread is baking will entice you to eat a slice warm from the oven (or bread machine) without even thinking of spreading margarine on top.

1	TABLESPOON (1 ENVELOPE) ACTIVE DRY YEAST
1 1/4	CUPS WARM WATER (105°F)
2	CUPS ALL-PURPOSE FLOUR
2	TABLESPOONS ACCEPTABLE STICK MARGARINE
1	TEASPOON DRIED DILLWEED
1	TEASPOON ONION POWDER
1/2	TEASPOON GARLIC POWDER
1/2	TEASPOON DRIED OREGANO, CRUMBLED
1/2	TEASPOON SALT
1 1/2	CUPS ALL-PURPOSE FLOUR
	VEGETABLE OIL SPRAY

In a medium bowl, dissolve the yeast in the water. Let stand for 5 minutes.

PER SERVING

CALORIES 115	CHOLESTEROL 0 mg
TOTAL FAT 1.5 g	SODIUM 91 mg
SATURATED 0.5 g	CARBOHYDRATES 21 g
POLYUNSATURATED 0.5 g	FIBER 1 g
MONOUNSATURATED 0.5 g	PROTEIN 3 g

Meanwhile, in a large bowl, combine 2 cups flour, margarine, dillweed, onion powder, garlic powder, oregano, and salt.

Pour the yeast mixture into the flour mixture, stirring with a sturdy spoon for about 30 seconds.

Stir in small amounts of the remaining 1 1/2 cups flour until the dough starts to pull away from the sides of the bowl

Turn the dough onto a floured surface. Knead in enough remaining flour for the dough to become smooth and elastic, about 7 to 8 minutes. (You may or may not knead in all the flour.) Shape into a ball.

Wipe out the flour mixture bowl with a paper towel; spray the bowl with vegetable oil spray. Put the dough in the bowl, turning to coat all sides. Cover the bowl with a dish towel and put in a warm, draft-free place. Let the dough rise for 1 hour, or until doubled in bulk.

Lightly spray a baking sheet with vegetable oil spray. Punch the dough down and shape it into a round loaf. Place on the prepared baking sheet. Flatten the loaf slightly with your hands. Using a serrated knife, cut an X into the top of the loaf. Cover with a dish towel. Let the dough rise for 30 minutes, or until doubled in bulk.

Near the end of the rising cycle, preheat the oven to 375°F. Remove the dish towel from the loaf.

Bake for 35 to 40 minutes, or until the loaf sounds hollow when tapped. Cool on a wire rack for 15 minutes before cutting.

Cook's Tip on Bread Dough

Getting a feel for when bread dough reaches the proper consistency gets easier with practice, and it's fun too. Adding too much flour or overworking the dough will make it dry and stiff. Using too little flour or not kneading the dough enough will leave you with a loaf that won't retain its shape while baking.

The point of kneading is to develop the gluten in the flour, which produces a bread that has a strong structure. Try not to punch the dough completely down to your counter or board. When you do, the dough tends to become sticky. You'll probably think you should add more flour, but the dough may not need it.

honey-nut bread

serves 20; 1 slice per serving

Freeze single slices of this delicious bread for a lunch-box addition. When packed frozen, a slice will thaw in less than an hour.

VEGETABLE OIL SPRAY

1 CUP FAT-FREE MILK

1 CUP HONEY

1 1/4 CUPS WHOLE-WHEAT FLOUR

1 1/4 CUPS ALL-PURPOSE FLOUR

1 TABLESPOON BAKING POWDER

1/2 TEASPOON SALT

1/4 CUP LIGHT STICK MARGARINE

EGG SUBSTITUTE EQUIVALENT TO 1 EGG, OR 1 EGG WHITES OF 2 EGGS, LIGHTLY BEATEN

1/4 CUP FINELY CHOPPED WALNUTS, DRY-ROASTED

Preheat the oven to 325°F. Lightly spray two 9 x 5 x 3-inch loaf pans with vegetable oil spray.

In a small saucepan, heat the milk and honey over medium-high heat until very warm (120°F to 130°F).

PER SERVING

CALORIES 133	CHOLESTEROL 0 mg
TOTAL FAT 2.5 g	SODIUM 166 mg
SATURATED 0.5 g	CARBOHYDRATES 27 g
POLYUNSATURATED 1.0 g	FIBER 1 g
MONOUNSATURATED 0.5 g	PROTEIN 3 g

In a large bowl, combine the whole-wheat and all-purpose flours, baking powder, and salt.

Stir the liquid mixture into the dry mixture until just moistened.

Add the margarine, egg substitute, and egg whites; stir just until blended. (Overmixing will produce a rubbery texture.)

Fold in the nuts.

Pour the bread mixture into the prepared pans.

Bake for 50 to 60 minutes, or until a cake tester inserted into the center of the loaf comes out moist but not wet. Cool on a wire rack.

To store, wrap each loaf in aluminum foil to preserve moisture.

zucchini bread

serves 16, 1 slice per serving

A perfect luncheon bread is hard to find, but this comes close. It's hard to beat good nutrition and great taste rolled into one!

	VEGETABLE OIL SPRAY
1 1/2	CUPS ALL-PURPOSE FLOUR
1/2	CUP FIRMLY PACKED LIGHT BROWN SUGAR
1 1/2	TEASPOONS BAKING POWDER
1/2	TEASPOON GROUND CINNAMON
1/4	TEASPOON BAKING SODA
1/8	TEASPOON SALT
1	CUP SHREDDED ZUCCHINI (ABOUT 4 OUNCES)
1/4	CUP RAISINS (OPTIONAL)
1	TABLESPOON FINELY CHOPPED WALNUTS, DRY-ROASTED
1/2	CUP PINEAPPLE JUICE
	EGG SUBSTITUTE EQUIVALENT TO 1 EGG, OR 1 EGG
1	TABLESPOON ACCEPTABLE VEGETABLE OIL
1	TABLESPOON CORN SYRUP
1/2	TEASPOON VANILLA EXTRACT

PER SERVING

CALORIES 91	
TOTAL FAT 1.5 g	CHOLESTEROL 0 mg
SATURATED 0.0 g	SODIUM 96 mg
POLYUNSATURATED 0.5 g	CARBOHYDRATES 18 g
MONOUNSATURATED 0.5 g	FIBER 1 g
	PROTEIN 2 g

Preheat the oven to 350°F. Spray a 9 x 5 x 3-inch loaf pan with vegetable oil spray.

In a large bowl, combine the flour, brown sugar, baking powder, cinnamon, baking soda, and salt. Stir in the zucchini, raisins if desired, and nuts.

In a small bowl, beat together the remaining ingredients. Pour the liquid mixture into the zucchini-flour mixture; stir just until moistened. Pour the batter into the prepared pan.

Bake for 50 minutes to 1 hour, or until a cake tester inserted into the center of the loaf comes out clean. Let cool in the pan for 10 minutes, then turn out onto a wire rack and cool completely.

To store, wrap the loaf in plastic wrap and refrigerate for up to seven days.

speckled spoon bread

This soufflélike bread requires a spoon for serving, hence its name. It will deflate slightly when it comes out of the oven, but still be light and fluffy.

VEGETABLE OIL SPRAY

1 CUP WATER

1/2 CUP CORNMEAL

1/2 CUP CANNED NO-SALT-ADDED OR FROZEN WHOLE-KERNEL CORN

1/4 CUP SNIPPED FRESH PARSLEY

2 TABLESPOONS CHOPPED PIMIENTO

1 TABLESPOON LIGHT STICK MARGARINE

2 MEDIUM GARLIC CLOVES, MINCED

3/4 CUP FAT-FREE MILK

EGG SUBSTITUTE EQUIVALENT TO 1 EGG, OR 1 EGG

1 TEASPOON BAKING POWDER

WHITES OF 3 EGGS

Preheat the oven to 325°F. Lightly spray a 1 1/2-quart casserole dish with vegetable oil spray.

PER SERVING	
CALORIES 92	CHOLESTEROL 1 mg
TOTAL FAT 1.5 g	SODIUM 162 mg
SATURATED 0.0 g	CARBOHYDRATES 15 g
POLYUNSATURATED 0.5 g	FIBER 1 g
MONOUNSATURATED 0.5 g	PROTEIN 5 g

In a medium saucepan, bring the water and cornmeal to a boil over high heat. Reduce the heat to medium-low. Cook and stir for about 1 minute, or until very thick. Remove from the heat.

Stir in the corn, parsley, pimiento, margarine, and garlic, then stir in the milk.

In a small bowl, stir together the egg substitute and baking powder. Stir into the cornmeal mixture.

Using an electric mixer, beat the egg whites until stiff peaks form.

Fold the beaten whites into the cornmeal mixture. Spoon the cornmeal mixture into the prepared dish.

Bake, uncovered, for 50 to 60 minutes, or until a knife inserted near the center comes out clean.

southern-style corn bread

serves 12

This corn bread has a crispy crust and a flavorful, moist center. For a simple yet satisfying meal, serve it with black-eyed peas and Sautéed Greens and Cabbage (page 361).

1 1/2   TEASPOONS ACCEPTABLE VEGETABLE OIL

1 1/2   CUPS YELLOW CORNMEAL (WHOLE-GRAIN PREFERRED)

1 1/2   CUPS WHOLE-WHEAT FLOUR

1/3   CUP NONFAT DRY MILK

1   TO 3 TABLESPOONS SUGAR (OPTIONAL)

1 1/2   TABLESPOONS BAKING POWDER

1/2   TEASPOON SALT

WHITES OF 3 LARGE EGGS

1 1/2   CUPS FAT-FREE MILK

Preheat the oven to 450°F for cast iron or 425°F for glass.

PER SERVING

CALORIES 134

TOTAL FAT 1.5 g

   SATURATED 0.0 g

   POLYUNSATURATED 0.5 g

   MONOUNSATURATED 0.5 g

CHOLESTEROL 1 mg

SODIUM 326 mg

CARBOHYDRATES 26 g

FIBER 3 g

PROTEIN 6 g

Pour the oil into a 10 1/2-inch cast-iron skillet or 11 x 9-inch glass casserole dish and swirl to coat the bottom.

In a large bowl, combine the cornmeal, flour, dry milk, sugar if desired, baking powder, and salt.

In a small bowl, using a wire whisk, beat the egg whites until slightly frothy. Whisk in the milk. Stir the liquid mixture into the dry mixture, leaving some lumps. Do not overmix.

Put the skillet in the oven for 1 to 2 minutes to heat the oil. *Be careful not to let it burn!* Watch the time carefully. Pour the batter into the hot skillet.

Bake for 20 minutes. Immediately remove the corn bread from the pan by turning it onto a cutting board.

buttermilk biscuits

serves 8

A drizzle of honey instead of lots of margarine is perfect for these fluffy biscuits. Don't overmix the dough, or the biscuits will be tough.

VEGETABLE OIL SPRAY

1 CUP ALL-PURPOSE FLOUR

2 TEASPOONS BAKING POWDER

1 TEASPOON SUGAR

1/8 TEASPOON BAKING SODA

1/8 TEASPOON SALT

1 TABLESPOON ACCEPTABLE STICK MARGARINE

1/3 CUP LOW-FAT BUTTERMILK

1/4 CUP FAT-FREE PLAIN YOGURT

FLOUR

Preheat the oven to 425°F. Lightly spray an 8-inch round cake pan with vegetable oil spray.

In a medium bowl, combine 1 cup flour, baking powder, sugar, baking soda, and salt.

Using a pastry blender or fork, cut in the margarine until it is in small pieces throughout the flour mixture.

PER SERVING

CALORIES 81	CHOLESTEROL 1 mg
TOTAL FAT 1.5 g	SODIUM 211 mg
SATURATED 0.5 g	CARBOHYDRATES 14 g
POLYUNSATURATED 0.5 g	FIBER 0 g
MONOUNSATURATED 0.5 g	PROTEIN 2 g

Using a fork, stir the buttermilk and yogurt into the flour mixture until just moistened.

Turn the dough out onto a lightly floured board. Sprinkle the dough with a small amount of flour and shape into a disk. Using your hands or a rolling pin, pat out the dough until it is about 1/2 inch thick. Cut out the biscuits with a 2 1/2-inch round cutter. Place the biscuits in the prepared cake pan.

Bake for 10 to 12 minutes, or until the biscuits are done through the middle and golden-brown on the bottom. Remove from the pan. Serve warm.

oat bran muffins

serves 18

You've heard about the healthfulness of oat bran—now taste how good it can be. The almond extract "stretches" the nutty flavor of the pecans. Make an extra batch to freeze so you can enjoy these moist muffins at breakfast, lunch, or snack time.

2 1/2	CUPS UNCOOKED OAT BRAN
1/4	CUP FIRMLY PACKED LIGHT BROWN SUGAR
1/4	CUP CURRANTS (1 TO 2 OUNCES)
2	TABLESPOONS CHOPPED PECANS OR OTHER NUTS, DRY-ROASTED
1	TABLESPOON BAKING POWDER
1/4	TEASPOON SALT (OPTIONAL)
	WHITES OF 4 LARGE EGGS, LIGHTLY BEATEN
3/4	CUP FAT-FREE MILK
1/4	CUP HONEY
2	TABLESPOONS ACCEPTABLE VEGETABLE OIL
1	TEASPOON ALMOND EXTRACT
1	TEASPOON VANILLA EXTRACT
	VEGETABLE OIL SPRAY

PER SERVING

CALORIES 93

TOTAL FAT 3.0 g

  SATURATED 0.5 g

  POLYUNSATURATED 1.0 g

  MONOUNSATURATED 1.5 g

CHOLESTEROL 0 mg

SODIUM 101 mg

CARBOHYDRATES 18 g

FIBER 2 g

PROTEIN 4 g

Preheat the oven to 350°F.

In a large bowl, combine the oat bran, sugar, currants, nuts, baking powder, and salt if desired.

In a small bowl, stir together the remaining ingredients except the vegetable oil spray.

Stir the liquid mixture into the dry mixture until just moistened.

Lightly spray a 12-cup muffin pan and a 6-cup muffin pan with vegetable oil spray or use paper bake cups. Spoon the mixture evenly into the muffin pans.

Bake for 20 to 25 minutes, or until light brown. Serve warm or at room temperature.

oatmeal-fruit muffins

serves 12

What a find: oats, wheat germ, milk, and fruit—so many healthful ingredients in such tasty muffins!

VEGETABLE OIL SPRAY

1 CUP ALL-PURPOSE FLOUR

3/4 CUP UNCOOKED QUICK-COOKING OR REGULAR ROLLED OATS

1/3 CUP TOASTED WHEAT GERM

2 TEASPOONS BAKING POWDER

1 TEASPOON GROUND CINNAMON

1/2 TEASPOON BAKING SODA

1/8 TEASPOON SALT

3/4 CUP FAT-FREE MILK

1/2 CUP FIRMLY PACKED LIGHT BROWN SUGAR

EGG SUBSTITUTE EQUIVALENT TO 1 EGG, OR 1 EGG

1/4 CUP UNSWEETENED APPLESAUCE

1/2 TEASPOON VANILLA EXTRACT

1/2 CUP SNIPPED DRIED FIGS OR APRICOTS

PER SERVING

CALORIES 136	CHOLESTEROL 0 mg
TOTAL FAT 1.0 g	SODIUM 181 mg
SATURATED 0.0 g	CARBOHYDRATES 29 g
POLYUNSATURATED 0.5 g	FIBER 2 g
MONOUNSATURATED 0.0 g	PROTEIN 4 g

Preheat the oven to 400°F. Line a 12-cup muffin pan with paper bake cups or lightly spray with vegetable oil spray.

In a medium bowl, combine the flour, oats, wheat germ, baking powder, cinnamon, baking soda, and salt. Make a well in the center.

In another medium bowl, stir together the remaining ingredients except the figs.

Stir the liquid mixture into the dry mixture until just moistened (batter should be lumpy). Fold in the figs.

Spoon the batter into the muffin cups, using about 1/4 cup batter for each cup.

Bake for 10 to 12 minutes, or until a wooden toothpick inserted in the center comes out clean. Cool on a wire rack for 5 minutes. Remove the muffins from the bake cups. Serve warm or at room temperature.

Cook's Tip on Cutting Dried Fruit

To prevent your scissors or knife from becoming sticky when you snip or chop dried fruit, lightly spray the utensil with vegetable oil spray or dip it in hot water or sugar before using.

cardamom-lemon muffins

serves 24

Cardamom adds a distinctive flavor and enhances the sweetness of these muffins. Instead of using a lot of fat for moistness, this recipe calls on applesauce. Oat bran contains soluble fiber that may help lower blood cholesterol.

	VEGETABLE OIL SPRAY
2 1/2	CUPS UNCOOKED OAT BRAN
2	CUPS ALL-PURPOSE FLOUR
2	TEASPOONS BAKING POWDER
1 1/2	TEASPOONS BAKING SODA
1	TEASPOON GROUND CARDAMOM
2	CUPS UNSWEETENED APPLESAUCE
	WHITES OF 4 LARGE EGGS
1/2	CUP PINEAPPLE JUICE
1/2	CUP HONEY
2	TABLESPOONS ACCEPTABLE VEGETABLE OIL
1/4	TEASPOON ALMOND EXTRACT
	GRATED ZEST OF 1 LEMON

PER SERVING

CALORIES 109	CHOLESTEROL 0 mg
TOTAL FAT 2.0 g	SODIUM 130 mg
SATURATED 0.0 g	CARBOHYDRATES 24 g
POLYUNSATURATED 0.5 g	FIBER 2 g
MONOUNSATURATED 1.0 g	PROTEIN 3 g

Preheat the oven to 400°F. Lightly spray two 12-cup muffin pans with vegetable oil spray or use paper bake cups.

In a medium bowl, combine the oat bran, flour, baking powder, baking soda, and cardamom.

In a large bowl, stir together the remaining ingredients.

Stir the dry mixture into the wet mixture until just moistened (batter should be lumpy).

Fill the prepared muffin cups to almost full. Put in the oven and reduce the heat to 375°F.

Bake for 18 to 20 minutes, or until golden-brown. Serve warm or at room temperature.

spanish-style scrambled eggs

serves 3

Eggs with peppy personality, this recipe is perfect for a jump start of flavor in the morning. For a quick and tasty lunch or dinner, wrap the warm mixture in a tortilla and enjoy.

1 **TEASPOON ACCEPTABLE VEGETABLE OIL**

1 **SMALL TOMATO, FINELY CHOPPED**

1 **GREEN ONION (GREEN AND WHITE PARTS), FINELY CHOPPED**

EGG SUBSTITUTE EQUIVALENT TO 6 EGGS, OR WHITES OF 6 LARGE EGGS

1 **TABLESPOON SALSA OR PICANTE SAUCE**

PEPPER TO TASTE

1 **TABLESPOON FINELY SNIPPED FRESH CILANTRO OR PARSLEY**

FRESH CILANTRO OR PARSLEY SPRIGS (OPTIONAL)

1 **TOMATO, CUT INTO WEDGES (OPTIONAL)**

Heat a large nonstick skillet over medium-high heat. Pour the oil into the skillet and swirl to coat

PER SERVING

CALORIES 83	CHOLESTEROL 0 mg
TOTAL FAT 1.5 g	SODIUM 277 mg
SATURATED 0.0 g	CARBOHYDRATES 4 g
POLYUNSATURATED 0.5 g	FIBER 1 g
MONOUNSATURATED 1.0 g	PROTEIN 12 g

the bottom. Cook the tomato and green onion for 1 to 2 minutes, or until the green onion is tender. Reduce the heat to low.

In a medium bowl, beat the egg substitute, salsa, and pepper until frothy.

Pour the egg mixture into the skillet. Cook until almost set, stirring occasionally. Add the cilantro; cook until the eggs are fully set, stirring constantly.

Garnish with the cilantro sprigs and tomato if desired.

gingerbread pancakes with apple-berry topping

You don't need cold weather to enjoy these pancakes. In fact, they're so good, you'll look for excuses to eat them for dinner! Look for boysenberry syrup near the pancake syrup at the supermarket.

- 1 CUP ALL-PURPOSE FLOUR
- 2 TABLESPOONS SUGAR
- 2 TEASPOONS BAKING POWDER
- 1/2 TEASPOON GROUND CINNAMON
- 1/4 TEASPOON GROUND GINGER
- 1/4 TEASPOON GROUND ALLSPICE
- 3/4 CUP FAT-FREE MILK
- EGG SUBSTITUTE EQUIVALENT TO 1 EGG, OR 1 EGG
- 2 TABLESPOONS MOLASSES
- 1 TABLESPOON ACCEPTABLE VEGETABLE OIL
- 8 OUNCES LIGHT APPLE PIE FILLING
- 1/2 CUP BOYSENBERRY, BLUEBERRY, OR STRAWBERRY SYRUP
- 4 TABLESPOONS DRIED CRANBERRIES (OPTIONAL)

Heat a nonstick griddle over medium heat.

In a medium bowl, combine the flour, sugar, baking powder, cinnamon, ginger, and allspice.

In a small bowl, stir together the milk, egg substitute, molasses, and vegetable oil.

Stir the wet mixture into the dry mixture until just combined. (Do not overmix or pancakes will be tough.)

Test the griddle by sprinkling a few drops of water on it. If the water evaporates quickly, the griddle is ready. Pour about 1/4 cup of the batter onto the griddle. Cook for 2 to 3 minutes, or until bubbles appear all over the surface. Flip over; cook for 2 minutes, or until the bottom is golden-brown. Repeat until all the batter is used.

Meanwhile, in a small saucepan, heat the apple pie filling over low heat for 2 to 3 minutes, or until the filling is warmed through.

To serve, place two pancakes on a plate. Spoon about 2 tablespoons of the syrup on the pancakes. Spread 1/4 cup apple pie filling on top. Sprinkle with 1 tablespoon dried cranberries if desired. Repeat with the remaining ingredients.

PER SERVING	
CALORIES 343	CHOLESTEROL 1 mg
TOTAL FAT 4.0 g	SODIUM 310 mg
SATURATED 0.5 g	CARBOHYDRATES 71 g
POLYUNSATURATED 1.0 g	FIBER 2 g
MONOUNSATURATED 2.0 g	PROTEIN 6 g

breakfast tortilla wrap

serves 4

This hearty breakfast sandwich combines fluffy scrambled eggs, Canadian bacon, hash browns, red bell pepper for color, and a bit of cheese for flair. It makes an easy meal for busy people on the go.

VEGETABLE OIL SPRAY

EGG SUBSTITUTE EQUIVALENT TO 2 EGGS, OR 2 EGGS

1/8 TEASPOON PEPPER

4 6-INCH CORN TORTILLAS

1 CUP FROZEN FAT-FREE SHREDDED POTATO (ABOUT 3 OUNCES)

1/2 MEDIUM RED BELL PEPPER, DICED

1/4 CUP CHOPPED CANADIAN BACON (ABOUT 1 OUNCE)

1/8 TEASPOON PEPPER

1 OUNCE FAT-FREE OR REDUCED-FAT CHEDDAR CHEESE, SHREDDED

Preheat the oven to 350°F.

Heat a small nonstick skillet over medium-low heat. Remove the skillet from the heat and lightly

PER SERVING

CALORIES 92	CHOLESTEROL 4 mg
TOTAL FAT 0.5 g	SODIUM 221 mg
SATURATED 0.0 g	CARBOHYDRATES 14 g
POLYUNSATURATED 0.0 g	FIBER 2 g
MONOUNSATURATED 0.5 g	PROTEIN 8 g

spray with vegetable oil spray (being careful not to spray near a gas flame). Return the skillet to the heat and cook the egg substitute and 1/8 teaspoon pepper for 3 to 4 minutes, or until the eggs are cooked through, stirring occasionally. Set aside.

Wrap the tortillas in aluminum foil. Warm in the oven for 5 minutes.

Meanwhile, in a medium bowl, stir together the potato, bell pepper, bacon, and 1/8 teaspoon pepper.

Heat a medium nonstick skillet over medium-high heat. Remove the skillet from the heat and lightly spray with vegetable oil spray.

Spread the potato mixture evenly over the bottom of the skillet. Return the skillet to the heat and cook for 6 to 7 minutes on one side, or until the potatoes are a light golden-brown. Using a spatula, turn the potato mixture over; cook for 5 to 6 minutes.

To assemble, layer the ingredients horizontally across the middle of a tortilla as follows: one quarter of the scrambled eggs, one quarter of the potato mixture, and one quarter of the cheese. Roll like a jelly roll, starting at the bottom. Secure each wrap with a toothpick if desired. Repeat with the remaining tortillas.

Serve immediately, keep in an airtight container, or store individually in plastic wrap. To reheat, place one or two wraps on a microwave-safe plate. Microwave on 100 percent power (high) for 1 to 1 1/2 minutes.

beverages

Orange-Strawberry Froth

Fruit Lassi

Spiced Apple Cider

Chocolate Cappuccino

orange-strawberry froth

When you crave something sweet, try this thick and fruity blend.

2	**CUPS FRESH ORANGE JUICE**
1 1/2	**CUPS APRICOT NECTAR**
1	**CUP FROZEN UNSWEETENED STRAWBERRIES**

In a food processor or blender, process all the ingredients for 20 seconds, or until smooth and frothy. Serve immediately.

PER SERVING

CALORIES 81	CHOLESTEROL 0 mg
TOTAL FAT 0.0 g	SODIUM 3 mg
SATURATED 0.0 g	CARBOHYDRATES 20 g
POLYUNSATURATED 0.0 g	FIBER 1 g
MONOUNSATURATED 0.0 g	PROTEIN 1 g

fruit lassi

Traditionally served with spicy Indian cuisine, this yogurt drink is a delicious way to bring the benefits of fat-free dairy into your diet. Not only is it good for you, it's also refreshing and satisfying.

- 1   CUP FAT-FREE OR LOW-FAT PLAIN YOGURT
- 3/4   CUP MANGO OR BANANA, COARSELY CHOPPED
- 3   TABLESPOONS SUGAR
- 12   ICE CUBES

In a food processor or blender, process all the ingredients until the ice is crushed and the drink is frothy. Strain through a mesh sieve to remove the mango fiber if desired.
Serve immediately.

PER SERVING

CALORIES 181

TOTAL FAT 0.5 g
   SATURATED 0.0 g
   POLYUNSATURATED 0.0 g
   MONOUNSATURATED 0.0 g

CHOLESTEROL 3 mg
SODIUM 96 mg
CARBOHYDRATES 39 g
FIBER 1 g
PROTEIN 7 g

spiced apple cider

A warm fire. A cozy room. A comfy chair. This cold-weather favorite completes the scene.

2	QUARTS UNSWEETENED APPLE JUICE OR APPLE CIDER
1	QUART WATER
3	TEA BAGS (REGULAR OR DECAFFEINATED)
1/2	ORANGE WITH PEEL, THINLY SLICED
1/2	LEMON WITH PEEL, THINLY SLICED
12	WHOLE ALLSPICE
6	WHOLE CLOVES
2	CINNAMON STICKS
	GROUND ALLSPICE TO TASTE
1	ORANGE WITH PEEL, THINLY SLICED (OPTIONAL)
1	LEMON WITH PEEL, THINLY SLICED (OPTIONAL)

In a large saucepan, bring apple juice, water, tea bags, orange slices, lemon slices, whole allspice, cloves, and cinnamon sticks to a boil over high heat. Reduce the heat and simmer for 3 minutes.

PER SERVING

CALORIES 58

TOTAL FAT 0.0 g

  SATURATED 0.0 g

  POLYUNSATURATED 0.0 g

  MONOUNSATURATED 0.0 g

CHOLESTEROL 0 mg

SODIUM 6 mg

CARBOHYDRATES 15 g

FIBER 0 g

PROTEIN 0 g

Remove the tea bags, orange and lemon slices, allspice, and cloves. Simmer for 5 minutes. Stir in the ground allspice.

Serve hot or chilled. Garnish with fresh slices of orange and lemon if desired.

Cook's Tip on Bouquet Garni

For easy removal of the allspice and cloves from the juice mixture, make a bouquet garni. Tie the spices in cheesecloth or put them in a tea ball. When the cider is ready, you won't have to round up the spices, piece by piece. Most often made of parsley, thyme, and bay leaf, bouquets garnis are time-savers in soups and stews also.

chocolate cappuccino

serves 4

Cappuccino is a mixture of espresso, steamed milk, and the foam from the milk. Add chocolate syrup or cocoa powder and you have chocolate cappuccino, also known as mocha. Besides tasting terrific, this cappuccino is convenient—you don't need an espresso/cappuccino machine. A blender produces amazing results when frothing the milk. (See the Cook's Tip if you do own an espresso/cappuccino machine.)

2 CUPS FAT-FREE MILK

1 1/3 CUPS STRONG BREWED COFFEE (DARK ROAST PREFERRED)

1/4 CUP FAT-FREE OR LOW-FAT CHOCOLATE SYRUP

4 TEASPOONS SUGAR

1/4 CUP FAT-FREE OR LOW-FAT FROZEN WHIPPED TOPPING, THAWED (OPTIONAL)

1/4 TEASPOON UNSWEETENED COCOA POWDER

In a medium saucepan, heat the milk over medium heat for 2 to 3 minutes, or until warm (do not boil). No stirring is needed.

PER SERVING

CALORIES 116

TOTAL FAT 0.0 g

SATURATED 0.0 g

POLYUNSATURATED 0.0 g

MONOUNSATURATED 0.0 g

CHOLESTEROL 3 mg

SODIUM 78 mg

CARBOHYDRATES 24 g

FIBER 0 g

PROTEIN 5 g

Pour the milk into a blender; blend on high speed for 1 minute.

Pour 1/3 cup hot coffee into each of four coffee mugs or cappuccino mugs. Stir 1 tablespoon chocolate syrup and 1 teaspoon sugar into each mug.

Pour 1/2 cup milk into each mug (do not stir). Top each serving with a dollop of whipped topping if desired and a sprinkle of cocoa powder.

Cook's Tip

If you have an espresso/cappuccino machine, brew the coffee, and steam and froth the milk according to the manufacturer's directions. Add the chocolate syrup, sugar, and whipped topping as directed in the recipe.

desserts

Chocolate Custard Cake with Raspberries

Lemon Poppy Seed Cake

Cream-Cheese Banana Cake

Cappuccino Torte

Orange Angel Food Cake

Mocha Cheesecake

Key Lime Tart with Tropical Fruit

Gingersnap and Graham Cracker Crust

Apple-Cranberry Tarts with Ice Cream

Peach-Raspberry Cobbler

Apple-Rhubarb Crisp

Cocoa-Almond Meringue Kisses

Mock Baklava

Sugar-Dusted Mocha Brownies

Coconut Cornflake Cookies

Gingerbread Bars

Chocolate Soufflé with Vanilla Sauce

Honey-Baked Pecan Peaches

Bananas Foster Plus

Strawberries Romanoff

Mango Brûlée with Pine Nuts

Very Berry Sorbet

Strawberry Margarita Ice

Berry Sauce

Apple-Raisin Sauce

Creamy Dessert Topping

chocolate custard cake with raspberries

serves 10

You'll love the richness and creamy texture of this cake. Serve it warm or chilled with a double dose of raspberries.

VEGETABLE OIL SPRAY

CAKE

14-OUNCE CAN FAT-FREE SWEETENED CONDENSED MILK

EGG SUBSTITUTE EQUIVALENT TO 5 EGGS

1/2 CUP FAT-FREE MILK

1/2 CUP SUGAR

1/4 CUP UNSWEETENED COCOA POWDER

1/4 CUP FAT-FREE OR LOW-FAT CHOCOLATE SYRUP

◆

1 1/4 CUP SEEDLESS ALL-FRUIT RASPBERRY PRESERVES

10 OUNCES FRESH OR FROZEN RASPBERRIES, THAWED

1 TABLESPOON CONFECTIONERS' SUGAR (OPTIONAL)

PER SERVING	
CALORIES 264	CHOLESTEROL 2 mg
TOTAL FAT 0.5 g	SODIUM 121 mg
SATURATED 0.0 g	CARBOHYDRATES 57 g
POLYUNSATURATED 0.0 g	FIBER 4 g
MONOUNSATURATED 0.0 g	PROTEIN 7 g

Preheat the oven to 350°F. Lightly spray an 8-inch nonstick round cake pan with vegetable oil spray. Cut a circle of parchment paper or wax paper to fit the bottom of the pan; place in the pan. If using wax paper, spray the top with vegetable oil spray.

In a large bowl, whisk together the cake ingredients. Pour into the prepared pan.

Place the pan in the middle of a 17 x 12 x 1-inch rimmed baking sheet and fill the baking sheet half full with warm water, or place the cake pan in a baking pan (the bottom of a broiler pan works well) and add warm water to a depth of 1 inch.

Bake for 40 to 45 minutes, or until a cake tester or wooden toothpick inserted in the center comes out clean. Remove the cake pan from the water. Let cool on a wire rack for 10 minutes. Carefully invert onto a plate (it is not necessary to loosen sides first) and remove the paper. Let cool for 15 minutes.

Meanwhile, in a small saucepan, heat the preserves over low heat, stirring occasionally.

Top the cake with a thin coating of the preserves. Sprinkle with half the raspberries. Cut the cake into 10 slices. Spoon the remaining preserves on each of 10 dessert plates. Place a cake slice on the preserves. Top with the remaining raspberries; dust lightly with confectioners' sugar if desired.

For a more formal presentation, place the raspberries in a ring around the top of the cake before cutting. Sprinkle any remaining berries on the dessert plates.

Cook's Tip

This flanlike cake isn't a high riser because it doesn't contain any flour or leavening agent.

lemon poppy seed cake

serves 10

Perfect with an afternoon cup of tea, this moist cake has a bold lemon flavor accented with the delicate crunch of poppy seeds.

	VEGETABLE OIL SPRAY
2	CUPS ALL-PURPOSE FLOUR
3/4	CUP SUGAR
1	TABLESPOON POPPY SEEDS
2	TEASPOONS BAKING POWDER
1/4	TEASPOON BAKING SODA
1/4	TEASPOON SALT
3/4	CUP UNSWEETENED APPLESAUCE
1	TEASPOON GRATED LEMON ZEST
1/4	CUP FRESH LEMON JUICE
2 1/2	TABLESPOONS ACCEPTABLE VEGETABLE OIL
2	TABLESPOONS CORN SYRUP
1	TEASPOON LEMON EXTRACT
	WHITES OF 4 EGGS

Preheat the oven to 350°F. Lightly spray a 9-inch round cake pan with vegetable oil spray.

PER SERVING

CALORIES 214	CHOLESTEROL 0 mg
TOTAL FAT 4.0 g	SODIUM 215 mg
SATURATED 0.5 g	CARBOHYDRATES 41 g
POLYUNSATURATED 1.5 g	FIBER 1 g
MONOUNSATURATED 2.0 g	PROTEIN 4 g

In a medium bowl, combine the flour, sugar, poppy seeds, baking powder, baking soda, and salt.

In another medium bowl, stir together the applesauce, lemon zest, lemon juice, vegetable oil, corn syrup, and lemon extract. Stir the applesauce mixture into the flour mixture until just combined.

In a large bowl, beat the egg whites with an electric hand or stand mixer until they form stiff peaks.

Using a rubber scraper, fold the flour-applesauce mixture into the beaten egg whites. Pour the mixture into the prepared pan; smooth the top with a spatula.

Bake for 30 minutes, or until a cake tester or wooden toothpick inserted in the center comes out clean. Cool in the pan for 10 minutes. Loosen the sides of the cake with a thin metal spatula, and invert the cake onto a cooling rack. The cake can be served warm, at room temperature, or chilled.

Cook's Tip on Poppy Seeds and Sesame Seeds

You can intensify the flavor of both poppy and sesame seeds by dry-roasting.

Store these popular seeds in the refrigerator. Otherwise, the oil in the seeds will turn rancid after a few months.

cream-cheese banana cake

serves 24

If banana pudding is a favorite in your family, try this cake . . . it's easy to serve and even easier to eat! You don't have to worry about the bananas discoloring because they're tucked away under the topping.

VEGETABLE OIL SPRAY

18.25-OUNCE BOX SPICE CAKE MIX

1 CUP WATER

EGG SUBSTITUTE EQUIVALENT TO 3 EGGS

1/2 CUP MASHED RIPE BANANA (ABOUT 1 MEDIUM)

2 CUPS FAT-FREE MILK

8 OUNCES FAT-FREE OR REDUCED-FAT CREAM CHEESE

1 OUNCE PACKAGE SUGAR FREE VANILLA PUDDING MIX

8 OUNCES FAT-FREE FROZEN WHIPPED TOPPING, THAWED

1 TEASPOON VANILLA EXTRACT

3 MEDIUM RIPE BANANAS, SLICED

1/4 TO 1/2 TEASPOON GROUND NUTMEG

Preheat the oven to 350°F. Lightly spray a 15 x 10-inch rimmed baking sheet with vegetable oil spray.

PER SERVING	
CALORIES 151	CHOLESTEROL 8 mg
TOTAL FAT 2.5 g	SODIUM 266 mg
SATURATED 1.0 g	CARBOHYDRATES 27 g
POLYUNSATURATED 0.0 g	FIBER 1 g
MONOUNSATURATED 1.0 g	PROTEIN 4 g

In a medium bowl, combine the cake mix, water, egg substitute, and mashed banana. Using an electric mixer, beat on low speed for 30 seconds, or until moistened. Increase the speed to medium and beat for 2 minutes.

Pour the batter into the prepared baking sheet. Using a spatula, smooth the batter evenly.

Bake for 20 to 25 minutes, or until a cake tester or wooden toothpick inserted in the center comes out clean. Put on a wire rack to cool completely.

Meanwhile, in a medium bowl, stir together the milk, cream cheese, and pudding mix. Beat on medium speed until well blended. Using a rubber spatula, fold in the whipped topping and vanilla until well blended. Cover and refrigerate until ready to use.

When the cake is completely cool, arrange the banana slices evenly over the top. Using a spatula or the back of a spoon, spread the cream-cheese mixture over all. Sprinkle lightly with nutmeg.

Cover with plastic wrap and refrigerate until ready to serve.

Cook's Tip

Be sure to use ripe bananas for peak flavor and sweetness.

cappuccino torte

This elegant cake is the dessert version of a cup of foamy cappuccino: Dark chocolate cake flavored with coffee and cinnamon is layered with fluffy whipped topping mixture.

	18.25-OUNCE BOX CHOCOLATE CAKE MIX
	18.25-OUNCE BOX CHOCOLATE CAKE MIX
3/4	CUP WATER
1/2	CUP STRONG COFFEE
	EGG SUBSTITUTE EQUIVALENT TO 3 EGGS
1/3	CUP UNSWEETENED APPLESAUCE
1	TEASPOON CINNAMON
3	CUPS FROZEN FAT-FREE OR LIGHT WHIPPED TOPPING, THAWED (ABOUT 8 OUNCES)
2	TEASPOONS INSTANT ESPRESSO POWDER (OR 2 TEASPOONS INSTANT COFFEE POWDER, OR 1/3 CUP COFFEE)
1/2	TEASPOON CINNAMON
1	TABLESPOON UNSWEETENED COCOA POWDER (DUTCH PROCESS PREFERRED)

Prepare the chocolate cake using the package directions for two 9-inch round cakes, substituting

---

PER SERVING

CALORIES 224

TOTAL FAT 4.0 g

   SATURATED 1.5 g

   POLYUNSATURATED —

   MONOUNSATURATED —

CHOLESTEROL 0 mg

SODIUM 313 mg

CARBOHYDRATES 43 g

FIBER 1 g

PROTEIN 4 g

the water and coffee for the liquid, the egg substitute for whole eggs, and the applesauce for oil. Add 1 teaspoon cinnamon before mixing.

In a medium bowl, whisk together the whipped topping, instant espresso powder, and 1/2 teaspoon cinnamon. Set aside.

Using a sharp knife, cut one cake layer in half horizontally. With a large spatula or dinner-size plate, remove and set aside the top half of the cake. Place the bottom half on a serving plate.

Spread one quarter of the whipped topping mixture on the bottom half. Place the top half on the bottom half. Spread one quarter of the whipped topping mixture on the top half. Repeat with the remaining cake layer, stacking the halves. (You will have four layers of cake and four layers of whipped topping mixture.)

Sprinkle the cake with the cocoa powder.

orange angel food cake

serves 10

Light and refreshing, this dessert is also pretty and festive. It makes a perfect finish for a rich meal. The best surprise, however, is how easy it is to make.

- 2 ENVELOPES UNFLAVORED GELATIN (2 TABLESPOONS)
- 1/2 CUP COLD WATER
- 1 CUP BOILING WATER
- 1 CUP SUGAR

   6-OUNCE CAN FROZEN ORANGE JUICE CONCENTRATE, THAWED

   10-INCH PREPARED ANGEL FOOD CAKE

- 4 11-OUNCE CANS MANDARIN ORANGES IN WATER OR LIGHT SYRUP, DRAINED, DIVIDED USE
- 8 OUNCES FROZEN FAT-FREE OR LIGHT WHIPPED TOPPING, THAWED

In a small bowl, stir together the gelatin and cold water until dissolved. Stir in the boiling water, sugar, and orange juice. Set aside to cool, but do not allow the mixture to set.

PER SERVING	
CALORIES 334	CHOLESTEROL 0 mg
TOTAL FAT 0.0 g	SODIUM 325 mg
SATURATED 0.0 g	CARBOHYDRATES 78 g
POLYUNSATURATED 0.0 g	FIBER 1 g
MONOUNSATURATED 0.0 g	PROTEIN 6 g

Meanwhile, cut the cake into 2-inch cubes.

Pack the cake cubes and 3 cans of drained oranges into a 13 x 9 x 2-inch baking pan.

Fold the whipped topping into the gelatin mixture. Pour over the cake and oranges, allowing the mixture to run down between the cubes. Top with the remaining 1 can of mandarin oranges.

Cover and refrigerate until set.

mocha cheesecake

serves 10

Indulge yourself! Yogurt Cheese and fat-free or low-fat ricotta cheese replace the high-fat cream cheese found in most cheesecakes. Also, egg whites and cocoa powder are used instead of whole eggs and chocolate. The result is a delectable cake that tastes sinful but isn't. It freezes well if wrapped tightly before freezing. Plan ahead to allow enough time for the yogurt cheese to thicken.

CRUST

	VEGETABLE OIL SPRAY
4	SLICES WHOLE-WHEAT BREAD, TOASTED
1/4	CUP HONEY
	WHITES OF 2 LARGE EGGS
3	TABLESPOONS WHEAT GERM
2	TABLESPOONS UNSWEETENED COCOA POWDER
1 1/2	TEASPOONS VANILLA EXTRACT
1 1/2	TEASPOONS COFFEE LIQUEUR

FILLING

2	CUPS YOGURT CHEESE (PAGE 473)
2	CUPS FAT-FREE OR LOW-FAT RICOTTA CHEESE
2/3	CUP SUGAR
	WHITES OF 2 LARGE EGGS
2	TABLESPOONS ALL-PURPOSE FLOUR

2 **TABLESPOONS UNSWEETENED COCOA POWDER**

1 **TABLESPOON VANILLA EXTRACT**

1 **TABLESPOON COFFEE LIQUEUR**

GRATED ZEST OF 1/2 ORANGE

◆

FRESH FRUIT, THINLY SLICED (OPTIONAL)

Preheat the oven to 300°F. Lightly spray a 9-inch springform pan with vegetable oil spray.

Break the bread into quarters. In a food processor, process the bread into fine crumbs.

In a medium bowl, stir the bread crumbs into the remaining crust ingredients until coarse and moist. Using a fork, press the mixture evenly into the bottom of the prepared pan.

Bake in the center of the oven for 10 minutes, or until firm to the touch. Let cool on a wire rack.

In a food processor, process the filling ingredients until fully blended, scraping the sides of the bowl as needed. Pour the filling over the cooled crust.

PER SERVING

CALORIES 219	CHOLESTEROL 5 mg
TOTAL FAT 1.0 g	SODIUM 214 mg
SATURATED 0.5 g	CARBOHYDRATES 37 g
POLYUNSATURATED 0.5 g	FIBER 2 g
MONOUNSATURATED 0.5 g	PROTEIN 14 g

Bake in the center of the oven for 1 hour. Turn off the heat and leave the cake in the oven for 15 minutes. Remove the cake and let cool. Cover and refrigerate for at least 3 hours, preferably overnight, before removing the sides of the pan.

Garnish with the fresh fruit if desired. Serve chilled or at room temperature.

Cook's Tip

To make a vanilla cheesecake with a hint of orange flavor, omit the cocoa and the coffee liqueur.

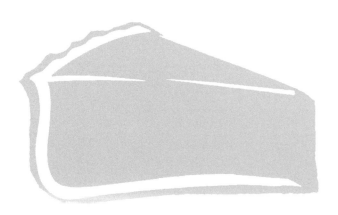

key lime tart with tropical fruit

serves 8

Serve this tropical treat after a spicy meal to cool down the heat.

VEGETABLE OIL SPRAY

1 1/4 CUPS LOW-FAT GRAHAM CRACKER CRUMBS (ABOUT 20 SQUARES)

1/4 CUP UNSWEETENED APPLESAUCE

14-OUNCE CAN FAT-FREE SWEETENED CONDENSED MILK

3 OUNCES FAT-FREE OR LIGHT CREAM CHEESE, SOFTENED

1 TEASPOON GRATED LIME ZEST

1/2 CUP FRESH OR BOTTLED KEY LIME JUICE OR FRESH LIME JUICE

1/4 TEASPOON ALMOND EXTRACT

2 CUPS FAT-FREE OR LIGHT FROZEN WHIPPED TOPPING, THAWED

1 CUP MANGO SLICES

1 MEDIUM BANANA, CUT CROSSWISE INTO THIN SLICES

1/2 CUP FRESH OR CANNED PINEAPPLE CHUNKS, IN THEIR OWN JUICE IF CANNED

Preheat the oven to 350°F. Lightly spray a 9–inch pie pan with vegetable oil spray.

In a medium bowl, stir together the graham cracker crumbs and applesauce. Transfer to the pie pan. Lay a piece of plastic wrap on top to keep the crumbs from sticking to your hands. Press the mixture onto the bottom and up the sides of the pie pan. Remove the plastic wrap.

Bake for 8 minutes, or until toasted. Let cool completely on a cooling rack.

In a large bowl, whisk together the canned milk, cream cheese, lime zest, lime juice, and almond extract until smooth. Using a rubber spatula, fold in the whipped topping until well blended. Spoon into the crust; smooth with the spatula.

Cover and refrigerate for at least 1 hour, or until the filling is chilled and thickened.

Arrange the mango, banana, and pineapple in a decorative pattern on top.

PER SERVING

CALORIES 188	CHOLESTEROL 2 mg
TOTAL FAT 1.0 g	SODIUM 199 mg
SATURATED 0.0 g	CARBOHYDRATES 38 g
POLYUNSATURATED 0.0 g	FIBER 2 g
MONOUNSATURATED 0.5 g	PROTEIN 6 g

gingersnap and graham cracker crust

makes one 9-inch piecrust

The flavorful pairing of gingersnaps and graham crackers makes this crust almost a dessert in itself. The corn syrup and apple juice bind the dough and make it easy to shape the piecrust. Fill the crust with your favorite fruits or fat-free frozen yogurt and top with frozen whipped topping.

3/4	CUP CRUSHED LOW-FAT GRAHAM CRACKERS (ABOUT 9 SQUARES)
3/4	CUP CRUSHED LOW-FAT GINGERSNAPS (ABOUT 18 COOKIES)
2	TABLESPOONS LIGHT CORN SYRUP
2	TABLESPOONS UNSWEETENED APPLE JUICE

In a medium bowl, stir together all the ingredients. Using your fingers, press the mixture evenly into a 9-inch pie pan.

The crust is ready to fill and bake. If you need a prebaked crust, bake it at 350°F for 10 minutes, then cool and fill.

NUTRITIONAL ANALYSIS IS BASED ON **1/8** OF PIECRUST.

PER SERVING

CALORIES 105	CHOLESTEROL 0 mg
TOTAL FAT 2.0 g	SODIUM 98 mg
SATURATED 0.5 g	CARBOHYDRATES 21 g
POLYUNSATURATED 0.0 g	FIBER 0 g
MONOUNSATURATED 1.0 g	PROTEIN 1 g

apple-cranberry tarts with ice cream

serves 12

Want the pleasure of dessert without feeling like you're cheating? Enjoy these delectable but low-guilt treats.

CRUST

2/3 CUP ALL-PURPOSE FLOUR

3 TABLESPOONS SUGAR

2 TABLESPOONS ACCEPTABLE STICK MARGARINE, DICED

1 1/2 TABLESPOONS FAT-FREE MILK

1 TEASPOON ALL-PURPOSE FLOUR

FILLING

1/2 CUP WATER

1 POUND GRANNY SMITH APPLES, DICED (ABOUT 4 CUPS)

1/2 CUP DRIED SWEETENED CRANBERRIES

2 TEASPOONS CORNSTARCH

1/3 CUP WATER

2 TABLESPOONS FIRMLY PACKED DARK BROWN SUGAR

1/2 TEASPOON GROUND CINNAMON

1/2 TEASPOON VANILLA EXTRACT

1/4 TEASPOON ALMOND EXTRACT

◆

3 CUPS FAT-FREE VANILLA ICE CREAM OR FROZEN YOGURT

In a food processor, process all crust ingredients except 1 teaspoon flour until the dough begins to stick together. Form the dough into a disk about 4 inches in diameter. Cover with plastic wrap and refrigerate for 15 minutes.

Meanwhile, preheat the oven to 425°F.

Place a sheet of plastic wrap on a flat surface. Sprinkle with 1 teaspoon flour. Put the dough on the floured surface, press lightly, and turn the dough over (this allows some flour to stick to both sides). Cover the dough with another sheet of plastic wrap. Roll the dough into an 8 x 12-inch rectangle. Remove the top sheet of plastic wrap.

Using a 3-inch biscuit cutter, cut 12 circles from the pie dough. (Piece together and reroll the remaining dough to cut the last few circles, if needed.) Put one dough round in each cup of a 12-cup nonstick muffin pan. Press down gently with fingertips to form the dough to the bottom of each cup.

Bake for 8 to 9 minutes, or until golden.

PER SERVING

CALORIES 153	CHOLESTEROL 0 mg
TOTAL FAT 2.0 g	SODIUM 57 mg
SATURATED 0.5 g	CARBOHYDRATES 33 g
POLYUNSATURATED 0.5 g	FIBER 2 g
MONOUNSATURATED 1.0 g	PROTEIN 3 g

For the filling, in a large skillet, bring 1/2 cup water to a boil over high heat. Stir in the apples and cranberries; cook for 3 minutes, or until the apples are just tender–crisp.

Put the cornstarch in a cup. Add 1/3 cup water, stirring to dissolve. Stir into the apple mixture with the brown sugar. Cook for 1 minute, or until thickened, stirring constantly. Remove from the heat. Stir in the cinnamon, vanilla extract, and almond extract.

Spoon 1/4 cup of the apple mixture into each tart crust. Serve with 1/4 cup ice cream on top or to the side of each tart.

peach-raspberry cobbler

serves 8

Cobblers get their names from the cobbled or
bumpy appearance of the biscuitlike topping that
bakes on a bubbly fruit filling. Serve this one
warm on its own or with a scoop of fat-free or
low-fat vanilla frozen yogurt or ice milk.

TOPPING

- 1/3 CUP ALL-PURPOSE FLOUR
- 1/4 CUP WHOLE-WHEAT FLOUR
- 2 TABLESPOONS LIGHT BROWN SUGAR
- 1 TABLESPOON WHEAT GERM
- 1 TEASPOON BAKING POWDER
- 2 TABLESPOONS LIGHT STICK MARGARINE

FILLING

- 1/2 CUP SUGAR
- 2 TABLESPOONS ALL-PURPOSE FLOUR
- 1/2 TEASPOON GROUND GINGER
- 3 CUPS FRESH OR FROZEN UNSWEETENED SLICED PEACHES OR NECTARINES
- 3 CUPS FRESH OR FROZEN RASPBERRIES
- 3 TABLESPOONS WATER

- EGG SUBSTITUTE EQUIVALENT TO 1 EGG, OR 1 EGG
- 2 TABLESPOONS FAT-FREE MILK

Preheat the oven to 400°F.

In a medium bowl, stir together all the topping ingredients except the margarine.

Using a pastry blender, cut in the margarine until the mixture resembles coarse crumbs. Make a well in the center. Set aside.

For the filling, in a small bowl, stir together the sugar, 2 tablespoons all-purpose flour, and ginger.

In a large saucepan, bring the peaches, raspberries, and water to a boil over high heat (it's not necessary to thaw frozen fruit). Reduce the heat and simmer, covered, for 5 minutes, or until soft, stirring often.

Stir in the flour-ginger mixture. Cook until thickened and bubbly, stirring constantly. Reduce the heat; keep the filling hot.

In a small bowl, stir together the egg substitute and milk. Using a fork, stir into the topping mixture just until moistened.

PER SERVING	
CALORIES 172	CHOLESTEROL 0 mg
TOTAL FAT 2.0 g	SODIUM 99 mg
SATURATED 0.5 g	CARBOHYDRATES 38 g
POLYUNSATURATED 0.5 g	FIBER 5 g
MONOUNSATURATED 0.5 g	PROTEIN 3 g

Pour the hot filling into an ungreased 1 1/2-quart baking pan. Immediately spoon the topping in small mounds onto the hot filling.

Bake, uncovered, for 20 to 25 minutes, or until a wooden toothpick inserted into one of the biscuit mounds comes out clean. Serve warm.

apple-rhubarb crisp

serves 8

The apples give sweetness and the rhubarb contributes tartness to this fruit crisp. Like most baked fruit desserts, this one tastes best when eaten warm, but let it cool a bit after you remove it from the oven.

FILLING

- 2 CUPS FRESH OR FROZEN UNSWEETENED SLICED RHUBARB, THAWED IF FROZEN AND DRAINED
- 2 MEDIUM COOKING APPLES, CORED, PEELED, AND SLICED (ABOUT 2 CUPS)
- 1/2 CUP SUGAR
- 1 TABLESPOON CORNSTARCH

TOPPING

- 2/3 CUP UNCOOKED REGULAR OR QUICK-COOKING ROLLED OATS
- 1/2 CUP ALL-PURPOSE FLOUR
- 1/4 CUP FIRMLY PACKED LIGHT BROWN SUGAR
- 3 1/2 TABLESPOONS LIGHT TUB MARGARINE

PER SERVING

CALORIES 173	CHOLESTEROL 0 mg
TOTAL FAT 2.5 g	SODIUM 44 mg
SATURATED 0.0 g	CARBOHYDRATES 37 g
POLYUNSATURATED 0.5 g	FIBER 2 g
MONOUNSATURATED 1.0 g	PROTEIN 2 g

In a large bowl, stir together the filling ingredients to mix well. Let stand for 1 hour. Spoon into an ungreased 8-inch square baking pan or 1-quart casserole dish.

Preheat the oven to 375°F.

In a medium bowl, stir together the topping ingredients except the margarine.

Using a pastry blender, cut the margarine into the topping until the mixture resembles coarse crumbs. Sprinkle the topping over the apple-rhubarb mixture.

Bake, uncovered, for 30 to 40 minutes, or until the topping is light brown. Let cool for about 20 minutes before serving.

Cook's Tip on Cooking Apples

Apples that retain their shape and flavor are especially good for baking. Among the best are Rome Beauty, Baldwin, Winesap, Granny Smith, Jonathan, and Cortland.

Cook's Tip on Rhubarb

When buying fresh rhubarb, look for crisp, brightly colored stalks. The leaves (which are inedible) should look fresh and be free of blemishes. To store rhubarb, wrap it tightly in plastic wrap or a plastic bag and refrigerate it for up to three days. Remove and discard the leaves just before using the stalks.

cocoa-almond meringue kisses

serves 14

These meringues are crisp on the outside and chewy on the inside.

      VEGETABLE OIL SPRAY

      WHITES OF 3 LARGE EGGS

1/8 TEASPOON CREAM OF TARTAR

3/4 CUP SUGAR

  3 TABLESPOONS UNSWEETENED COCOA POWDER

1/2 TEASPOON VANILLA EXTRACT

1/4 CUP SLICED ALMONDS

Preheat the oven to 325°F. Lightly spray two large baking sheets with vegetable oil spray.

In a large bowl, beat the egg whites and cream of tartar until stiff peaks form. Add the sugar, 2 tablespoons at a time, beating well after each addition. Add the cocoa and vanilla; beat well to blend. Fold in the almonds.

Drop the mixture by tablespoonfuls onto the prepared baking sheets.

PER SERVING	
CALORIES 60	CHOLESTEROL 0 mg
TOTAL FAT 1.0 g	SODIUM 13 mg
SATURATED 0.0 g	CARBOHYDRATES 12 g
POLYUNSATURATED 0.0 g	FIBER 1 g
MONOUNSATURATED 0.5 g	PROTEIN 1 g

Bake for 25 minutes, or until the meringues are crisp on the outside. Remove from the baking sheets immediately and let cool on a wire rack. Store in an airtight container.

Cook's Tip on Cocoa Powder

Cocoas are different colors and have different acidities and different tastes. Dutch-process cocoa has less acid than other cocoas, so its taste is mellower. Combine various cocoas to experience different flavors.

mock baklava

Traditional baklava usually is full of butter and therefore loaded with saturated fat. Through the wonders of modern technology—in the form of butter-flavor vegetable oil spray—here is a revamped and guilt-free version of this Greek sweet.

- **1 CUP RAISINS**
- **1/3 CUP FINELY CHOPPED PECANS OR WALNUTS, DRY-ROASTED**
- **8 SHEETS FROZEN PHYLLO DOUGH, THAWED**
- **BUTTER-FLAVOR VEGETABLE OIL SPRAY**
- **1/2 CUP HONEY**
- **2 TEASPOONS GROUND CINNAMON**
- **1 TABLESPOON ACCEPTABLE STICK MARGARINE, MELTED**

Preheat the oven to 350°F.

In a small bowl, combine the raisins and nuts.

Lightly spray every other sheet of phyllo with vegetable oil spray, stacking all the sheets. Spread the raisin-nut mixture over the phyllo, leaving a

PER SERVING

CALORIES 154	CHOLESTEROL 0 mg
TOTAL FAT 4.0 g	SODIUM 77 mg
SATURATED 0.5 g	CARBOHYDRATES 30 g
POLYUNSATURATED 1.0 g	FIBER 2 g
MONOUNSATURATED 2.5 g	PROTEIN 2 g

1-inch border on all sides. Drizzle with the honey and sprinkle with cinnamon.

Starting on a long side, roll lengthwise, jelly-roll fashion. Place with seam side down on a nonstick baking sheet, tucking the ends of the roll under.

Brush the top lightly with the margarine. Cut shallow slashes through the pastry to the raisin-nut mixture at 1 1/2-inch intervals so steam can escape.

Bake for 20 to 30 minutes, or until light golden-brown. Slice, using the vent lines as guides.

Cook's Tip

This dish freezes well. Prepare as above but omit brushing with margarine and baking. (Do cut the steam vents.) Freeze overnight on a baking sheet, then wrap in freezer paper or aluminum foil. Place, still frozen, on a baking sheet, brush with margarine, and bake at 350°F for 35 to 45 minutes, or until golden-brown.

sugar-dusted mocha brownies

serves 12

This light, yet fudgy, version of the ever-popular favorite features a touch of coffee and a pretty confectioners'-sugar top.

VEGETABLE OIL SPRAY

1/2 CUP ALL-PURPOSE FLOUR

1/2 CUP UNSWEETENED COCOA POWDER

1/2 TEASPOON BAKING POWDER

4 TABLESPOONS LIGHT STICK MARGARINE

1 TABLESPOON INSTANT COFFEE CRYSTALS

1 CUP SUGAR

EGG SUBSTITUTE EQUIVALENT TO 2 EGGS, OR 2 EGGS

1/4 CUP PRUNE BABY FOOD

2 TEASPOONS VANILLA EXTRACT

2 TABLESPOONS CONFECTIONERS' SUGAR

Preheat the oven to 350°F. Lightly spray an 8-inch square cake pan with vegetable oil spray.

PER SERVING	
CALORIES 131	CHOLESTEROL 0 mg
TOTAL FAT 2.0 g	SODIUM 69 mg
SATURATED 0.5 g	CARBOHYDRATES 25 g
POLYUNSATURATED 0.5 g	FIBER 1 g
MONOUNSATURATED 0.5 g	PROTEIN 3 g

In a small bowl, combine the flour, cocoa powder, and baking powder. Set aside.

In a medium saucepan, melt the margarine over medium-low heat.

Stir in the coffee crystals until dissolved. Remove from the heat and let cool slightly.

Using a wooden spoon, stir the sugar, egg substitute, prune baby food, and vanilla into the coffee mixture.

Fold the cocoa mixture into the sugar mixture until well combined.

Spoon the batter into the prepared pan.

Bake, uncovered, for 18 to 20 minutes, or until a wooden toothpick inserted in the center comes out almost clean (it should have a few fudgy crumbs on it).

Cool the brownies in the pan on a wire rack. Sift the confectioners' sugar over the brownies.

Cook's Tip

For a decorative topping, place a doily on top of the brownies before sifting the confectioners' sugar. Remove the doily before cutting the brownies.

coconut cornflake cookies

Cookies for breakfast? The thought will be tempting when you try these crunchy, fruity cookies. Easy to mix with just a bowl and a spoon, these healthful treats will please kids and moms alike.

VEGETABLE OIL SPRAY

1 CUP SUGAR

2/3 CUP LIGHT TUB MARGARINE, SOFTENED

EGG SUBSTITUTE EQUIVALENT TO 2 EGGS

1 TEASPOON VANILLA EXTRACT

1 TEASPOON COCONUT EXTRACT

3 CUPS ALL-PURPOSE FLOUR

1 TEASPOON BAKING POWDER

1/2 TEASPOON BAKING SODA

1 CUP DRIED MIXED FRUIT BITS (APRICOTS, APPLES, RAISINS, CRANBERRIES, PLUMS)

2 CUPS COARSELY CRUSHED CORNFLAKE CEREAL

PER SERVING	
CALORIES 120	CHOLESTEROL 0 mg
TOTAL FAT 2.0 g	SODIUM 112 mg
SATURATED 0.0 g	CARBOHYDRATES 24 g
POLYUNSATURATED 0.5 g	FIBER 1 g
MONOUNSATURATED 1.0 g	PROTEIN 2 g

Preheat the oven to 375°F. Lightly spray two baking sheets with vegetable oil spray.

In a large mixing bowl, stir together the sugar, margarine, egg substitute, and vanilla and coconut extracts until smooth.

In a small bowl, combine the flour, baking powder, and baking soda. Using a spoon, gradually stir the flour mixture into the margarine mixture until the flour is incorporated (dough will be slightly sticky). Gently stir in the fruit bits to distribute evenly throughout the dough.

Put the crushed cornflakes in a shallow bowl or on a large platter. Drop a teaspoon-sized portion of dough onto the cornflakes and roll to coat with cornflakes. Place the cookie on a baking sheet and flatten slightly with the bottom of a juice glass. Repeat with the remaining dough, leaving 2 inches between cookies.

Bake for 10 to 11 minutes, or until the cookies feel slightly soft when lightly pressed in the middle.

Transfer the cookies to wire cooling racks. Let cool completely, about 30 minutes.

gingerbread bars

serves 30

The family will line up to get these cookies fresh from the oven.

VEGETABLE OIL SPRAY

6 TABLESPOONS ACCEPTABLE STICK MARGARINE, AT ROOM TEMPERATURE

1 CUP FIRMLY PACKED DARK BROWN SUGAR

WHITES OF 2 LARGE EGGS

1/4 CUP MOLASSES

1 1/4 CUPS ALL-PURPOSE FLOUR

1 CUP WHOLE-WHEAT FLOUR

1/4 CUP NONFAT DRY MILK

3/4 TEASPOON BAKING POWDER

3/4 TEASPOON BAKING SODA

3/4 TEASPOON GROUND GINGER

1/2 TEASPOON GROUND CINNAMON

1/2 TEASPOON GROUND NUTMEG

1/8 TEASPOON GROUND CLOVES

1/4 CUP FINELY CHOPPED WALNUTS

PER SERVING

CALORIES 98

TOTAL FAT 3.0 g

   SATURATED 0.5 g

   POLYUNSATURATED 1.5 g

   MONOUNSATURATED 1.0 g

CHOLESTEROL 0 mg

SODIUM 81 mg

CARBOHYDRATES 17 g

FIBER 1 g

PROTEIN 2 g

Preheat the oven to 350°F. Spray a 13 x 9 x 2-inch baking pan with vegetable oil spray.

In a large bowl, beat the margarine at medium speed until creamy.

Add the brown sugar and beat at high speed for 1 to 2 minutes, or until light.

Beat in the egg whites. Add the molasses and beat until no lumps remain.

In a separate bowl, sift together the remaining ingredients except the nuts. Stir the sifted ingredients into the margarine mixture and blend thoroughly.

Stir in the nuts. The dough will be sticky.

Place the dough in the center of the prepared pan. Using a spatula or clean, wet hands, spread the dough evenly.

Bake for 25 minutes. Let cool for at least 5 minutes. Cut into 30 bars.

chocolate soufflé with vanilla sauce

serves 6

This wonderful soufflé uses cocoa instead of chocolate. You'll think this classic dessert tastes just like its high-fat counterpart.

VEGETABLE OIL SPRAY

1/3 **CUP FRESH ORANGE JUICE**

1/3 **CUP SUGAR**

WHITES OF 4 LARGE EGGS

1/4 **CUP UNSWEETENED COCOA POWDER (DUTCH-PROCESS PREFERRED)**

2 **TABLESPOONS ORANGE LIQUEUR**

3/4 **CUP VANILLA ICE MILK, SOFTENED**

Preheat the oven to 300°F. Lightly spray six 5-ounce custard cups with vegetable oil spray.

In a small saucepan, cook the orange juice and sugar over medium-high heat for 3 to 4 minutes, or until the mixture has a syrupy consistency, stirring occasionally. Remove from the heat.

PER SERVING	
CALORIES 109	CHOLESTEROL 2 mg
TOTAL FAT 1.0 g	SODIUM 46 mg
SATURATED 0.5 g	CARBOHYDRATES 19 g
POLYUNSATURATED 0.0 g	FIBER 1 g
MONOUNSATURATED 0.5 g	PROTEIN 4 g

In a large bowl, beat the egg whites until stiff, but stop before dry peaks form.

Pour the syrup over the egg whites; beat for 2 minutes.

Add the cocoa and liqueur; beat only until well mixed. Pour into the prepared custard cups.

Bake for 12 minutes, or until the soufflés have puffed. Do not overbake or the soufflés will become tough.

To serve, spoon 2 tablespoons softened ice milk into the center of each soufflé. Serve immediately.

honey-baked pecan peaches

serves 8

Self-made contentment—luscious fruit is cut in half, baked upside down over honey and pecans, then flipped and served in the sauce that it makes as it cooks.

VEGETABLE OIL SPRAY

2 TABLESPOONS HONEY

1 OUNCE PECAN PIECES

1/4 TEASPOON GROUND CINNAMON

4 LARGE RIPE PEACHES OR NECTARINES (ABOUT 6 OUNCES EACH), HALVED

2 TABLESPOONS LIGHT TUB MARGARINE

1/4 TEASPOON VANILLA EXTRACT

2 CUPS FAT-FREE VANILLA ICE CREAM (OPTIONAL)

Preheat the oven to 350°F.

Lightly spray a 9-inch round cake or pie pan with vegetable oil spray. Pour the honey into the pan and heat in the oven for 2 minutes to soften the honey. Remove the pan from the oven. Tip

PER SERVING	
CALORIES 85	CHOLESTEROL 0 mg
TOTAL FAT 3.5 g	SODIUM 23 mg
SATURATED 0.0 g	CARBOHYDRATES 14 g
POLYUNSATURATED 1.0 g	FIBER 2 g
MONOUNSATURATED 2.0 g	PROTEIN 1 g

the pan to coat it evenly with the honey. Sprinkle the pecans evenly over the honey.

Sprinkle the cinnamon over the cut sides of the peaches. Place the peaches with cut side down over the pecans. Using a fork, pierce each peach half several times for faster cooking.

Bake, uncovered, for 20 minutes, or until tender. Place the peaches with cut side up on a platter.

Add the margarine and vanilla to the honey-pecan drippings in the pan, stirring until the margarine has melted. Spoon evenly over the peaches. Let stand for 10 minutes to absorb flavors.

Serve warm or at room temperature. Serve with ice cream if desired.

WITH ICE CREAM

PER SERVING	
CALORIES 135	CHOLESTEROL 0 mg
TOTAL FAT 3.5 g	SODIUM 56 mg
SATURATED 0.0 g	CARBOHYDRATES 25 g
POLYUNSATURATED 1.0 g	FIBER 2 g
MONOUNSATURATED 2.0 g	PROTEIN 3 g

bananas foster plus

This 1950s specialty of Brennan's restaurant in New Orleans has been updated for the modern cook with a pretty trio of fruit and significantly less saturated fat.

- 2 TABLESPOONS LIGHT STICK MARGARINE
- 3 TABLESPOONS LIGHT BROWN SUGAR
- 1/4 TEASPOON GROUND CINNAMON
- 1/8 TEASPOON GROUND NUTMEG
- 2 MEDIUM BANANAS, CUT INTO 1/2-INCH SLICES
- 2 KIWIFRUIT, PEELED AND CUT INTO 1/2-INCH SLICES
- 1 MEDIUM PEACH OR NECTARINE, CUT INTO 1/2-INCH SLICES, OR 1/2 CUP DRAINED CANNED SLICED PEACHES IN FRUIT JUICE (ABOUT 4 OUNCES)
- 1 TABLESPOON DARK RUM OR 1/4 TEASPOON RUM EXTRACT
- 1 PINT FAT-FREE OR LOW-FAT VANILLA FROZEN YOGURT OR ICE MILK

In a medium skillet, melt the margarine over medium heat.

PER SERVING	
CALORIES 255	CHOLESTEROL 2 mg
TOTAL FAT 3.5 g	SODIUM 108 mg
SATURATED 0.5 g	CARBOHYDRATES 52 g
POLYUNSATURATED 1.0 g	FIBER 3 g
MONOUNSATURATED 1.0 g	PROTEIN 0 g

Stir in the brown sugar, cinnamon, and nutmeg. Cook for 3 to 5 minutes, or until the sugar melts, stirring constantly.

Add the bananas, kiwifruit, and peach; cook for 1 minute, or until heated through, stirring gently.

Stir in the rum. Cook for 1 minute, stirring gently.

Serve warm with the frozen yogurt.

strawberries romanoff

serves 6

This dreamy dessert brings a hint of cinnamon to sweet fresh berries. It can be served as a breakfast treat; just leave out the liqueur and top with crunchy whole-grain cereal. For flavor variety, try substituting other fruits and complementary liqueurs. Also, be sure to plan enough time for the Yogurt Cheese to thicken and become creamy.

SAUCE

- 1 CUP YOGURT CHEESE (RECIPE FOLLOWS)
- 1/4 CUP FIRMLY PACKED LIGHT BROWN SUGAR
- 2 TABLESPOONS FRUIT-FLAVORED LIQUEUR, SUCH AS ORANGE OR STRAWBERRY (OPTIONAL)
- 1 TEASPOON VANILLA EXTRACT
- 1/2 TEASPOON GROUND CINNAMON

    ◆

- 2 PINTS FRESH STRAWBERRIES
- 2 TABLESPOONS FINELY CHOPPED PECAN PIECES, DRY-ROASTED (OPTIONAL)

PER SERVING	
CALORIES 95	CHOLESTEROL 1 mg
TOTAL FAT 0.5 g	SODIUM 33 mg
SATURATED 0.0 g	CARBOHYDRATES 20 g
POLYUNSATURATED 0.0 g	FIBER 2 g
MONOUNSATURATED 0.0 g	PROTEIN 4 g

In a small bowl, whisk together the sauce ingredients until thoroughly combined. Cover and refrigerate for at least 1 hour, or until the sauce is slightly firm.

Meanwhile, discard the stems from the strawberries. Cut the strawberries into bite-size pieces.

Spoon the berries into six dessert dishes. Top each serving with equal amounts of sauce and a sprinkling of pecans if desired. Serve immediately.

yogurt cheese

makes about 2 cups

**1 QUART FAT-FREE OR LOW-FAT PLAIN YOGURT
WITHOUT GELATIN**

Place a double-thick layer of fine-mesh cotton cheesecloth or paper coffee filters inside a rust-proof colander. Put the colander in a bowl, leaving enough space for about 2 cups of whey (watery liquid) to drain out of the colander. (The collected whey shouldn't touch the bottom of the colander.) Pour the yogurt into the prepared colander, cover loosely with plastic wrap, and refrigerate for at least 8 hours. This will yield about 2 cups of firm yogurt and 2 cups of drained whey.

Cook's Tip

You can use Yogurt Cheese almost anywhere a recipe calls for plain yogurt or sour cream. It can be used as a base for any number of sauces, both savory and sweet. Try the whey as a substitute for fat-free milk in recipes such as Honey-Nut Bread (page 397).

mango brûlée
with pine nuts

serves 4

Easy, elegant, and fast, too, this very special dessert requires only four ingredients.

 2 **CUPS CUBED FRESH MANGO, PAPAYA, OR PEACHES (ABOUT 3 MANGOES, 2 MEDIUM PAPAYAS, OR 4 MEDIUM PEACHES)**
2/3 **CUP FAT-FREE OR LOW-FAT SOUR CREAM**
 2 **TABLESPOONS PINE NUTS**
 2 **TABLESPOONS DARK BROWN SUGAR**

Preheat the broiler.

Place the fruit in the bottom of a 9-inch pie pan.

Stir the sour cream and dollop over the fruit. Using a spatula or the back of a spoon, spread the sour cream evenly.

Sprinkle with the pine nuts and brown sugar.

Broil 4 to 6 inches from the heat for 1 to 2 minutes, or until the sugar melts and the pine nuts

PER SERVING

CALORIES 146	CHOLESTEROL 7 mg
TOTAL FAT 2.0 g	SODIUM 38 mg
SATURATED 0.5 g	CARBOHYDRATES 29 g
POLYUNSATURATED 1.0 g	FIBER 2 g
MONOUNSATURATED 1.0 g	PROTEIN 4 g

toast (watch the nuts closely to avoid burning).
Serve immediately.

Cook's Tip

If fresh fruit is out of season, you can use frozen
unsweetened fruit that's been thawed, fruit in a
jar, or fruit canned in natural juice.

very berry sorbet

To freeze or not to freeze, that is the question. With this slightly tart dessert, either answer is correct. Try both ways and see which you prefer.

1 1/2	CUPS FROZEN UNSWEETENED BLACKBERRIES, SLIGHTLY THAWED (6 TO 8 OUNCES)
2	TEASPOONS WATER
1	TEASPOON FROZEN ORANGE JUICE CONCENTRATE
1	TEASPOON BRANDY OR COGNAC (OPTIONAL)
	FRESH MINT SPRIGS (OPTIONAL)

In a food processor or blender, process all ingredients except the mint until smooth, scraping sides as needed.

Sorbet can be served immediately or frozen. If the sorbet is frozen, remove it from the freezer about 15 minutes before serving to defrost until soft enough to serve.

Garnish with the mint sprigs if desired.

PER SERVING

CALORIES 77	CHOLESTEROL 0 mg
TOTAL FAT 0.5 g	SODIUM 1 mg
SATURATED 0.0 g	CARBOHYDRATES 19 g
POLYUNSATURATED 0.5 g	FIBER 6 g
MONOUNSATURATED 0.0 g	PROTEIN 1 g

strawberry margarita ice

serves 6

This frosty dessert reflects the popularity of the slushy drink called a frozen margarita. You can adjust the level of sugar in this recipe depending on the sweetness of your strawberries and how tart you like your margaritas.

2 CUPS FRESH OR FROZEN UNSWEETENED STRAWBERRIES, THAWED

2/3 CUP FRESH LIME JUICE

1/2 TO 2/3 CUP SUGAR

1 TABLESPOON TEQUILA OR FRESH LIME JUICE

1 TABLESPOON ORANGE LIQUEUR OR FRESH ORANGE JUICE

In a food processor or blender, process all the ingredients until smooth.

Pour the mixture into a 9 x 5 x 3-inch loaf pan. Cover and freeze for 4 hours, or until firm but not frozen solid.

Put a large bowl in the refrigerator to chill.

PER SERVING

CALORIES 111	CHOLESTEROL 0 mg
TOTAL FAT 0.0 g	SODIUM 1 mg
SATURATED 0.0 g	CARBOHYDRATES 26 g
POLYUNSATURATED 0.0 g	FIBER 1 g
MONOUNSATURATED 0.0 g	PROTEIN 0 g

When the mixture is firm, break it into chunks and put it in the chilled bowl. Using an electric mixer, beat until smooth but not melted. Serve immediately or return the mixture to the loaf pan, cover, and freeze until serving time.

To serve when frozen, scrape across the surface with a spoon and mound the shavings in dessert dishes.

Cook's Tip

If you leave the strawberry mixture in the freezer until it becomes frozen solid, let it stand at room temperature for about 15 minutes before breaking it into chunks and beating with an electric mixer.

berry sauce

serves 6; 1/4 cup per serving

This topping is as easy to make as it is colorful and flavorful. It's great on French toast, waffles, fruit salads, sorbet, fat-free or low-fat yogurt, or even fat-free or low-fat cottage cheese.

16-OUNCE PACKAGE FROZEN UNSWEETENED STRAWBERRIES, RASPBERRIES, OR OTHER BERRIES

1 TEASPOON CORNSTARCH

Defrost the berries.

In a food processor or blender, puree the berries.

In a medium saucepan, bring the berry puree and cornstarch to a boil over medium-high heat, stirring frequently. Cook until the mixture thickens, stirring frequently.

Cover and refrigerate. Serve chilled.

PER SERVING	
CALORIES 28	CHOLESTEROL 0 mg
TOTAL FAT 0.0 g	SODIUM 2 mg
SATURATED 0.0 g	CARBOHYDRATES 7 g
POLYUNSATURATED 0.0 g	FIBER 2 g
MONOUNSATURATED 0.0 g	PROTEIN 0 g

apple-raisin sauce

serves 6; 1/2 cup per serving

Instead of apple strudel à la mode, try this delicious fruit sauce over fat-free or low-fat ice cream or frozen yogurt. You'll enjoy the same taste combination without the fat and calories.

3	MEDIUM APPLES
2	CUPS UNSWEETENED APPLE JUICE
1/4	CUP RAISINS OR DRIED CRANBERRIES
1	TEASPOON GROUND CINNAMON
1	TABLESPOON CORNSTARCH
2	TABLESPOONS COLD WATER

Peel the apples if desired. Core and chop coarsely.

In a large saucepan, bring the apples, juice, raisins, and cinnamon to a boil over medium-high heat. Reduce the heat and simmer for 15 minutes, or until the apples are tender.

Meanwhile, put the cornstarch in a cup. Add the water, stirring to dissolve.

Stir the cornstarch mixture into the apple mixture. Cook for 1 to 2 minutes, or until thick and smooth, stirring constantly.

Serve warm.

PER SERVING

CALORIES 102	CHOLESTEROL 0 mg
TOTAL FAT 0.5 g	SODIUM 5 mg
SATURATED 0.0 g	CARBOHYDRATES 26 g
POLYUNSATURATED 0.0 g	FIBER 2 g
MONOUNSATURATED 0.0 g	PROTEIN 0 g

creamy dessert topping

serves 8; 2 tablespoons per serving

Reminiscent of cheesecake, this topping is luscious when drizzled over fruit, spread on muffins, or poured on a slice of angel food cake.

- 1/2 CUP FAT-FREE OR LOW-FAT PLAIN YOGURT
- 1/2 CUP FAT-FREE OR LOW-FAT COTTAGE CHEESE
- 2 TABLESPOONS HONEY
- 1/2 TO 3/4 TEASPOON VANILLA EXTRACT (OPTIONAL)

In a food processor or blender, process all the ingredients until light and creamy.

Cover and refrigerate. Serve chilled.

PER SERVING

CALORIES 35	CHOLESTEROL 1 mg
TOTAL FAT 0.0 g	SODIUM 60 mg
SATURATED 0.0 g	CARBOHYDRATES 6 g
POLYUNSATURATED 0.0 g	FIBER 0 g
MONOUNSATURATED 0.0 g	PROTEIN 3 g

appendix a

Eat Wisely, Eat Well: TLC for Your Heart

Researchers learn more every day about how you can control the cholesterol that puts your heart at risk. Nutrition experts continue to carefully analyze the results of new studies to make recommendations on how to stay as healthy as possible and how to reduce harmful cholesterol levels.

A DIET TO HELP CONTROL CHOLESTEROL

The Therapeutic Lifestyle Change (TLC) Diet is based on the latest information we have about how diet affects your health. We recommend the TLC Diet for adults who need to control their cholesterol or who have coronary heart disease. It follows the basic principles of healthy eating to help prevent blood cholesterol from accumulating in your arteries and reduce your risk for heart disease. The American Heart Association has endorsed and adopted the TLC Diet as outlined by the National Cholesterol Education Program Expert Panel. The TLC Diet also provides the basis of treatment plans to lower unhealthy cholesterol levels. If you've had a heart attack or have more than two risk factors, your doctor may recommend additional treatment options.

For the general population and children over age two, the American Heart Association recommends the Eating Plan for Healthy Americans to help prevent future problems. (For more specific information, visit *www.americanheart.org.*)

THE GOALS OF THE THERAPEUTIC LIFESTYLE CHANGE (TLC) DIET ARE:

- Limit intake of saturated fat

- Limit intake of dietary cholesterol

- Keep intake of trans fat at a minimum

- Control calorie intake to maintain a desirable weight and prevent weight gain

- Include enough physical activity to burn at least 200 calories per day

For people at immediate risk, use other treatment options as recommended by a physician. These may include dietary options, such as plant stanols/sterols, soluble fiber, soy products, or cholesterol-lowering medications.

TO ACHIEVE THE GOALS OF THE TLC DIET:

- Eat six or more servings per day of a variety of grain products, especially whole grains.

- Eat three to five servings per day of a variety of vegetables, without added fats or salt.

- Eat two to four servings per day of a variety of fruits.

- Eat two to three servings per day of fat-free and low-fat dairy products.

- Eat no more than two egg yolks per week.

- Eat 5 ounces or less per day of cooked lean meats, poultry, and fish.

- Limit your intake of foods high in saturated fat, trans fat, and cholesterol. (For more information on these foods, see pages 14 to 17.)

- Adjust your intake of fats and oils to fit the number of calories you should be eating. Choose unsaturated oils, soft or liquid margarines and vegetable oil spreads, salad dressings, seeds, and nuts. (For a list of sources of recommended fats and those to avoid, see pages 17 to 21.)

- Eat fewer than 6 grams of salt per day (2,400 milligrams of sodium).

- Maintain a level of physical activity that keeps your weight in a desirable range and matches the number of calories you eat. To lose weight, be active enough to burn more calories than you eat every day.

By following the eating plan outlined in the TLC Diet, you will receive the recommended proportions of nutrients listed below.

Recommendations of the TLC Diet to Lower Cholesterol

SATURATED FATS	LESS THAN 7% OF TOTAL CALORIES
POLYUNSATURATED FATS	UP TO 10% OF TOTAL CALORIES
MONOUNSATURATED FATS	UP TO 20% OF TOTAL CALORIES
TOTAL FAT	25% TO 35% OF TOTAL CALORIES
TRANS FATS	KEPT TO A MINIMUM
DIETARY CHOLESTEROL	LESS THAN 200 MG PER DAY
CARBOHYDRATES*	50% TO 60% OF TOTAL CALORIES
DIETARY FIBER	20 TO 30 GRAMS PER DAY
PROTEIN	ABOUT 15% OF TOTAL CALORIES

*CARBOHYDRATES SHOULD COME PRIMARILY FROM WHOLE GRAINS, FRUITS, AND VEGETABLES.

DAILY INTAKE OF SATURATED FAT VERSUS TOTAL FAT

Much attention has been paid to total fat intake over the last decade. Saturated, monounsaturated, and polyunsaturated fats, however, have different effects on cholesterol levels. The important thing to remember is that reducing the intake of saturated fats is crucial to your heart health. Remember that this reduction applies to *saturated fats,* not all fats. By reducing your intake of total fat, you will probably also lower the amounts of harmful saturated and trans fats you eat. It is not necessary to overly restrict total fat intake to reduce LDL levels, but do remember that total fat is a large part of total calories consumed.

The following table shows the amounts of saturated and unsaturated fats in a variety of fats and oils. The most healthful oils have the least saturated fat.

PUTTING THEORY INTO PRACTICE

You know *why* eating wisely will keep your blood cholesterol level under control. But you might need a little help to know *how* to put the theory into practice. We're all creatures of habit, and habits are acquired slowly. You will learn to fit your new eating pattern into your lifestyle by making changes a little at a time. For example, if you prefer to have lunch in the cafeteria, you don't have to bring a lunch from home; just start making more careful selections. Soon you will find that new eating habits become just as firmly established as old ones. Meanwhile, consider the following suggestions to help lower blood cholesterol. Many of the same strategies can also work if your goal is to lose weight.

What Is Your Motivation for Change?

Examine your old eating habits to understand your behaviors, attitudes, and motivations. Begin with some personal reflection and a frank discussion with members of your family. Keep a written record of your eating habits for at least a few

Percentages of Saturated and Unsaturated Fats in Commonly Used Oils and Fats

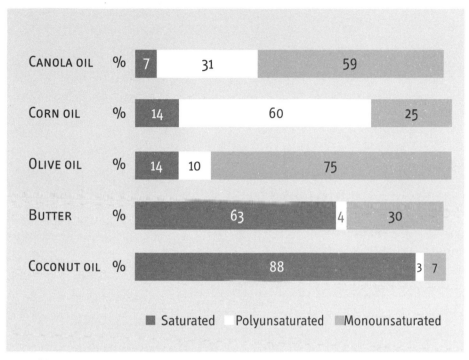

		Saturated	Polyunsaturated	Monounsaturated
CANOLA OIL	%	7	31	59
CORN OIL	%	14	60	25
OLIVE OIL	%	14	10	75
BUTTER	%	63	4	30
COCONUT OIL	%	88	3	7

VALUES MAY NOT ADD UP TO 100 PERCENT BECAUSE OF OTHER FATTY ACIDS NOT REPRESENTED.

days. As you reflect on these habits, look for signs of subconscious behavior. For instance, do you use high-fat "comfort" foods to relieve anxiety or depression? Do you feel pressure from family or friends to eat foods that are wrong for you? What you learn from your answers can be eye-opening—and can help you change your eating behaviors.

ASSESS YOUR INTAKE OF SATURATED FAT AND CHOLESTEROL

Ask yourself how much you eat of the foods that raise cholesterol levels. Be honest and pinpoint the foods you can live without to help reduce your risk for heart disease.

Dairy fats (whole milk, 2% milk, ice cream, cream, whole-fat cheese, and whole-fat yogurt)

Animal fats (ground meat, hot dogs, cold cuts, fried foods, fatty cuts of meat)

Restaurant meals high in fat, either take-out or eaten in restaurants

Extra fat from commercial products (pastries, pies, doughnuts, cookies, chips)

Your family's support—or lack of it—can have a major effect on your eating habits. Explain to them how important it is to your health to make some changes. If you consult a registered dietitian or a licensed nutritionist, take your spouse or other family members along so they'll understand exactly what your eating plan requires. Your whole family should know about the potential health problems related to high blood cholesterol and adopt a cholesterol-lowering eating plan, too. Even if they don't join you, encourage them to support your efforts to eat a healthful diet.

Keeping Cholesterol Low

After you reduce your cholesterol level, you face a very important task—keeping it low. Start by realizing that you will face lapses and relapses on the way to a safe cholesterol level. A *lapse* is a slight error or return to your unhealthy habits. After a bad day, you might eat several foods high in saturated fat or skip a week of exercise. Just get back on track as soon as you can to prevent a *relapse,* which is returning to your former habits for several days or skipping exercise for weeks. This is your signal to stop, take stock, and begin your new eating and exercise habits afresh.

A lapse or a relapse should not be seen as a failure. Instead, see it as a challenge to overcome, a wake-up call. Setbacks are a natural part of the change process. Be persistent. It will take time to get your cholesterol to the level you want it.

TIPS FOR MAINTAINING YOUR BEST CHOLESTEROL LEVEL

- Analyze your environment and eliminate those things that stimulate you to eat foods that you shouldn't.

- Find friends, neighbors, and coworkers who support and encourage your new lifestyle changes.

- Social engagements, holidays, and business luncheons will always happen. So will depressing or upsetting episodes in life. You can always find an excuse for not eating right or not getting enough exercise. Instead of letting these temptations control you, plan the kind of life you really want, and live it every day.

- Learn to tell the difference between hunger (gnawing in your stomach and lightheadedness) and urges (mental cravings for comfort foods). Hunger tells you it's time to eat, either a meal or perhaps a small piece of fruit or glass of fat-free milk. Urges come from using food to satisfy an emotional need (for example, eating a snack high in saturated fat to reward yourself after a stressful incident).

- Depriving yourself of special treats only makes you crave them. You can enjoy a treat now and then. It's better to eat a little of a food you crave than to avoid it for so long that you gorge when you finally indulge yourself.

Finally, realize that eating wisely doesn't mean eating tasteless foods—it means eating delicious, healthful foods prepared with creativity. We hope that the recipes and information in this book will be just what you need to feed your commitment. As you make the connection between health and a healthful diet, your good choices will be the basis of your success in taking control of your cholesterol level.

appendix b

Planning Your Meals with TLC

You—and your heart—deserve a little tender, loving care. It's great to know that even on a cholesterol-lowering eating plan, you can still have most of your favorite foods—as long as you make a few key substitutions. To stock your kitchen, start with a grocery list that covers all the food groups. Aim for a variety of nonfat or low-fat, no- or low-cholesterol foods for breakfast, lunch, dinner, and snacks. Grocery stores can be full of temptation, so know what you need before you go. A shopping game plan will help you fill your cart with foods that are taste tempting but low in saturated and trans fats and cholesterol.

- Stock up on good, fresh foods that make you look forward to meals.

- Plan your weekly menus using the TLC Diet as a guide. If you're running short on time, plan just the entrées.

- Make a shopping list before you go out. This helps cut down the impulse to buy items that may not fit into your eating plan.

- Never go shopping on an empty stomach. Hunger may tempt you to reach for the wrong foods.

- Buy specials or sale items only if they fit into your food plan for the week and into your overall cholesterol-lowering program.

- Read the nutrition labels on all the items you buy—even low-fat or low-cholesterol products—so you know they fit into your eating plan. Just because a food is low in fat doesn't mean it's low in calories or sodium.

HEALTHY FOOD CHOICES BY FOOD GROUP

The following chart is based on the recommendations of the TLC Diet (for an overview of the TLC Diet, see pages 482 to 490). Use this chart for guidance on what kind of foods to buy and the serving sizes to plan for in each major food group. The information that follows is organized by food group. Each section explains how different foods fit into a healthy eating plan and gives you some shopping tips to make your planning easier.

Foods to Choose More Often

RECOMMENDED SERVINGS PER DAY	SERVING SIZE
BREADS AND CEREALS	
AT LEAST 6 SERVINGS PER DAY, DEPENDING ON YOUR CALORIC NEEDS	1 SLICE BREAD 1/2 BUN, BAGEL, MUFFIN 1 OUNCE DRY CEREAL
	(CONTINUED ON NEXT PAGE)

RECOMMENDED SERVINGS PER DAY	SERVING SIZE
BREADS AND CEREALS	
BREADS, CEREALS, AND PASTA PASTA, ESPECIALLY (ESPECIALLY WHOLE-GRAIN); RICE; LEGUMES SUCH AS BEANS AND PEAS; POTATOES; LOW-FAT CRACKERS AND COOKIES	1/2 CUP COOKED CEREAL OR WHOLE-GRAIN; DRIED BEANS OR PEAS; POTATOES; OR RICE OR OTHER GRAINS 1/2 CUP TOFU
VEGETABLES	
3 TO 5 SERVINGS PER DAY FRESH, FROZEN, CANNED, WITHOUT ADDED FAT, SAUCE, OR SALT	1 CUP LEAFY OR RAW 1/2 CUP COOKED 3/4 CUP JUICE
FRUITS	
2 TO 4 SERVINGS PER DAY FRESH, FROZEN, CANNED, OR DRIED	1 PIECE FRUIT 1/2 CUP DICED FRUIT 3/4 CUP FRUIT JUICE
DAIRY PRODUCTS	
2 TO 3 SERVINGS PER DAY FAT-FREE, 1/2%, 1% MILK, , BUTTERMILK YOGURT, AND COTTAGE CHEESE; FAT-FREE AND LOW-FAT CHEESES	1 CUP MILK 1 CUP YOGURT 1 OUNCE CHEESE WITH 3 OR FEWER GRAMS OF FAT PER SERVING 1/2 CUP COTTAGE CHEESE
EGGS	
NO MORE THAN 2 YOLKS PER WEEK	1/4 CUP EGG SUBSTITUTE = 1 EGG

(CONTINUED ON NEXT PAGE)

RECOMMENDED SERVINGS PER DAY	SERVING SIZE
Eggs	
Egg whites or egg substitute as desired	
Meat, Poultry, and Fish	
No more than 5 ounces per day (cooked weight) Lean cuts of loin, leg, round; lean ground meat; cold cuts made with lean meat or soy protein; skinless poultry; fish	About the size of a deck of cards or a computer mouse
Fats and Oils, Nuts	
Amount per day depends on your caloric needs. Choose unsaturated oils, soft or liquid margarine and vegetable oil spreads, salad dressings, and nuts	1 teaspoon soft margarine or vegetable oil 1 ounce nuts
TLC Diet Options	
Stanol/sterol-containing margarines and viscous fiber food sources such as barley, oats, psyllium, apples, bananas, berries, citrus fruits, nectarines, peaches, pears, plums, prunes, broccoli, brussels sprouts, carrots, dry beans, peas, soy products (tofu and miso).	

Foods to Choose Less Often

BREADS AND CEREALS

MANY BAKERY PRODUCTS, INCLUDING DOUGHNUTS, BISCUITS, ROLLS, MUFFINS, CROISSANTS, CAKES, PIES, COFFEE CAKES, COOKIES

VEGETABLES

FRIED OR PREPARED WITH BUTTER, CHEESE, OR CREAM SAUCE

FRUITS

FRIED OR SERVED WITH BUTTER OR CREAM

DAIRY PRODUCTS

WHOLE MILK, 2% MILK

WHOLE-MILK YOGURT, ICE CREAM, CREAM, CHEESE

EGG YOLKS

MEAT, POULTRY, AND FISH

HIGHER-FAT MEAT CUTS: RIBS, T-BONE STEAK, REGULAR GROUND BEEF, BACON, SAUSAGE

COLD CUTS: SALAMI, BOLOGNA, HOT DOGS

ORGAN MEATS: LIVER, BRAINS, SWEETBREADS

POULTRY WITH SKIN

FRIED MEAT, POULTRY, OR FISH

FATS AND OILS

BUTTER, SHORTENING, STICK MARGARINE, CHOCOLATE, COCONUT

Carbohydrates

Carbohydrates are the foundation of a healthy eating plan and offer a wide variety of food choices ranging from grains to fruits. Carbohydrates contain no cholesterol and are generally low in total fat. Most of the carbohydrates in your diet should come from whole-grain products, vegetables, fruits, and fat-free and low-fat dairy products. Your daily intake of carbohydrates should be no more than 60 percent of total calories. People with the metabolic syndrome (see page 4) who have high triglyceride levels or low levels of HDL cholesterol should consider a lower intake of about 50 percent.

GRAIN PRODUCTS AND LEGUMES

Whole-grain breads, cereals, and pasta as well as potatoes, whole-grain rice, and legumes such as dried peas and beans are rich in complex carbohydrates. Beans and dried peas provide plant protein and are rich in fiber. As you plan your meals, use these carbohydrates as substitutes for foods high in saturated fat, cholesterol, and total fat. Be sure to check the ingredient labels on processed breads, cereals, pastas, and rice and other grains to avoid those with added saturated fat, cholesterol, or sodium.

VEGETABLES AND FRUITS

Vegetables and fruits can also contain carbohydrates. They provide important vitamins, minerals, and fiber. In general, fresh produce is always an excellent choice. When you use frozen or canned vegetables, look for items without added sodium, fats, or sauces. Some produce can surprise you, however. Coconut meat, for example, is high in saturated fat. Olives and avocados also are high in fat, but it's mostly beneficial unsaturated fat. You will also want to check the calorie content of these foods; some, like avocados, are high in calories.

SHOPPING TIPS FOR CARBOHYDRATES

- Check cracker labels for fats and oils. Choose Scandinavian-style rye crackers and other whole-grain crackers that are made without fats or oils and with little or no salt.

- Try brown rice, bulgur wheat, millet, and other whole grains. Cook them in low-sodium seasoned broth for a side dish. They're high in fiber, relatively low in calories, and economical.

- Use pasta, rice, dried peas or beans, and lentils as entrées, or substitute them for meats in casseroles, stews, and soups. They're excellent protein sources and very economical.

- Substitute brown rice for white rice in recipes and as a side dish to add fiber to your diet.

- Check the ingredients lists on packaged cereals. Most of these are low in saturated fat, but avoid those that contain large quantities of sugar, salt, and fat. Try to avoid the so-called natural cereals and granolas that contain all three, including coconut or coconut oil.

- Look for reduced-salt versions of canned soups and canned vegetables. You can find them either in the diet section or on the shelves with their "regular" counterparts. Look for canned or dehydrated varieties of soup lowest in sodium, saturated fat, and cholesterol. You may be surprised at the amount of sodium in many soups.

- Choose frozen vegetables without added sauce, sodium, and fat.

- Avoid buying fried vegetables: They have several times more fat and calories than do vegetables prepared without fat.

- Fruits that are fresh or canned in water are lower in calories and are better choices than fruits canned in juice or in syrup. If you buy fruits canned in syrup, drain them and discard the syrup before using the fruit.

BAKERY GOODS

Cakes, pies, doughnuts, and cookies offer very little benefit to a cholesterol-lowering diet. They're typically high in calories and low in important nutrients. Plus, many commercial baked goods are made with saturated or trans fats, which will hamper your cholesterol-lowering efforts. Try baking at home using unsaturated oils and substituting egg whites or egg substitutes for whole eggs to control the fat and cholesterol. Don't go overboard, however. Baked goods of any kind add lots of calories without the important nutrients you need.

Proteins

Like most Americans, you probably eat much more protein than you actually need. You should eat no more than 5 ounces (cooked weight) of lean meat, skinless poultry, and fish per day, served in one or two portions. It's also important to get protein from a variety of foods, including dried peas and beans, meat, seafood, poultry, and soy products, such as tofu. Both plant and animal proteins give you a wide range of vitamins, minerals, fiber, and other nutrients.

MEATS

A cholesterol-lowering diet doesn't mean giving up meat. A 3-ounce portion contains about 70 to 75 milligrams of cholesterol and an acceptable level of saturated fat—if you choose carefully. First, make sure the meat is lean (see "Shopping Tips for Proteins," page 500). Second, before cooking the meat, remove all visible fat.

POULTRY

Poultry is one of the most popular protein sources for health-conscious consumers. It's in special demand as a substitute for red meat. Since much of the fat in poultry is in the skin, removing it greatly reduces the fat content. Remember too that the white meat is lower in saturated fat than the dark meat.

SEAFOOD

Fish contains less saturated fat than red meat, so it is a good choice when you're eating to lower your cholesterol. We recommend eating fish at least two times a week, particularly fatty fish that contain omega-3 fatty acids.

Shellfish is low in fat but varies in cholesterol content. Some, such as shrimp and squid, are fairly high in cholesterol. Others, including scallops, mussels, and clams, are low. Shellfish have little saturated fat and total fat. You can eat shellfish as part of a cholesterol-lowering diet, but make sure you stay within the limits of your dietary cholesterol for each day.

EGGS

One large egg yolk contains about 213 milligrams of cholesterol. Keep in mind that the recommended daily limit for people trying to lower their cholesterol is 200 mg. Egg whites and egg substitute, on the other hand, contain no fat or cholesterol and are an excellent source of protein. You can also substitute two egg whites for one whole egg in most recipes.

SHOPPING TIPS FOR PROTEINS

- USDA "prime" grades of meat are heavily marbled, making them high in saturated fat. "Choice" grades are less fatty than prime but are still high in saturated fat. Choose "select" grades instead—they're lower in saturated fat.

- Look for the words "lean" and "extra lean" on beef, lamb, pork, and processed meats.

- Organ meats, such as liver, brains, kidney, and sweetbreads, are extremely high in cholesterol, so eat them sparingly.

- Choose lean cuts of beef, such as eye of round, top round, tenderloin, sirloin, or flank.

- Select lean pork, such as tenderloin, loin chops, sirloin, center-cut ham (fresh and cured), and Canadian bacon.

- Most cuts of veal are lean. Chops and roast are leaner than breast and ground or cubed cutlets.

- The leanest cut of lamb is the leg or shank.

- Some wild game, such as venison, rabbit, squirrel, and pheasant, is very lean.

- Chicken and turkey are good choices. Avoid goose, duck, and processed poultry products, which are high in saturated fat.

- Limit processed meats, such as bacon, hot dogs, bologna, salami, and sausage. They're high in saturated fat and total fat. Reduced-fat, low-fat, and nonfat versions of these meats are available, but watch out for high sodium. Compare labels to find the brands that are lowest in fat, saturated fat, and sodium.

- Try fresh ground turkey or chicken made from white meat. Choose packages that say "white meat," "light meat," or "breast." Others may include the skin and dark meat, making them higher in saturated fat.

- Salmon, tuna, mackerel, carp, halibut, smelt, and trout are rich in omega-3 fatty acids, which may reduce the risk of heart disease.

- Canned tuna packed in water is another good choice.

- Try uncreamed or smoked herring, as well as sardines canned in tomato sauce or rinsed.

Dairy Products

Dairy foods are an important part of a healthful diet. Even though many milk products traditionally are high in saturated fats and cholesterol, there are now many low-cholesterol and low-fat options in the dairy case.

MILKS: WHOLE, LOW-FAT, AND FAT-FREE

Many people don't realize that 49 percent of the calories in whole milk comes from fat, and most of that is saturated. In fat-free milk, on the other hand, less than 1 percent of calories comes from fat. Even 2 percent reduced-fat milk gets an amazing 35 percent of its total calories from fat. On the other hand, fat-free and low-fat milk are rich in protein, calcium, and other nutrients without much fat. Switching to fat-free milk will dramatically help you cut your saturated fat intake. (See the table comparing whole milk to fat-free on page 511.)

CHEESES

For decades, people have considered cheese to be an acceptable high-protein substitute for meat.

Unfortunately, many cheeses contain large amounts of saturated fat. In fact, 60 to 70 percent of the calories in whole-milk cheese comes from butterfat, about the same percentage as in ice cream. Fortunately, a wide selection of nonfat, low-fat, or part-skim cheeses is now available. In the past, fat-free cheese was often criticized for not melting well. Recently, however, manufacturers have found new ways to produce fat-free cheese that melts well. Cheese can contain a significant amount of sodium, so check the nutrition labels of different cheeses and choose those lowest in sodium.

SUBSTITUTES FOR HIGH-CHOLESTEROL, HIGH-FAT DAIRY PRODUCTS

Butter, cream, and ice cream contain much more fat than does whole milk. The good news is that margarine, fat-free evaporated milk and half-and-half, and nonfat or low-fat ice cream and frozen yogurt are readily available. For example, margarine substitutes nicely for butter and is much lower in saturated fat. (It does contain the same total fat, though.)

Although it can be tricky to bake with fat-free and reduced-fat margarines, you can put them to good use in cooking, on vegetables, dotted on casseroles, and in many other ways. Another word to the wise: Butter and cream are often "hidden" in foods, especially in baked goods and desserts. Read ingredient lists carefully to be sure you're not getting unwanted fat.

SHOPPING TIPS FOR DAIRY PRODUCTS

- Choose nonfat or low-fat milk products. Buy fat-free or 1 percent low-fat milk. Remember that buttermilk is very low in fat, despite its name and rich taste, since it is made from cultured fat-free milk.

- If you like cream in your coffee, try fat-free or low-fat evaporated milk. Also try fat-free half-and-half.

- Look for fat-free, reduced-fat, low-fat, light, or part-skim cheeses. Good examples are nonfat or part-skim mozzarella or ricotta or dry cheese such as Parmesan or sapsago. Imitation cheeses with 2 to 5 grams of fat per ounce are another alternative. Limit your intake of creamy cheeses, such as Brie or processed cheese spreads, which are high in saturated fats.

- Don't forget nonfat or low-fat cottage cheese and cream cheese.

- For dessert, choose nonfat or low-fat yogurt, frozen yogurt, ice milk, or ice cream.

- Some dairy substitutes, such as sour cream substitutes and whipped toppings, often contain coconut, palm, or palm kernel oil and are high in saturated fat. Instead, try nonfat or low-fat versions.

A Comparison of Chicken, Beef, and Cheese

FOOD (per serving)	SATURATED FAT (g)	DIETARY CHOLESTEROL (mg)	TOTAL FAT (g)
CHICKEN— WITHOUT SKIN, WHITE MEAT, ROASTED (3 OZ)	1.0	72	3.0
BEEF— TOP ROUND, BROILED (3 OZ)	2.5	72	7.0
NATURAL CHEDDAR CHEESE (1 OZ)	6.0	30	9.5

Fats and Oils

Saturated fats are found in animal products and in some plant products. Fats and oils high in saturated fat tend to become hard at room temperature. On the other hand, oils that stay liquid at room temperature are high in *unsaturated fats,* such as polyunsaturated and monounsaturated fats. You can use these oils in place of saturated fats to help lower your blood cholesterol while keeping your meals tasty. Choose salad dressings, spreads, and cooking oils made of polyunsaturated or monounsaturated fats.

Hydrogenated and *partially hydrogenated oils* have been processed to change them from a liquid to a solid form. This processing creates the *trans fats* that researchers believe act to increase cholesterol levels in the blood. Use liquid vegetable oil, soft margarines, and trans-fat-free margarine instead of butter, stick margarine, or shortening.

SHOPPING TIPS FOR FATS AND OILS

- Buy margarine instead of butter. Always look for a margarine that has unsaturated liquid vegetable oil listed as the first ingredient. It should have fewer than 2 grams of saturated fat per tablespoon. Choose spray, tub, or liquid margarine or vegetable oil spreads. The softer the margarine, the less hydrogenated it is and the less trans fat it contains. Because diet and nonfat margarines contain water, they are not recommended for baking. They do work well for other cooking and for flavoring vegetables and casseroles, however.

- When shopping for unsaturated vegetable oil, choose unhydrogenated oils such as canola or olive oil. Safflower, corn, sunflower, and soybean oils are also good choices. Peanut oil is a little higher in saturated fat, but you can use it for a flavor change occasionally.

- Stay away from solid shortenings, lard, and fatback. They're high in saturated fat. Use vegetable oils instead.

- Nonstick vegetable oil sprays—plain or flavored—are great to use in place of butter or oil on equipment such as pans, baking sheets, and casserole dishes. (Note: Certain nonstick cookware manufacturers advise against using commercial sprays, which contain propellant. Be sure to check your warranty information.)

- Buy nonfat or light mayonnaise dressing instead of the regular kind, which is high in fat and cholesterol.

- Beware of chocolate, coconut, coconut oil, palm kernel oil, and palm oil. They contain more saturated than unsaturated fat. When choosing manufactured food items containing these ingredients, look on the label to find out the kinds of fat included and use those with saturated fat less often.

RECOMMENDED	FOR OCCASIONAL USE ONLY
CANOLA OIL	PEANUT OIL
OLIVE OIL	VEGETABLE SHORTENING
SAFFLOWER OIL	REGULAR STICK MARGARINE
SUNFLOWER OIL	BUTTER
CORN OIL	BACON, SALT PORK
SESAME OIL	CHICKEN OR TURKEY FAT, MEAT FAT
SOYBEAN OIL	CHOCOLATE
POLYUNSATURATED MARGARINE	

Nuts and Seeds

Nuts and seeds contain no cholesterol and are a healthful addition to your diet. They're good sources of protein and, to some degree, can replace other high-protein foods. Most nuts and any variety of seeds are high in the beneficial unsaturated fats. But if you're watching your weight, remember that nuts are also high in calories.

Snacks and Sweets
What would life be without the occasional snack? Luckily, we can have healthy hearts and tasty snacks, too. Before you reach for any snack food, though, consider how it fits into your cholesterol-lowering eating plan. Whenever possible, snack on a piece of fruit, a variety of vegetables, or non-fat or low-fat yogurt. You'll get important nutrients and fiber as you satisfy your hunger. Avoid any snack or dessert high in saturated fat, trans fat, and cholesterol. If you're watching calories, look closely at the calorie count on the product label. Many low-fat items contain as many calories as (and sometimes more than) the high-fat versions.

SHOPPING TIPS FOR SNACKS AND SWEETS

- Savory snacks, such as most chips and rich crackers, are high in saturated or trans fats. However, you can find chips and crackers made with unsaturated oil and others that are baked and are fat free or lower in fat. Choose only those labeled as having more polyunsaturated than saturated fats.

- Many commercially prepared cookies, such as fruit-bar cookies, graham crackers, animal crackers, and gingersnaps, are low in saturated fat. In addition, food manufacturers have produced nonfat and low-fat versions of a huge variety of cookies, cakes, and pastries. Check labels carefully, and avoid products that are high in hydrogenated oils. Remember to watch the serving size. Eating five cookies at one sitting is probably not a good idea—even when the cookies are low in fat.

- Any help-your-heart dessert list should include nonfat or low-fat frozen yogurt, fruit ices, ice milk, sherbet, and sorbet.

Beverages

WATER
Good foods aren't the only things your body needs—water is an essential. You need water to carry nutrients to the cells and for elimination of wastes.

FRUIT JUICES
Fruit juices offer an easy and delicious way to add nutrients to your daily diet. They are especially useful if you find it difficult to eat the recommended number of fruit servings each day. If you're watching your weight, however, don't forget to consider the calories you drink in juices. Use sweetened juices sparingly.

COFFEE AND TEA
You can enjoy a cup or two of coffee or tea a day as long as you don't add cream, whole milk, or high-fat creamers. Instead, opt for fat-free milk or half-and-half or fat-free evaporated milk.

ALCOHOL
Studies have shown that drinking a moderate amount of alcohol may have a protective effect on

your heart. If you drink more, however, you may not only lose the protective effect, you run many well-established risks. If you do not drink alcohol, do not start. If you do drink, keep your alcohol intake to no more than two drinks per day if you are a man and one drink per day if you are a woman. One drink is defined as 5 ounces of wine, 12 ounces of beer, or 1 1/2 ounces of .80-proof liquor. It's always a good idea to talk to your doctor before deciding what is best for you.

SHOP SMART

To make good choices as you stock your pantry, take the time to know what you are buying. New products appear on the shelves every day. The best way to find the best foods is to compare product labels and key words on packaging. It's easy to identify the products that contain saturated fat and cholesterol and those that you can substitute to help your heart. The labeling on packaged foods gives you all the information you need to put together delicious meals that will help you lower your cholesterol level.

Read Nutrition Labels
The U.S. Food and Drug Administration (FDA) requires that all U.S. food manufacturers put a nutrition label on their products. This label states how much total fat, saturated fat, cholesterol, sodium, carbohydrate, fiber, sugar, and protein each serving contains. The label also gives serving size and the number of calories per serving.

Nutrition Facts

Serving Size ½ cup (114g)
Servings Per Container 4

Amount Per Serving

Calories 90   Calories from Fat 30

% Daily Value*

Total Fat 3g	**5%**
Saturated Fat 0g	**0%**
Cholesterol 0mg	**0%**
Sodium 300mg	**13%**
Total Carbohydrate 13g	**4%**
Dietary Fiber 3g	**12%**
Sugars 3g	
Protein 3g	

Vitamin A	00%	Vitamin C	60%
Calcium	4%	Iron	4%

* Percent Daily Values are based on a 2,000 calorie diet. Your daily values may be higher or lower depending on your calorie needs:

		Calories	2,000	2,500
Total Fat	Less than		65g	80g
Sat Fat	Less than		20g	25g
Cholesterol	Less than		300mg	300mg
Sodium	Less than		2,400mg	2,400mg
Total Carbohydrate			300g	375g
Fiber			25g	30g

Calories per gram:
Fat 9 • Carbohydrate 4 • Protein 4

(Remember that if you eat double the serving size listed, you need to double the amount of calories, fats, cholesterol, and other nutrients listed in your calculations, too.)

Compare the nutrient information for whole and fat-free milks:

PER 1-CUP SERVING	WHOLE MILK	FAT-FREE MILK
CALORIES	149	86
PROTEIN	8 G	8 G
CARBOHYDRATES	11 G	12 G

PER 1-CUP SERVING	WHOLE MILK	FAT-FREE MILK
TOTAL FAT	8.0 G	0.5 G
SATURATED	5.0 G	0.5 G
POLYUNSATURATED	0.5 G	0.0 G
MONOUNSATURATED	2.5 G	0.0 G
CHOLESTEROL	34 MG	5 MG

As you read labels, focus on these important nutrient values:

- Fats and Cholesterol. Look at the grams of total fat, saturated fat, and cholesterol. The lower the amounts of saturated fat and cholesterol, the better. Keep your intake of trans fat as low as possible.

- Sodium. Pay attention to the amount of sodium listed. You should keep your total daily intake at or below 2,400 mg a day.

- Carbohydrates. When you look at the carbohydrate value, also consider the dietary fiber. Soluble fiber can help reduce levels of LDL cholesterol, so look for high-fiber carbohydrates. Examples are whole-grain foods, beans, peas, vegetables, and fruits.

- Protein. Remember that a daily maximum of 5 ounces of cooked lean meat, poultry, or seafood is recommended in the TLC Diet.

Understand Daily Values

The nutrition label also lists the percentages of daily value. That shows how much of your daily need for that nutrient is provided by one serving of that product. These percentages are based on an intake of 2,000 calories each day. Using the product our sample label describes, if you eat 2,000 calories a day, the amount of fat it contains would be just 5 percent of the total you can eat for the day.

Identify Sources of Cholesterol, Saturated Fat, and Trans Fat

When reading food labels, also look at the list of ingredients. Ingredients are listed in order, with the greatest amount first and the least amount last. What you find might surprise you. For example, in many cereals, the first ingredient listed is sugar, meaning the cereal contains more sugar than wheat, oats, or other grains.

When looking for cholesterol and saturated and trans fats in foods, watch for the ingredients listed below. Be aware that the term "vegetable oil" can mean coconut, palm, or palm kernel oil, each of which is high in saturated fat. Look for products that list a specific polyunsaturated or monounsaturated vegetable oil, such as corn oil or canola oil. Trans fats also occur naturally in foods such as meat and whole milk. However, by eating fewer than 5 ounces of cooked lean meat per day and using fat-free or low-fat dairy products, you can easily stay within the recommended limit for both trans and saturated fats combined.

SATURATED FAT AND CHOLESTEROL	SATURATED FAT	TRANS FAT
• Animal fats (bacon, beef, chicken, lamb, pork, turkey)	• Cocoa butter	• Hydrogenated vegetable oil
• Butter	• Coconut	• Vegetable shortening
• Cheese	• Coconut oil	
• Cream	• Palm kernel oil	
• Egg and egg yolk solids	• Palm oil	
• Lard	• Vegetable oil (could be coconut, palm or palm kernel oil)	
• Whole-milk solids		

Understand Key Words on Food Packaging
The FDA has strict guidelines for the descriptors food manufacturers are allowed to put on their packages. It's important to know what those terms mean. For example, low fat does not necessarily mean low calorie. Many people gain weight because they eat more of a low-fat version of a high-fat food without paying attention to how the calories add up. Whether you're reducing your blood cholesterol level, watching your weight, or both, it pays to read food labels carefully.

Note that the key words on packaging follow a consistent pattern:

- "Free" has the least amount.

- "Very Low" and "Low" have a little more.

- "Reduced" or "Less" means that the food has 25 percent less of that nutrient than the reference (or standard) version of the food.

Food packages can also carry certain health claims related to heart disease and cancer. The FDA has defined exactly what a food must offer to make these claims.

American Heart Association
Food Certification Program
Many foods now display the heart-check mark of the American Heart Association Food Certification Program. This symbol means that the food meets the American Heart Association criteria for saturated fat and cholesterol for healthy people over the age of two. This program was begun in 1995 to help consumers identify grocery-store foods that can be part of a balanced, heart-healthy eating plan. You can find more information about the American Heart Association Food Certification Program at *www.americanheart.org*.

**American
Heart
Association**

Meets American Heart
Association food criteria
for saturated fat and
cholesterol for healthy
people over age 2.

appendix c

Cooking for a Healthy Heart

As you prepare the tempting recipes in this book, your time in the kitchen will be well spent. With each satisfying and delicious meal, you will be helping your heart. To create these heart-healthy dishes, we rely on certain principles that allow us to cut out the saturated fat without losing flavor and appeal. You can apply the same technique to all the foods you cook at home.

HIGH-FLAVOR, LOW-FAT PREPARATION

You can avoid an astounding amount of fat by grilling, baking, roasting, or steaming instead of deep-fat frying or pan frying. You'll find that these lower-fat cooking methods can be faster, easier, and tastier than their higher-fat counterparts. Best of all, cooking with more healthful methods will help you lower your cholesterol.

Help-Your-Heart Cooking Techniques

Many meat, seafood, poultry, and vegetable dishes can be cooked in an open skillet with little or no fat. Use nonstick cookware, nonstick vegetable spray, or a tiny bit of polyunsaturated oil rubbed on the pan with a paper towel. Try a small amount of low-sodium broth or wine. A relatively high cooking temperature and stirring food as it cooks will prevent sticking.

ROASTING

The slow, dry heat of this method keeps fat to a minimum. Trim away visible fat before roasting. Place the meat on a rack in a roasting pan to prevent the meat from sitting in its own fat drippings. Roast at a moderate temperature, 325°F or 350°F, to avoid searing, which seals in the fat. If needed, baste with fat-free liquids, such as wine, fruit juice, or low-sodium broth. An instant-read meat thermometer is a convenient way to tell when meat is fully cooked. Plan on removing a roast from the oven 15 to 20 minutes before serving. Letting the meat "rest" makes it easier to carve.

BAKING

Add a little liquid to poultry, seafood, and meat, then bake the food in covered cookware. The moisture and flavor from the liquid makes this method particularly good for fish or chicken breasts, which can be a little dry.

BRAISING OR STEWING

These slow-cooking methods use more liquid than baking and are great ways to tenderize tougher cuts of meat. For braising, first brown the food on all sides in a small amount of vegetable oil or vegetable oil spray. Next, slowly cook the food in a covered container on top of the stove or in the oven. Stewing doesn't require the browning step. Simply add enough liquid to cover the food, then cook it slowly in a covered pot. Because braising or stewing meat or poultry cooks the fat out into the sauce, begin a day ahead. Prepare the dish, then refrigerate it overnight. Once the chilled fat has hardened at the top, you can easily remove it. Braising is also an excellent way to cook vegetables.

POACHING

Poaching is especially good for preparing fish or chicken. To poach food, immerse it in a pan of simmering liquid, such as fat-free broth or milk, wine, or water. After the food is cooked, reduce the liquid to make a delicious sauce.

STEAMING

When food is cooked in a basket over simmering water in a covered pan, the natural flavor, color, and nutrients remain. Add herbs to the steaming water or use broth instead of water to add even more flavor to the finished dish.

STIR-FRYING

Quickly stirring food in a minimum of hot oil seals in the natural juices of meats and seafood and preserves the texture and color of vegetables. Stir-frying is often done in a wok, although a large skillet also works well. The high temperature and the constant movement of the food keep it from sticking and burning.

GRILLING OR BROILING

When you cook meat or poultry on a rack, the fat drips away, but the flavor remains. Grilling or broiling is also a good way to cook fish steaks or whole fish. For extra flavor, try marinating food before putting it over the coals or under the broiler. Vegetables, fruit, and even bread also taste great when browned over an open flame.

MICROWAVE COOKING

Fast and easy, microwave cooking requires no added fat because foods don't stick in the moist heat of the microwave. In fact, you can drain the fat off some foods as they cook by microwaving the food between two paper towels. If you want to adapt a recipe for the microwave oven, cut the cooking time to one fourth to one third of the conventional time. If that isn't enough, gradually increase the cooking time. You can also try to find a microwave recipe similar to the one you want to adapt.

MICROWAVE COOKING TIPS

- Choose foods that cook well in moist heat: chicken, fish, ground meat, vegetables, sauces, and soups.
- Choose a microwave-safe container slightly larger than the dish required for cooking the recipe in a conventional oven.

- Pieces that are about equal in size and shape will cook more uniformly.
- Reduce the liquid used in cooking beverages, soups, vegetables, fruits, and main dishes by about one third because less liquid evaporates in microwave cooking.
- Add nonfat or low-fat cheese and other toppings near the end of cooking to keep the top of your food from becoming tough or soggy.

Help-Your-Heart Cooking Tips
Here are more ways to help trim cholesterol, fat, salt, and calories from your dishes—without trimming taste.

MEATS, POULTRY, AND SEAFOOD

- Remove all visible fat before cooking meat or poultry.

- After you roast meat or poultry, refrigerate the drippings. Once chilled, the fat will rise to the top and harden. You can remove the fat easily and discard it, saving the stock to use in stews, sauces, and soups.

- If you're using leftover marinade in a sauce or for basting, you'll need to take precautions to kill any harmful bacteria that the raw food might have transmitted. Boiling the marinade for at least 5 minutes will do the trick, as will not basting the food during the final 15 minutes of cooking time.

- Buy only the leanest ground meat and poultry (no more than 15 percent fat). After browning, put the ground meat or poultry into a strainer or colander and rinse under hot water to remove even more fat. Ground meat is generally higher in fat than nonground meat. Instead of buying prepackaged ground beef, have your butcher grind a sirloin steak for you. Before grinding, ask the butcher to remove all visible fat and clean the grinder to remove any fat from previous grindings.

- When figuring serving sizes, remember that meat loses about 25 percent of its weight during cooking. (For example, 4 ounces of raw meat will weigh about 3 ounces when cooked.)

- Before cooking most chicken dishes, remove the skin and all visible fat. The skin will be easier to remove if you use paper towels or a clean cloth. (Be sure to scrub the cutting surface and utensils well with hot, sudsy water after preparing poultry for cooking.) If you're roasting a chicken, leave the skin on to prevent the meat from drying out. Remove the skin before serving the chicken.

- Buy turkeys that are not self-basting. Self-basting turkeys are high in saturated fat.

- Baste meats and poultry with fat-free ingredients, such as wine, fruit juice, or defatted beef or chicken broth.

- Try grilling or broiling fish, either directly on the grill or broiler pan or wrapped in foil. A few herbs and citrus juice will let you enjoy the wonderful flavor of the fish itself – instead of the sometimes overwhelming flavors of the batter and oil in fried fish.

VEGETABLES

- To retain natural juices, wrap food in foil before grilling or baking. Or try wrapping food in edible pouches made of steamed lettuce or cabbage leaves.

- Cook vegetables just long enough to make them tender-crisp. Overcooked vegetables lose both flavor and important nutrients.

- Cut down on cholesterol by using more vegetables and less poultry, seafood, or meats in soups, stews, and casseroles. Finely chopped vegetables are great for stretching ground poultry or meat.

- Use small amounts of lean meats instead of salt pork or fatback to flavor vegetables.

- When you make stuffing, substitute chopped vegetables for some of the bread.

SOUPS, SAUCES, AND GRAVIES

- After making soups and sauces, refrigerate them and skim the hardened fat off the top.

- Thicken soups, stews, or sauces with pureed cooked vegetables.

- Another nonfat way to thicken food is to blend a tablespoon of cornstarch, flour, or ground left-over rice with a cup of room-temperature low-sodium broth by shaking the two in a jar with a tight-fitting lid. Add the blended liquid to the soup, sauce, or gravy and simmer until thickened.

- Reduced-fat tofu that's been processed in a blender or a food processor is creamy and works wonderfully as a thickener.

GENERAL

- Substitute herbs, spices, and salt-free seasonings for salt as you cook and at the table.

- Substitute onion or garlic flakes or powder for onion salt and garlic salt.

- Add a drop of lemon juice to the water you cook pasta in, and eliminate the salt and oil.

- Reduce or omit salt in baking recipes that don't use yeast.

- Since most recipes include more sugar than necessary, you can usually reduce the amount of sugar by one fourth to one third.

- Use a blend of whole-wheat flour and all-purpose flour in recipes that call for regular flour.
- Use wheat germ, bran, and whole-wheat bread crumbs in place of buttered crumbs to top casseroles.
- Cut down on fat in creamy salad dressing by mixing the dressing with nonfat or low-fat buttermilk, plain yogurt, or sour cream.
- Instead of croutons, fried bacon, or onion rings in salads and casseroles, try water chestnuts or wheat berry sprouts.

ADAPTING RECIPES

If you're afraid you'll have to give up your favorite recipes to lower your cholesterol, don't worry. You can still enjoy many dishes simply by making a few easy substitutions.

WHEN YOUR RECIPE CALLS FOR	USE
ALL-PURPOSE FLOUR	2 TEASPOONS OF CORNSTARCH FOR EVERY 1 TABLESPOON OF FLOUR (SAVES 30 CALORIES).
BROTH OR BOUILLON	LOW-SODIUM BOUILLON GRANULES OR CUBES, RECONSTITUTED ACCORDING TO PACKAGE DIRECTIONS; HOMEMADE OR COMMERCIALLY PREPARED FAT-FREE, LOW-SODIUM BROTH.

(continued on next page)

WHEN YOUR RECIPE CALLS FOR	USE
BUTTER; MELTED BUTTER OR SHORTENING	ACCEPTABLE MARGARINE OR ACCEPTABLE OIL. WHEN POSSIBLE, USE FAT-FREE OR LIGHT TUB, LIGHT STICK, OR FAT-FREE SPRAY MARGARINE. HOWEVER, IF THE TYPE OF FAT IS CRITICAL TO THE RECIPE, ESPECIALLY IN BAKED GOODS, YOU MAY NEED TO USE AN ACCEPTABLE STICK MARGARINE (SEE PAGE 506).
BUTTER OR OIL FOR SAUTÉING	FAT-FREE, LOW-SODIUM BROTH; VEGETABLE OIL SPRAY; WINE; FRUIT OR VEGETABLE JUICE.
CREAM	POLYUNSATURATED NONDAIRY COFFEE CREAM; UNDILUTED FAT-FREE EVAPORATED MILK; FAT-FREE HALF-AND-HALF.
EGGS	CHOLESTEROL-FREE EGG SUBSTITUTES; 2 EGG WHITES FOR 1 WHOLE EGG.
EVAPORATED MILK	FAT-FREE EVAPORATED MILK.
FLAVOR SALTS, SUCH AS ONION SALT, GARLIC SALT, AND CELERY SALT	ONION POWDER, GARLIC POWDER, CELERY SEEDS OR FLAKES. USE ABOUT ONE FOURTH OF THE AMOUNT OF FLAVORED SALT INDICATED IN THE RECIPE.
ICE CREAM	FAT-FREE, LOW-FAT, OR LIGHT ICE CREAM; NONFAT OR LOW-FAT FROZEN YOGURT; SORBET; SHERBET.
OIL IN BAKING	UNSWEETENED APPLESAUCE.
SALT	NO-SALT-ADDED SEASONING BLENDS.

(continued on next page)

WHEN YOUR RECIPE CALLS FOR	USE
TOMATO JUICE	NO-SALT-ADDED TOMATO JUICE; 6-OUNCE CAN OF NO-SALT-ADDED TOMATO PASTE DILUTED WITH 3 CANS OF WATER.
TOMATO SAUCE	6-OUNCE CAN OF NO-SALT-ADDED TOMATO PASTE DILUTED WITH 1 CAN OF WATER.
UNSWEETENED BAKING CHOCOLATE	3 TABLESPOONS COCOA POWDER PLUS 1 TABLESPOON POLYUNSATURATED OIL OR UNSATURATED, UNSALTED MARGARINE FOR EVERY 1-OUNCE SQUARE OF CHOCOLATE.
VEGETABLE OIL FOR SAUTÉING OR TO PREPARE PAN	VEGETABLE OIL SPRAY; FAT-FREE OR LIGHT TUB, LIGHT STICK, OR FAT-FREE SPRAY MARGARINE; ACCEPTABLE MARGARINE. HOWEVER, IF THE TYPE OF FAT IS CRITICAL TO THE RECIPE, ESPECIALLY IN BAKED GOODS, YOU MAY NEED TO USE AN ACCEPTABLE STICK MARGARINE (SEE PAGE 506).
WHIPPING CREAM	CREAMY DESSERT TOPPING (SEE RECIPE ON PAGE 481). FAT-FREE EVAPORATED MILK (THOROUGHLY CHILLED BEFORE WHIPPING).
WHOLE MILK	FAT-FREE MILK.

appendix d

Dining Out

If you're like most Americans, more than half the time, you don't make dinner. You make reservations, or you head out for a quick bite. Instead of forgoing the pleasure or worrying about the effect of restaurant food on your heart, learn how to eat out with your heart in mind.

WHEN YOU ORDER

- If you're familiar with the restaurant's menu, decide what you'll order before you arrive. You will avoid the temptation of ordering something that is not part of your eating plan.

- If you're trying a new place, take time to study the menu to avoid making split-second—and often unhealthy—decisions.

- Feel free to ask the waiter about ingredients or preparation methods for dishes you're not familiar with. You deserve to know what you're eating.

- Order first. You'll be less likely to be swayed by your dining partners' choices.

- Choose seafood, chicken, or lean meat. Avoid fatty meats. If you order a chicken dish, don't eat the skin. If you order meat, remove all visible fat.

- Choose broiled, baked, grilled, steamed, or poached entrées over the high-fat fried ones. Ask the waiter to have your food prepared without butter or cream sauces.

- Order vegetable side dishes. Ask the waiter to leave off any sauces or butter.

- If you love potatoes, order them baked, boiled, or roasted—not fried. Then leave off the butter and sour cream. Try pepper and chives instead.

- Order all dressings and sauces on the side so you can control your portions. Try a squeeze of lemon instead of ordering dressing for your salad.

- For dessert, see whether the restaurant offers any low-fat options, such as sorbet. If not, order fresh fruit.

- If virtually everything on the menu is high in fat, ask the waiter whether the chef could prepare a fruit or vegetable platter for you. Most chefs are eager to please.

BY CUISINE

ASIAN

- Choose a steamed main dish or try a stir-fried chicken or seafood and vegetable dish.

- Ask for brown rice instead of white and steamed instead of fried.

- Ask the chef to use a minimal amount of oil, and leave out the soy sauce, MSG, and salt.

- Choose entrées with lots of vegetables.

- Avoid the crispy fried noodles usually served as an appetizer.

- Instead of tempura-style vegetables, ask for steamed or stir-fried vegetables.

ITALIAN

- Opt for red marinara or marsala sauce instead of white cream sauce.

- Try a seafood selection or meatless pasta in place of an entrée with sausage or meatballs.

- If you order pizza, choose one with a thin crust. Opt for topping ingredients such as spinach, mushrooms, broccoli, and roasted peppers instead of sausage or pepperoni.

- Ask for plain Italian bread instead of buttery garlic bread.

- For dessert, choose an Italian ice.

MEXICAN

- Ask your waiter not to bring fried tortilla chips to the table.

- Ask him or her to hold the sour cream and guacamole from the entrées. Use salsa, pico de gallo, cilantro, and jalapeño peppers instead for flavor.

- Ask for a tomato-based sauce instead of a creamy or cheesy sauce.

- If you order a taco salad, don't eat the fried shell.

- Choose corn rather than flour tortillas.

- Instead of the ever-present refried beans, ask for frijoles a la charra or borracho beans instead.

- Chicken or beef fajitas and enchiladas with salsa, for example, are more heart healthy than chimichangas or burritos.

You can use the same principles to make similar choices wherever you eat and whatever cuisine is featured. No matter where you are, use your head to make wise choices for your heart.

appendix e

Ingredient Equivalents

INGREDIENT	MEASUREMENT
ALMONDS	1 OUNCE = 1/4 CUP SLIVERS
APPLE	1 MEDIUM = 3/4 CUP CHOPPED; 1 CUP SLICED
BASIL LEAVES, FRESH	2/3 OUNCE = 1/2 CUP CHOPPED, STEMS REMOVED
BELL PEPPER, ANY COLOR	1 MEDIUM = 1 CUP CHOPPED OR SLICED
CARROT	1 MEDIUM = 1/3 TO 1/2 CUP CHOPPED OR SLICED, 1/2 CUP SHREDDED
CELERY	1 MEDIUM RIB = 1/2 CUP CHOPPED OR SLICED
CHEESE, HARD, SUCH AS PARMESAN	4 OUNCES = 1 CUP GRATED 3 1/2 OUNCES = 1 CUP SHREDDED
CHEESE, SEMIHARD, SUCH AS CHEDDAR, MOZZARELLA, OR SWISS	4 OUNCES = 1 CUP GRATED
CHEESE, SOFT, SUCH AS BLUE, FETA, OR GOAT	1 OUNCE, CRUMBLED = 1/4 CUP
CUCUMBER	1 MEDIUM = 1 CUP SLICED
LEMON JUICE	1 MEDIUM = 3 TABLESPOONS
LEMON ZEST	1 MEDIUM = 2 TO 3 TEASPOONS
LIME JUICE	1 MEDIUM = 1 1/2 TO 2 TABLESPOONS
LIME ZEST	1 MEDIUM = 1 TEASPOON

INGREDIENT	MEASUREMENT
MUSHROOMS (BUTTON)	1 POUND = 5 CUPS SLICED OR 6 CUPS CHOPPED
ONIONS, GREEN	8 TO 9 MEDIUM = 1 CUP SLICED (GREEN AND WHITE PARTS)
ONIONS, WHITE OR YELLOW	1 LARGE = 1 CUP CHOPPED 1 MEDIUM = 2/3 CUP CHOPPED 1 SMALL = 1/3 CUP CHOPPED
ORANGE JUICE	1 MEDIUM = 1/3 TO 1/2 CUP
ORANGE ZEST	1 MEDIUM = 1 1/2 TO 2 TABLESPOONS
STRAWBERRIES	1 PINT = 2 CUPS SLICED OR CHOPPED
TOMATOES	2 LARGE, 3 MEDIUM, OR 4 SMALL = 1 1/2 TO 2 CUPS CHOPPED
WALNUTS	1 OUNCE = 1/2 CUP CHOPPED

appendix f

For Further Information

The American Heart Association and the American Stroke Association offer many resources to help you take care of your heart and your health. Call 1-800-AHA-USA1 (1-800-242-8721) or visit www.americanheart.org for access to the many programs and services we provide, as well as easy-to-understand and useful information.

- Learn the warning signs of heart disease and stroke.

- Follow a healthy lifestyle with updates on diet, nutrition, and exercise.

- Find clear and concise answers to your questions about diseases and conditions that affect the heart.

- Take a class on CPR and help save a life.

- Stay informed on the latest advances in medical research.

- Learn about important health issues, join our advocacy network, and let your voice be heard.

- Become a part of your local American Heart Association affiliate to help in the fight against heart disease and stroke.

As you address your individual health needs, be sure to work with your healthcare provider to find a long-term plan that is right for you and your family.

appendix g

American Heart Association National Center and Affiliates

For more information about our programs and services, call 1-800-AHA-USA1 (1-800-242-8721) or contact us online at *www.americanheart.org.* For information about the American Stroke Association, a division of the American Heart Association, call 1-888-4STROKE (1-888-478-7653).

NATIONAL CENTER

American Heart Association
7272 Greenville Avenue
Dallas, TX 75231-4596
214-373-6300

AFFILIATES

FLORIDA/PUERTO RICO AFFILIATE
St. Petersburg, FL

GREATER MIDWEST AFFILIATE
Illinois, Indiana, Michigan, Minnesota, North Dakota, South Dakota, Wisconsin
Chicago, IL

HEARTLAND AFFILIATE
Arkansas, Iowa, Kansas, Missouri, Nebraska, Oklahoma
Topeka, KS

HERITAGE AFFILIATE
Connecticut, Long Island, New Jersey, New York City
New York, NY

MID-ATLANTIC AFFILIATE
District of Columbia, Maryland, North Carolina, South
Carolina, Virginia
Glen Allen, VA

NORTHEAST AFFILIATE
Maine, Massachusetts, New Hampshire, New York State
(except New York City and Long Island), Rhode Island,
Vermont
Framingham, MA

OHIO VALLEY AFFILIATE
Kentucky, Ohio, West Virginia
Columbus, OH

PACIFIC/MOUNTAIN AFFILIATE
Alaska, Arizona, Colorado, Hawaii, Idaho, Montana, New
Mexico, Oregon, Washington, Wyoming
Seattle, WA

PENNSYLVANIA/DELAWARE AFFILIATE
Delaware, Pennsylvania
Wormleysburg, PA

SOUTHEAST AFFILIATE
Alabama, Georgia, Louisiana, Mississippi, Tennessee
Marietta, GA

TEXAS AFFILIATE
Austin, TX

WESTERN STATES AFFILIATE
California, Nevada, Utah
Los Angeles, CA

Index

saturated fat in, 505
Swedish Meat Loaf with
Dill Sauce, 265–67
Thai Chicken with Basil
and Vegetables,
197–98
chick-pea(s)
Marinated Vegetable
Salad, 105–6
Spinach, Chick-Pea, and
Olive Pasta, 313–14
chile peppers
Baked Beans with
Chipotle Peppers,
348–49
cook's tip on, 50
Edamame Stir-Fry,
339–40
Jícama and Grapefruit
Salad with Ancho-
Honey Dressing,
100–1
Southwestern Black Bean
Spread, 38–39
Stuffed Chile Peppers, 49
Chili, 263–64
chocolate
buying, 507
Cappuccino Torte,
437–38
Chocolate Cappuccino,
426–27
Chocolate Custard Cake
with Raspberries,
430–32

Chocolate Soufflé with
Vanilla Sauce, 465–66
Cocoa-Almond
Meringue Kisses,
455–56
low-fat substitute for,
526
Mocha Cheesecake,
441–43
Sugar-Dusted Mocha
Brownies, 459–60
cholesterol. *See* blood
cholesterol; dietary
cholesterol
chowder
Clam and Potato
Chowder with Fresh
Herbs, 72–73
chutney
Nectarine-Plum
Chutney, 238–41
cigarettes, and heart disease, 2
Cioppino, 184–85
clam(s)
Cioppino, 184–85
Clam and Potato
Chowder with Fresh
Herbs, 72–73
cocoa powder
Cocoa-Almond
Meringue Kisses,
455–56
cook's tip on, 456
replacing chocolate with,
526

Honey-Nut Bread,
397–98
Italian-Style Zucchini
Slices, 388–89
Mango Brûlée with Pine
Nuts, 474–75
Mock Baklava, 457–58
Oat Bran Muffins, 407–8
Praline Butternut Squash,
379–80
protein in, 507
Stuffed Mushrooms,
51–52
TLC Diet recommenda-
tions on, 494
Zucchini Bread, 399–400

O

oats and oat bran
Apple-Rhubarb Crisp,
453-54
Oat Bran Muffins, 407–8
Oatmeal-Fruit Muffins,
409-10
obesity, 5–7, 16
oils, cooking
acceptable vegetable, 27
best choices for, 27, 494,
506-7, 525, 526
types of fats in, 487
types to avoid, 495
okra
Gumbo with Greens and
Ham, 84-85

Red and Green Pilaf,
371–72
olive(s)
Broiled Salmon with
Pesto and Olives,
157–58
fat in, 496
Greek-Style Stewed
Chicken, 223-24
Moroccan Chicken,
219–20
Spinach, Chick-Pea, and
Olive Pasta, 313–14
Tilapia with Roasted
Red Bell Peppers and
Olives, 159–60
Tomato Bursts, 55
omega-3 fatty acids, 18, 20,
500, 502
omega-6 fatty acids, 18
Open-Face Turkey
Sandwiches, 234–35
orange(s)
Beets in Orange Sauce,
350–51
Boston Citrus Salad,
90–91
Fresh Fruit Salad with
Poppy Seed and
Yogurt Salad Dressing,
103–4
Herbed Chicken Salad,
122–23
Orange Angel Food
Cake, 439–40